*f*P

GLIMPSES

OF THE

DEVIL

*A Psychiatrist's Personal
Accounts of Possession,
Exorcism, and Redemption*

M. Scott Peck, M.D.

Free Press
NEW YORK   LONDON   TORONTO   SYDNEY

FREE PRESS

A Division of Simon & Schuster, Inc.
1230 Avenue of the Americas
New York, NY 10020

For information regarding special discounts for bulk purchases,
please contact Simon & Schuster Special Sales at 1-800-456-6798
or business@simonandschuster.com

Designed by Paul Dippolito

Manufactured in the United States of America

1   3   5   7   9   10   8   6   4   2

Library of Congress Cataloging-in-Publication Data is available.

ISBN 0-7432-5467-8

Dedicated to Malachi Martin
1921–1999

CONTENTS

———◆———

CONTENTS

HANDLE WITH CARE

Satan is spirit, and spirit is mysterious. Some things can be said about it; most cannot. Those things that can be said, I have tried to say with clarity, but take them with a grain of salt. That is how I take them myself. If and when it seems I am speaking with excessive certainty, I hope you will remember that had I expressed all of my own reservations, much of the book would have been unreadable. My only alternative would have been to write nothing at all. But that, I believe, would have been the greater sin. These things need to be talked of.

Satan is evil spirit. "Evil" is a dangerous word. Speak it carefully—full of care. It is not to be used lightly. Try your best to do no harm with it. Be gentle with yourself as well as others. Yet remember those three famous monkeys covering their eyes and ears and mouth: See no evil; hear no evil; speak no evil. I think the wise person who thought them up was trying to tell us they were stupid little monkeys, monkeys of denial.

The focus of this work has been Satan first, possession second, and only slightly on evil. Readers interested in the general phenomenon of evil should read my 1983 book, *People of the Lie.*

The pope recently directed that every Roman Catholic diocese should have a diocesan exorcist. People with a serious personal concern about possession in regard to themselves or others should seek out the exorcist in their diocese. How well trained or experienced that person might be I have no idea. Regrettably, on account of my health and retirement, I myself am no longer able to be of any assistance as a clinician or advisor except to the church. Remember that genuine possession is a very rare phenomenon. The diagnosis, like that of evil, is not one to be bandied about.

PREFACE

In large part, this is a book of personal history and, in particular, an account of two experiences I had during my forties. They constitute, so far as I know, the first full accounts of possession and exorcism by a modern psychiatrist—which is to say, a medical scientist.

Still, what I write is not autobiography. Here I am not the subject; the subject is Satan and I have included only those experiences of mine that relate to that subject.

To most in our culture the subject of Satan seems esoteric indeed. But then I am not sure how seriously most take God either, beyond a touch of superficial piety. The problem is that ours is a materialistic culture. Materialism is a philosophy or attitude that holds that what you can see and touch and measure is all you get, and anything else is not worth serious consideration. But both God and Satan are Spirit. Since spirit cannot be seen, touched, or measured, it is impossible to obtain hard evidence of its existence and thereby pin it down in our collection box like a captured butterfly.

The evidence of spirit is, at best, indirect. As one very early Christian theologian put it, in relation to God, "The most we can hope for is to get a glimpse of His footprints on the ramparts He has walked." *

---

* *De Mystica Theologia,* i.3. (paraphrased). Dionysius the Areopagite (1st century A.D.), a Greek follower of Saint Paul mentioned in Acts 17:34.

Because Satan's the lesser of the two spirits, it is even more unusual to obtain glimpses of Satan's manifestations. Still, if we pay attention, it is sometimes possible.

And for some, myself included, the notion of Satan is far from esoteric. In my book *People of the Lie,* after quoting a description from *Hostage to the Devil* by Malachi Martin in which a priest's struggle between good and evil was described in depth, I wrote that the issue of free will is a paradox. On the one hand, there is no question in my mind that we humans possess free will. Indeed, I believe this is the essence of what is meant when we say that God created us in His own image. He gave us free will. Like Himself, we are free to choose. But then I went on to state:

> On the other hand, we cannot choose freedom. There are two states of being: submission to God and goodness or the refusal to submit to anything beyond one's own will—which refusal automatically enslaves one to the forces of evil. We must ultimately belong either to God or the devil. This paradox was, of course, expressed by Christ when he said, "Whosoever will save his life shall lose it. And whosoever shall lose his life, for my sake, shall find it." * As C. S. Lewis put it, "There is no neutral ground in the universe: every square inch, every split second is claimed by God and counterclaimed by Satan." † I suppose the only true state of freedom is to stand exactly halfway between God and the devil, uncommitted either to goodness or to utter selfishness. But that freedom is to be torn apart. It is intolerable. As Martin indicates, we must choose. One enslavement or the other.

------◆------

* Matthew 10:39, 16:25; Mark 8:35; Luke 9:24.

† C. S. Lewis, "Christianity and Culture" contained in *Christian Reflections,* Walter Hooper, ed. Grand Rapids, Mich.: Wm. B. Eerdmans Publishing Co., 1967, p. 33.

PREFACE

In *People of the Lie* there was a brief chapter, "Of Possession and Exorcism," which was based on my experiences with two very different cases of satanic possession and their exorcisms. The subject of that book was the entirety of human evil. Because the phenomenon of demonic possession is such a tiny part of the "mystery of iniquity" (a phrase of St. Paul's), my two case descriptions were extremely condensed. While this condensation was appropriate to that book, it did not do justice to the extraordinary nature of both happenings. In the course of those happenings, I was privileged to witness things that very, very few other people have seen. It seemed to me that there should be a reasonably thorough historical record of these almost unique events.

The full account of these two cases, along with my commentaries on each case, constitutes this book. It should be noted that the entirety of both exorcisms was videotaped, and thus the characters' dialogue could be faithfully rendered.

GLIMPSES

OF THE

DEVIL

INTRODUCTION

———◆———

My Mentor, the Leprechaun

Perhaps like the ancient Roman god Janus, I always see at least two sides to everything. Consequently, there are always two sides to me. I do not think that either side is more important than the other.

One side, however, comes first. It is that of a scientist. The other side is that of a religious person. It is only somewhat more passionate. Whenever I approach a new issue, it is the scientist in me that begins the exploration. Yet the moment the scientist is done, my religious passion is unleashed upon the matter. If that matter is of major importance, eventually I'll be working on it with both sides simultaneously.

No matter how different my two identities have appeared to the world, I never felt them to be anything but me. In my mind, psychology and theology are so integrated as to be interdependent branches of the same science.

In 1971, a novel by William Peter Blatty entitled *The Exorcist* became a bestseller. I devoured the book during two consecutive stormy nights in a house on a New England hilltop, the bushes beating against the windowpanes. Intellectually I did not take the book seriously. It told of paranormal happenings so dramatic as to be beyond my experience; it also seemed to the scientist in me to have a glaring flaw. While it depicted a thirteen-year-old girl in Washington, D.C., who became wildly, demonically possessed, the book offered no explanation whatsoever for her condition—no reason at all why this one girl out of millions might have become possessed. By this flaw it indirectly suggested that someone perfectly normal might be walking down the street one day when a demon would, for no reason, jump out from behind a bush and simply dive into him or her. As a novel, a book of pure fiction, *The Exorcist* was a very good read on those stormy nights, but it was in no way believable by the light of day.

It was about the same time that I was beginning to confront a huge problem. Over the years I had deeply experienced not only human goodness and the existence of benign spirit—namely, God—but I had also experienced human evil. This left a glaring hole in my understanding of both psychiatry and theology: the obvious question of whether there was such a thing as an evil spirit or the devil. I thought not. In common with 99.9 percent of psychiatrists (and with 80 percent of Catholic priests polled confidentially in 1960) I did not believe in the devil.*

Priding myself on being an open-minded scientist, I felt it incumbent upon me to explore any possible evidence before drawing absolute conclusions. Specifically, it occurred to me that if I could see but one case of genuine demonic possession, it might change my mind. In seven years of busy psychiatric practice I had never seen anything faintly resembling a case of possession, so I doubted I would ever find one.

However, two things bothered me. One was that during my four years in medical school and one year as an intern, I had never seen a case of diabetic coma—a rather common condition in the experience of interns and medical students. The fact I'd never seen a case did not mean there was no such thing as dia-

---

* The statistic for psychiatrists is merely my own guess. The figure for Catholic priests, to the best of my recollection, is accurate, but I cannot recall where I read it.

betic coma; it meant only that a part of reality had been missing from my experience. Similarly, just because I had never seen a case of demonic possession did not mean that such a case never existed. Furthermore, I realized that I could well have walked right over such a case in previous years because we humans have a remarkable capacity to overlook things we don't believe in. Grappling with the issue of evil spirit, I therefore began to look for the possibility of possession as a routine part of making my diagnoses. I did not find a case. Still, I remained undeterred.

A few years later, in the winter of 1976 at the age of forty, I began to write my first book, *The Road Less Traveled*. It was accepted for publication, and in the spring of 1978, as is customary, the publisher sent around copies of the manuscript to some important people who might be willing to write a nice comment about it for the back of its dust jacket. Only one person wrote back with a promotional comment, and the publisher sent me a copy. The comment was made by one Dr. Malachi Martin, a person I had never heard of. But being pleased that anybody should look with favor on my baby, I wanted to know who this Dr. Martin might be. At first I guessed he might be a fellow psychiatrist, so I immediately looked his name up in a large tome in my office, a directory of all known psychiatrists in the United States. His name was not among them. I then thought of the possibility that he was a fellow author. I went to our local bookstore and thumbed through another huge tome entitled *Books in Print*. There I did find the name Malachi Martin among the authors and discovered he had written a number of books, the most recent of which was entitled *Hostage to the Devil* and subtitled *The Possession and Exorcism of Five Americans*. It was in stock and I quickly drove home with it.

Unlike *The Exorcist,* which was generally assumed to be fiction, *Hostage to the Devil* was clearly portrayed as nonfiction. The bulk of it described five separate cases of demonic possession and their treatment. The majority of space was devoted to describing the exorcisms, which seemed to me a bit over-dramatic (almost as much as Blatty's book). This excess of drama aroused my skepticism. That same skepticism was partly calmed, however, as I read how in each case, Dr. Martin suggested there was a reason the patient had become possessed—some flaw in his or her personality that attracted the victim toward possession. Dr. Martin put it clearly for me when he suggested that each of the five victims he described, because of their character flaw, had cooperated with the demonic. That made the possibility of possession considerably more real to me than the "jump out from behind a bush" theory.

Unlike Blatty's book, there was just enough in Dr. Martin's work to leave the scientist in me more open to the possibility of possession in the psychiatric patients I saw. And enough for me to want to meet this Dr. Martin.

I got his phone number from his publisher. I then learned that the man had the most elaborate set of telephonic protections I had encountered in my life. I was referred from answering service to answering service to answering service. Finally, after several days, he got in touch with me and, when he learned who I was, he seemed as eager as I to meet for lunch. He suggested an elegant Continental restaurant on the Upper East Side, and I drove the first of many drives down to New York City for lunch with Malachi.

———◆———

I remember Malachi as I first saw him sitting at a table in that restaurant waiting for me. He was a fine-featured diminutive man with a gigantic presence. It was only in the first five seconds that one perceived how small he was; thereafter, one would be overwhelmed by the size of his spirit. The contrast between his physical size and that of his spirit created a strange kind of beauty in the man.

By way of background he told me that he had been a Jesuit

priest and had worked for a number of years in the Vatican, where he had been unusually close to Pope Paul VI. It was Pope Paul who released him from his vows so that he might come to America as an undercover agent on a mission to rescue the Catholic church from the wild liberal excesses of the Second Vatican Council. I didn't believe a word of it. I recognized his spiel about being a plainclothesman as a remarkably unsubtle cover-up for the real reason he was no longer a Jesuit. Instinctively, I assumed he had been kicked out of the order for some reason, most probably a sexual one.

He told me he spoke seventeen languages, not including the most charming Irish brogue I've ever heard. Listening to him address various waiters in fluent Italian, French, and Spanish, I could believe him about the languages. He had the famous Irish gift for gab and could talk circles around any subject. Many a time I asked him a question and became so enthralled with his answer that it was only hours later I realized he had deliberately not addressed my query. Indeed, he was perhaps the most bald-faced liar I have ever known, yet I always had a sense when he was lying and recognized that his lies were always little ones, even if they were about his identity. In everything that deeply mattered to me and my quest for the devil, I knew him to speak only God's truth.

On our first meeting I made no bones about how my curiosity about possession and exorcism had brought me to him. I told him, "It seems to me that in the cases you wrote about in *Hostage to the Devil* you must have been the exorcist himself, at least in some of them." It was one of those occasions when he managed to divert me with his humor, and I never did hear him directly confess to the correctness of my assumption. It wasn't dishonest exactly; it just wasn't an answer to my question.

On the other hand, I also asked him, "What is the effect on the exorcist of performing an exorcism?" He didn't hesitate a moment before replying, "It will give you greater authority and make you more lonely." It would not be too long before I would learn just how powerful a truth that answer was.

I wondered whether exorcists ever sought psychiatric consultation. He was so enthusiastic he could hardly contain himself, explaining that in cases of suspected possession, priests were literally frantic to obtain competent psychiatric consultation, but usually were unable to do so. A competent psychiatrist in this regard, he noted, needed to at least be open to the possibility of possession. The situation was desperate, he continued, because psychiatrists who were open to the possibility were as rare as hen's teeth. I told him I thought I was open and would be happy to accept such referrals. He seemed most pleased. In my fantasies I imagined I would begin to receive referrals immediately. I did not. In fact, it would be almost two years before I saw my first such case.

During that first lunch I also made mention that I was thinking about becoming baptized, but was dragging my feet for a variety of reasons. He listened intently but otherwise seemed uninterested. Certainly he showed no desire to push me toward baptism.

At the conclusion of that first lunch, walking back to the car, I thought about the man I had just met—of how I did not trust his story about being some sort of special agent in plainclothes for the church; of how he could trick me in other ways; of how obviously brilliant he was; of his small stature yet great presence; and of that wonderful brogue that I could have listened to forever. I came half-seriously to the conclusion that Malachi Martin was a leprechaun.*

---

* Many lands have their "little people." According to myth or legend these "wee folk" are diminutive humanoid beings who in prehistoric times dwelled in the land before it was inhabited by ordinary people. The best known of the world's wee folk are the leprechauns of Ireland. Legend goes that there are not many of them left. Consequently, it is most rare for a human to ever see one,

———◆———

As I was reluctantly moving toward my baptism, I had a number of Catholic and Episcopalian clergy friends who were encouraging me. Idly at first, I mentioned to them my meeting with Malachi. It became immediately apparent that Malachi Martin was no stranger to these people. No, let me take that back, he was a stranger to them, but they all held passionate feelings about him. They told me to stay away from him.

Their judgment from afar was unanimous: Malachi Martin was a man who should not be trusted, a kind of sorcerer who had managed to sneak into the Upper East Side of Manhattan, worse than a wolf in sheep's clothing; in fact, much as they hated to use the word, he was downright evil and probably more possessed by the devil—if there was a devil—than anyone he had written about.

I usually write liars off very quickly. Yet I had a deep sense that Malachi Martin was hardly usual, that he was much more than his lies. I somehow knew the man I had met was neither evil nor dangerous. Initially, I was amazed by the fierce judgment my friends all shared. But over several years, I would realize that at the root of their misperception lay the terror they had—despite all their divinity-school training—of radical evil. It was not really Malachi they vilified; it was their own unacknowledged ignorance and the darker ghosts by which they themselves were haunted.

So I did not take their vilification seriously, and Malachi and

---

but there are occasional reports of sightings and even meetings. The typical leprechaun is a highly ambiguous little person. In a good mood he will be humorous, mischievous, and good company. But more often they seem a bit arrogant and irritable. They have a reputation of being untrustworthy tricksters. Of course we do not believe in the reality of leprechauns, yet few exist who have not heard of them. They are magical beings and most of us are glad that they still stay around.

I continued to dine together every six months or so. It was a strange relationship for me. Normally, I am not a person who left issues unaddressed. To the contrary, when something is obviously being avoided, I am like a dog with a bone, and I won't let go of it. Yet I never challenged Malachi about anything. I didn't ask him if he was aware of how he was vilified by his fellow clergy. I didn't push him to admit that he himself was the exorcist in at least some of the cases he wrote about. I didn't ask him any personal questions at all.

Nor did he pry into my life. I do recall that he hungrily asked me question after question about psychiatry, and I can remember asking him a few technical questions about the diagnosis of possession. One of the things that had impressed me about *Hostage to the Devil* was its conservatism. In it, for instance, Malachi had estimated that out of every one hundred cases in which the diagnosis of possession was somehow raised, no more than one of the hundred would turn out to be the genuine article. "But what about charismatics?" I enquired. "They seem to go around casting out spirits all over the place."

"They're generally just casting out their own fantasies," he said. "But very occasionally, usually by accident, they do catch a real fish."

I think Malachi enjoyed being a man of mystery, and I enjoyed letting him be one. Although I, myself, was usually a blabbermouth, I kept my secrets too. I volunteered myself as a psychiatric consultant, but I never told him why. I never spoke of my two-sided agenda for offering my services.

One side was my desire to prove scientifically that there was no such thing as the devil. If he referred me to enough patients with putative possession and they all had standard psychiatric diagnoses, then I imagined I would obtain my proof. On the other hand, if by some wild chance he did refer a case to me that truly seemed possession, my fantasy was that I would humbly ask him if I could be allowed to witness him perform the exorcism and take my scientific notes without becoming more deeply involved. While I never told him about these fantasies, I imagined even at the time he knew about them already. I also had a sense that when he questioned me about psychiatry that he was, in part, testing me. I always sensed I passed the test. Nonetheless, he still hadn't referred a case to me, but I didn't press him about this either. For some reason we were both being very patient with each other.

Although we both enjoyed each other's company, it was the most distant loving relationship I ever had before or since. None of the common psychodynamics were involved. Despite his attractiveness, I never looked to Malachi to be a father figure, and I never felt he was trying to make a son of me. Then what were we doing?

I think we were working quite hard, so hard there really wasn't room for intimacy. I am sure that Malachi was much more aware of what was going on than I, and I trusted that awareness. In talking about his capacity for unimportant lying, I spoke earlier about how superficially I never trusted him, but on the deepest level I have never trusted anyone more. Certainly I had never put myself so wholeheartedly into another person's hands. The word for "hand" in Latin is *manus,* and from it we get the word "manipulate."

I was dimly aware that I was allowing myself to be thoroughly manipulated by Malachi, and I was strangely confident that the reasons for all this would be revealed to me in good time. But I must admit I had no idea how soon it would be revealed to me or how deep a manipulation it would turn out to be.

———◆———

I mentioned how, even before meeting Malachi, I was struggling with the idea of getting baptized. My baptism represented a death for me on a number of levels, and no one likes to die. I used every rationalization in the book for my foot-dragging. The most effective one was that I couldn't decide whether to be baptized as an Orthodox Christian or a Roman Catholic or an

Episcopalian or a Presbyterian or Lutheran or Methodist or Congregationalist or American Baptist or even a Southern Baptist. This complex denominational decision was obviously going to take me twenty-five or thirty years of research to figure out.

Finally I did realize that it was a rationalization, and that baptism is not a specifically denominational celebration. Consequently, when I was finally drowned, it was by a North Carolina Methodist minister in the chapel of an upstate New York Episcopal convent in a deliberately nondenominational service. I have jealousy guarded my nondenominational status ever since.

I invited Malachi to come up from New York City to witness my baptism, but he had a more important competing obligation for the day (an exorcism, maybe?). I could tell from his voice on the phone he was deeply regretful. It was all of two weeks after my baptism that he referred the first case of putative possession to me for psychiatric evaluation. I found that the patient had a standard sort of psychiatric disorder without a hint of anything else. I proudly carved the first notch on the handle of my scientific pistol to signify the beginning of my accumulation of the final body of scientific evidence that would demonstrate that there was no such thing as demonic possession.

But I also wondered at the timing of this referral. Was it an accident that I had been waiting for two years for Malachi to refer a patient for consultation, but no one was sent until immediately following my baptism? I doubted it. I myself did not believe that my baptism had conferred upon me any magical protection, but I suspect that Malachi did. Like so much else, I never questioned him about the timing. I simply tucked the matter in the back of my mind. However, I did happen to have lunch with Malachi shortly after that referral and used the opportunity to ask him a slightly different question.

"Malachi, you've got this reputation for being a very right-wing archconservative Roman Catholic," I noted. "Why on earth would you want to have anything to do with the likes of me, a baby Christian who is not only not a Catholic, but such a left-wing liberal he won't even formally affiliate himself with any denomination?"

With one of the frequent twinkles in his eyes, he proceeded to teach me something about the religion business. "Those of us in the church," he answered, "often make a distinction between what we call the Church Visible and the Church Invisible. Ever since we first met I have known—even before your baptism—that you were, without question, a member of the Church Invisible."

It felt as if he had given me a benediction. I was not aware at the time that an even stronger and far more awesome blessing was to come.

Within the month he referred a second case to me. It was a man of about my age (forty-three) whose understanding of life was more like that of a five-year-old. I gave him a standard psychiatric diagnosis without finding, even though I looked hard, the slightest sign of anything like possession. With a touch of satisfaction I carved the second notch in the handle of my scientific pistol.

About a month later Malachi sent me yet a third patient, Jersey, a twenty-six-year-old woman. She had that interesting name given to her by her parents because she had been born prematurely in New Jersey while the family was away from their home in the Southwest. Almost against my will, Jersey turned out to be the real thing, an honest-to-God case of possession. In the process of dealing with her over the following year, I learned not only that Malachi Martin was an extremely loving mentor who, on the deepest level, spoke only the truth to me, but also, as far as I could ascertain, that he was the greatest expert on the subject of possession and exorcism in the English-speaking world. Additionally, I learned he was without question the English-speaking world's greatest manipulator.

PART I

Jersey

CHAPTER 1

DIAGNOSIS

———•———

"I feel sorry for them."

Jersey Babcock belonged to two strong, close-knit families living in the same southwestern city. At twenty-one she married Peter Babcock and quickly had two daughters. Peter's several brothers and sisters had migrated elsewhere, but they usually came home for family gatherings. The Babcock family were not exactly atheists, but certainly agnostic and distinctly secular.

Jersey's parents, the Lewises, and her siblings were active Christians, but theirs was a freewheeling brand of Christianity characterized by vagueness and tolerance. Their unspoken motto seemed to be "Live and let live." Their theology ranged across the map. Even if their belief systems were nebulous, it was evident that they all loved one another. The Lewises were a bit more psychologically sophisticated than most because they had a family psychiatrist, Dr. Philip Lieberman. Most of the Lewis family had used his services upon one occasion or another with the exception of Jersey, until the day before this story begins.

Until that day, as far as anyone knew, Jersey was mentally stable. She was a very caring mother to her young daughters. If she had any fascination, it was an interest in all manner of New Age varieties of spiritualism. She spent most of her free time visiting the scores of psychics in her city. This interest in spiritualism—

even in the occult—was nothing new. Her mother remembered Jersey reading all the works of Edgar Cayce the year she was twelve.

On the opening day of this story, Jersey, now twenty-five, went to see Dr. Lieberman for the first time, having made an appointment a week before. She was clear about why she was there. Almost her first words were "I'm possessed." Dr. Lieberman managed to keep his cool and inquired about what she meant, but he made little sense out of her answers. He suggested she might be helped by taking some Thorazine that he could prescribe. She declined that or any medicine. Dr. Lieberman then focused on building a relationship with her. Jersey did come for two more visits, but then quit. Dr. Lieberman had not been able to engage her in therapy.

The next external event in the story occurred six months later. At two o'clock in the morning, Jersey awoke from a terrifying nightmare. Peter tried to comfort her, but Jersey insisted upon calling her mother. Her mother and stepfather came right over, and it was then that Jersey told them all that she was possessed.

The family's response was to ask her to return to see Dr. Lieberman. She agreed. Once again she turned down Dr. Lieberman's offer of medication, and once again he was unable to engage her in therapy.

Mrs. Lewis was particularly concerned: she had noticed that Jersey was no longer attending to her young daughters as well as before. She seemed irritable with them and was requesting an ever-increasing number of baby-sitters so that she might attend psychic meetings. Thinking perhaps she ought to take her daughter's self-diagnosis seriously, Mrs. Lewis wondered where to turn. Although she had had no previous relationship with the Catholic church, she thought that the matter of possession probably was more a Catholic concern than a Protestant one. She called the nearest large Catholic church and explained the situation. Several days later the church sent a young priest to talk with Jersey. Later, he would tell me that Jersey had said something horrible to him—he couldn't remember what—and he had no other recollection of the visit. He did, however, refer Jersey to the diocesan exorcist with the recommendation that her case be taken seriously.

The diocesan exorcist, Father Terry O'Connor, and his assistant came a week later to visit Jersey. After spending four full hours with her and briefly conferring with each other, they told Mrs. Lewis they thought Jersey was indeed possessed, but that she was not yet psychologically ready for an exorcism and should first receive psychotherapy before they could see her again.

Understandably, Mrs. Lewis was dissatisfied with this recommendation. It put Jersey in a classical Catch-22 position, recommending that she be engaged in psychotherapy when, on two prior occasions, she had failed to become a psychotherapeutic candidate. Mrs. Lewis confided her dilemma to a Catholic friend who happened to have read Malachi Martin's *Hostage to the Devil* and suggested that she read it. Mrs. Lewis immediately did so and then, with equal dispatch, wrote to Malachi Martin for help. Malachi asked me if I would fly to the Southwest to evaluate the case. I said I would, and Malachi referred me to Mrs. Lewis to make the necessary arrangements.

When I first arrived, I spoke with Mrs. Lewis to get an account of the family constellation. What I thought would be a brief description turned out to be as complicated as any I had ever encountered. Mrs. Lewis had had four husbands, and her five children had three different fathers. Jersey was the second child.

Mrs. Lewis was married to her first husband, Sean Flannigan, a boat salesman, for six years. She divorced him because of his drinking when Jersey was only a year old and her brother five. Some years later Flannigan died at a relatively early age from his alcoholism.

Mrs. Lewis quickly remarried an independently wealthy clergyman, Caleb Lewis, by whom she had a daughter and son. Jersey and her brother took their new stepfather's name. Jersey had no memories of her biological father. She always thought of herself as a Lewis and referred to her stepfather as her father.

Bored with being a minister, Caleb decided to become a psychologist. After obtaining his Ph.D. in psychology, he soon developed a thriving psychotherapy practice out of his home. For the entirety of her late childhood and early adolescent years, Jersey could remember the stream of patients coming in and out of the house. When practicing, he always wore a long, starched white coat, traditional for physicians but extremely rare for psychologists. His patients respectfully called him "Dr. Lewis." Caleb Lewis died suddenly from a heart attack when Jersey was fifteen. Jersey grieved for him deeply.

Eighteen months after her second husband's death, Mrs. Lewis remarried another independently wealthy man, a mildly successful painter. A year later, they adopted a two-year-old boy. A year after that, the artist left Mrs. Lewis and their child for another woman. Mrs. Lewis quickly sued him for divorce and received a decent settlement without alimony. For the next few years Mrs. Lewis heard rumors that he was bisexual and flagrantly promiscuous. At the time I met her, Mrs. Lewis had no idea where he lived.

Two years after that divorce, Mrs. Lewis married her fourth husband, an engineer named Harry Anderson, but kept the name of her second husband and longest marriage. Harry had been an unusually good stepfather to all five of her children in the years since, Mrs. Lewis said, noting that Jersey adored him. I also got the impression that he was the most deeply religious person in the family, a man who attended church on Sunday without fail. Occasionally, Mrs. Lewis would accompany him. It was obvious to me that theirs was a good and solid marriage.

It took me an hour to obtain Jersey's complicated family history. Psychiatrists are not immune to prejudice. Initially, I imagined Mrs. Lewis might have some personality problem that would account for her many marriages. But I did not find one. To the contrary, by the end of the hour I reached the conclusion that she was a remarkably strong woman, capable of either firmness or flexibility as the occasion required. I judged her to be a fine mother who loved all her children well—a judgment that would be borne out in the months to come.

I then spent close to a half hour with Jersey's husband, Peter Babcock. A successful executive in his late twenties, I also found him to be a strong person, genuinely concerned about his young wife and his baby daughters. Perhaps a bit too strong, he struck me as being an overcontrolling sort of man. But if he was that way with Jersey she never seemed to mind—at least on the surface.

Tired from my flight, I waited until the next morning to speak with Jersey herself. The primary focus of our conversation was her experience with a variety of demons speaking to her, both in her dreams and when awake. The names of those demons seemed to keep changing, as if Jersey were making them up on the spot. Only one of them seemed constant—an entity she called the Lord Josiah.

Superficially, I found Jersey to be pleasant and vivacious, but obviously she was a young lady with psychiatric difficulties. She was slightly flirtatious, remarkably naive, and a bit overdramatic—all of which could suggest a diagnosis of hysteria. But she was also pressured, speaking rapidly with what we psychiatrists call flight of ideas, suggestive of a possible schizophrenic condition, only she had none of the emotional blunting characteristic of schizophrenia. If you take a bit of hysteria and add it to a mere hint of schizophrenia, what you get in psychiatry is a vague but well recognized and common condition called borderline personality disorder.

So after four quite friendly hours with her I had already diagnosed Jersey as a borderline and was in the process of mentally packing my bags and making a third notch in the handle of my scientific pistol, when Jersey blew the whole thing wide open with a single sentence. Referring to her demons, she said, "I feel sorry for them."

"You feel sorry for them?" I echoed, confused.

"Yes," she answered, "they're really rather weak and pathetic creatures."

The reason this stopped me dead in my tracks was that it did not fit with standard psychopathology. It seemed to me that if a young woman—particularly a somewhat hysterical one—had a need to invent demons, she would create great, strong, hairy demons, not weak and pathetic ones.

So I mentally unpacked my bags to explore things more deeply.

"Could I talk to your demons?" I asked.

"Oh, no," Jersey responded. "They would be much too afraid to do that."

I was already in utterly uncharted waters, so why not keep rowing ahead? "Perhaps they would talk to me under hypnosis," I said. "How would you feel about being hypnotized, Jersey?"

"That would be kind of fun," Jersey replied in her childlike manner, more like that of a twelve-year-old than a twenty-six-year-old mother of two. "I've never been hypnotized before. It sounds interesting. How do you go about it?"

I explained to her the standard techniques of inducing hypnosis, and she readily agreed to a session. She proved to be an unusually good hypnotic subject, and within a few minutes was in a deep trance. I then asked once again if I could speak to her demons. This time Jersey said, "Well, there are so many of them, but there are at least a couple in here that really do want to talk to you."

"Let them go ahead," I welcomed.

I cannot now, more than twenty years later, remember their names, and it doesn't matter anyway, as we shall eventually see.

They were both female and did indeed sound weak and pathetic. Each acknowledged that they did things to frighten or otherwise hurt Jersey, but each maintained that if they didn't, their "employer" would hurt them. They began to whimper at their bind and, speaking together now, asked, "Can you help us, Dr. Peck? Won't you try to help us?"

I clearly remember feeling like I was Alice in Wonderland, speaking to these supposed demons with Jersey under hypnosis. In one sense, I did know how to help them. A part of me felt like saying: "As always, your salvation lies in going to the cross by refusing to hurt Jersey. Yes, you then might be hurt, but you will be free, and it's obviously the only way to end this stupid game." Fortunately, through the clutter of my thoughts, my still, small voice told me that the supposed demons were using my tendency to be a compulsive helper to suck me into a place I didn't belong. I simply told them that I had to leave them, and I proceeded to bring Jersey out of her trance. Afterward, she was more lucid and mature than she had been at any time with me throughout the day.

Jersey had looked a little bit schizophrenic, and one of the reasons I was anxious about hypnotizing her was that schizophrenics tend to become more disorganized after hypnosis. Yet Jersey had become better organized. My mindset was beginning to change.

The dilemma the supposed demons complained about—that they would be hurt if they did not hurt Jersey—fit with the little I knew of demonology. The demonic hierarchy is so strict and merciless that lesser demons seem to have negligible freedom. Yet, as far as I could ascertain, Jersey had no knowledge of demonology. At this point, all I could do was tell her and her family that I was very uncertain about the case, and that, after I got home, I would be in further contact with Malachi Martin and probably Dr. Lieberman and Father O'Connor as well. After that, I would get back in touch with them.

As I flew back home that evening, three things came to mind.

One was the expression "poor devil," remembering how under hypnosis the *supposed* demons had whimpered about their predicament. For me there was meaning in the phrase for the first time. The second, remembering how Jersey had seemed more rather than less sane after I had listened to her supposed demons, was the expression "Give the devil his due." Perhaps doing that briefly had allowed the devil to step aside somewhat. Finally, I recalled a brief paragraph from *Hostage to the Devil* where Malachi had noted that an unusual percentage—not all but many—of possessed people had slightly strange faces in which their skin seemed tightly stretched so as to be smooth and relatively lacking in wrinkles. I cursed myself for not recognizing it at the time, but Jersey had just such a face.

When the day began I did not believe there was such a thing as possession. As a psychiatrist I was still in no way ready to pronounce Jersey possessed, but with the list of contradictions Jersey already posed to traditional psychiatry, mountains had been moved in my mind. I knew that when I called Malachi, I would be telling him my assessment was that there was a fifty-fifty chance Jersey was the genuine article and that the case deserved to be delved into more deeply.

———◆———

I did, of course, phone Malachi and recount my observations. I told him that Jersey did not quite fit the standard categories of psychopathology. It was conceivable to me she could be possessed, but I was hardly able to make such a diagnosis without knowing her better. I felt I needed to be more certain before turning the case over to him. He made no response to my intent to give him the case.

I suggested contacting Father O'Connor, the diocesan exorcist, to propose that he and I do some work together on Jersey's case. Indeed, I wanted to clarify for Father O'Connor the Catch-22 situation in which he had placed Jersey and her family and make him accountable for a better resolution. Malachi agreed with my strategy.

When I phoned Father O'Connor, he was perfectly receptive. I explained the extent to which Jersey did not fit the established categories of psychiatric diagnosis, which was why, as a scientific-minded psychiatrist, I thought she might be possessed. I further gave him my opinion that she was not amenable to psychotherapy in her current state and that insisting she get therapy before an exorcism was probably approaching the case backward. My instinct was that she likely required an exorcism before she could meaningfully participate in psychotherapy, though I did volunteer that these were shaky opinions. I couldn't say Jersey was possessed—only that she might be.

Father O'Connor was not threatened by my opinions in the least. I learned that he was unusually sophisticated in psychiatric matters, having spent several years studying psychiatry at a prominent clinic. By the end of the conversation we had not only become colleagues but friends. I called him Terry and he called me Scotty.

Accepting my uncertainty, Terry proposed attempting a deliverance with Jersey. Beyond assuming that a deliverance was a religious, healing process that stopped short of a full-scale exorcism, I knew nothing about the matter. But it was Terry's field of expertise. He had a team of another Christian man and woman with whom he worked, and he customarily did deliverances in a common room at the monastery where he lived, an hour's drive from Jersey's home. He suggested therefore that I return to the Southwest. We both looked at our calendars and came up with a date two months in the future. Terry was thinking in terms of only one day, but the prospect of flying back across the country for a single day didn't sit right with me. I imagined there might be pieces we would need to pick up one way or another. Terry agreed. We set aside two days, and I phoned Jersey and her husband to cement the engagement. At the same time I asked

23

Jersey for the phone number of her family's psychiatrist, Dr. Lieberman.

Dr. Lieberman proved to be a remarkable man. Typical of most psychiatrists, he was himself thoroughly secular, yet he had no problem working with us religious folk. After all, he acknowledged that his own approach with Jersey had twice failed. I asked him if he would arrange for Jersey to be psychologically tested before I came out for the deliverance. I also asked him if he could arrange for this testing under unusual circumstances. Most psychologists will insist upon having a history on the patient before they will do testing. In this case, however, I requested that the psychologist do the testing blind—that is, without any knowledge of why the patient was being tested. Dr. Lieberman thought that he could meet these unusual requirements, and so he did. It was to be but the first of a number of ways he would eventually make the rough places plain for everyone.

———◆———

When I returned to the Southwest two months later, Jersey superficially seemed the same. Her husband and mother told me, however, that her behavior appeared to be deteriorating. She was not only attending spiritualist events with even greater frequency, but in order to do so, she had begun to leave her two daughters—an infant and a toddler—unattended. Her husband and mother had chastised her for this neglect, but nothing changed her behavior.

I received the psychologist's evaluation of Jersey. Three things in the report were quite striking. First, the tests showed no abnormality whatsoever. Jersey's functioning on the tests was remarkably even. Such evenness, particularly on the intelligence test, is a strong indication of psychological health. Second, the intelligence test showed Jersey to have a full-scale IQ of 99. This essentially meant that 51 percent of the population was brighter than she was and 49 percent less bright. She could hardly have been more average. Third, the psychologist noted that throughout the testing there were frequent, split-second moments when Jersey's attention seemed to wander as if she had suddenly absented herself. He added that he had seen something similar in patients with petit mal epilepsy, but he did not think that such epilepsy was the cause of Jersey's lapses. He had no explanation to offer.

With this information in hand, Mrs. Lewis drove us out to the monastery where we were all introduced to Terry and his two associates, a man and a woman. Mrs. Lewis was shown to a waiting room and was told that we had no idea how long we would be with Jersey. She accepted this, as she did virtually everything, with a graceful equanimity. She too was to make the rough places plain. The others of us then went to the common room that served as Terry's deliverance place.

Terry explained to Jersey that there was no need for her to feel threatened; while we might talk to her occasionally, mostly we would simply pray and the man on Terry's team would also quietly strum a guitar and hum. And this we did for an hour, during which nothing happened. We had no intuitions, no insights, and no response to our prayers whatsoever.

At the end of this hour, Terry said to me that the deliverance was not working. He then made a bizarre suggestion. I had told him that Jersey was an excellent hypnotic subject and that I had talked with her supposed demons under hypnosis. Since we seemed to be getting nowhere through the usual means, he wondered how I would feel about hypnotizing Jersey and then proceeding with the deliverance while she was in a trance. This was utterly uncharted territory for me, and I would not have consented had Terry not said, with considerable authority, that he thought it would be safe. I remembered his years studying psychiatry at the clinic.

Uneasily, I hypnotized Jersey as before, and we began the deliverance all over again, only this time with some response. We talked with supposed demons, as I had with Jersey under hypnosis two months previously. They seemed apologetic for taking up our time and willing to take us deeper into their world. We turned the invitation down. Mostly we prayed. As we did, all four of us—Terry, his two assistants, and I—began to get increasingly strong feelings of a possible demonic presence in the room. As Terry's colleague gently strummed his guitar, this feeling became stronger. We then began to sense God's presence. We were encouraged, almost to the point of exhilaration. After an hour, we felt sure we were on the verge of a major breakthrough. The pace and loudness of the strumming guitar increased. It seemed as if success (however that might be defined) was no more than a minute away.

Then everything stopped. We no longer had any feeling of a presence in the room, demonic or holy. We were no longer on the verge of anything at all. It was as if we had collectively blown up a beautiful balloon, and then someone had come along with a needle and popped it. Everything just shriveled.

Terry and I agreed that we had failed once again, and I brought Jersey out of hypnosis. She seemed fine. Terry and I also agreed that we needed to talk alone. He dismissed his two colleagues and took Jersey out to the waiting room so she could be with her mother while we conferred.

Terry and I then spoke of how extraordinarily deflating the experience had been. I said I did not think it was an accident. Somehow I felt that Jersey had engineered this deflation. "I think she was toying with us, Terry," I commented.

Terry agreed it was possible that either Jersey or the supposed demons had been toying with us, but he expressed his bewilderment about how to proceed. Having no previous experience in these matters, I was just as bewildered. Praying out loud now, we both told God of our confusion. God's only answer was a feeling inside me that became ever more strong. It was a feeling akin to guilt, and the guilt was intertwined with a feeling of incompleteness. There was something I had left undone. As I thought (or prayed), it became clearer to me exactly what it was, how my visit was obviously incomplete.

"You know, Terry," I said, "I have never confronted Jersey. I have always been the sympathetic listener and never her critic. I've been gentle, gentle, gentle. She talks as if she were a loving mother, but the fact is that she is behaving ever more selfishly to the point of being guilty of child neglect, if not abuse. I wonder if it isn't the time for some tough love? But I am afraid to confront her alone. I do think she may well be possessed, but this is a whole new world for me. What would make me much more comfortable—yes, it feels really right—is if we could confront her together. Would you be willing to do this with me?"

Terry said that he would, even though he did not hold out much hope. It was mostly like a favor he was doing for me, but his extensive psychiatric training helped him to acknowledge that there might be some point to it. He agreed to spend the next afternoon in the same room with Jersey and me, without his colleagues. It would not be a religious event, as we thought of it. It would simply be a time that we got tough with Jersey.

———◆———

It was not difficult to get tough with Jersey the next afternoon. Terry and I took turns, each "punching" her, so to speak—trying to get her to admit her multiple faults. We told her how immature we thought she was; how she was an increasingly inadequate mother; how she was ignoring her husband and children in favor of spiritualist groups; how what was being taught at these groups was egregiously false; how she was naive and being taken in; how she blandly ignored all criticism from her husband and parents; how she demonstrated an extremely high opinion of herself with nothing to back it up. It went on this way for an hour. Jersey appeared totally unfazed by the onslaught. All our efforts were like water off a duck's back. Then, during the second hour, everything changed.

Terry had been trying to point out to her that she was acting as if she was extremely intelligent, even though there was no indication she was. Jersey responded, "It's you who are not bright enough to understand me. The truth is that I am brilliant."

"But that's not what your psychological tests demonstrated," I said. "They showed your intelligence to be only average at best."

Jersey looked visibly upset. "What do you mean they called me average?" she demanded.

Out of the folder I had assembled on her, I pulled out the psychologist's report and opened it to the relevant page. "It says here," I replied, "that you have a full-scale IQ of ninety-nine. The average score is one hundred, so it means that while just about half the population is less intelligent than you, it also means that half the people in this country are more intelligent than you."

The words were hardly out of my mouth when Jersey reached over and grabbed the test report off my lap. She could not miss the numbers printed there. After a few seconds, she threw the report to the floor at my feet. Then she began to speak extremely rapidly in words that made no sense whatsoever. Indeed, much of her speech seemed to be words she had just made up. As she spewed out all this nonsense at the rate of a .60-caliber machine gun, she also began to make a variety of compulsive, peculiar gestures with her hands, yet she did so without any expression or discernible emotion—a manner that psychiatrists call flatness of affect. There was now no doubt in my mind about her diagnosis: she was in an acute schizophrenic break. Indeed, I had seldom seen a case of schizophrenia so dramatically clear. And genuine. There was no sign of faking. I cursed myself inwardly as a terrible psychiatrist for making the mistake of confronting her so harshly that I had driven her into an obvious psychosis.

But then something strange happened in my own mind. I saw things with a bizarre clarity. Suddenly Jersey's psychosis, which looked so real, struck me as an act, and I blurted out something I would never have said in another similar situation. With an authority that seemed to come from someplace else, I snapped, "Jersey, cut it out! You're not schizophrenic. I don't buy it."

What happened next literally took our breath away.

Jersey snapped out of her schizophrenic psychotic breakdown as instantly as she had entered it. Her face steadily changed from one lacking emotion to one filled with the signs of emotion—but they were not nice emotions. A smile came to her face, only it was not a friendly smile, and her eyebrows lifted in scorn. The one word best describing the face was "haughty." I had never seen a human being look so haughty.

Her speech changed with equal suddenness. No longer incomprehensibly rapid and nonsensical, she began to speak with an unusual, slow deliberation.

"Well, you are right about some things, and you are wrong about some things. You are wrong about my intelligence. The truth is that I am one of the most brilliant beings on this planet. You have also been wrong when you have tried to portray me as emotionally immature, naive, and irresponsible. You just haven't gotten it, have you? The reality is that I am a saint. In fact, a great saint, and you have failed to recognize this.

"But you have been right about one thing," Jersey continued with slow, icy precision. "You have been right when you have accused me of cooperating with my demons. Oh yes, how I cooperate! In fact, the Lord Josiah is my lover. Not only that, but he and I will be meeting tonight." And now Jersey turned specifically to me. "Wouldn't you like to come along, Dr. Peck? We play together. You and I and the Lord Josiah could have a lot of fun with each other. Why don't you come along, Dr. Peck?"

The only thing I knew at this point was that I wanted nothing to do with this Lord Josiah, and certainly not in the way suggested. Otherwise, I was at a loss, and Terry seemed likewise. It occurred to both of us that this extraordinarily arrogant being might not be Jersey herself, but rather a demon. But whenever we asked it its name, it answered "Jersey." And whenever we asked Jersey whether there was a demon present, she informed us that it was only her in the room and that we were talking to the real Jersey. Terry and I were utterly confused and getting nowhere. The only thing we could do was pray.

We did not even know whether Jersey would have to leave the monastery in the form of this malignant personage. However, as we prayed, gradually the smirking expression left her face and she returned to being the normal Jersey, as we knew her: giggly and flirtatious, childlike and childish both, but not an immediate worry.

She was, however, a worry for us in the long term. We were so confused by her behavior that we still did not know whether she was possessed. Unfortunately, I was leaving that night to fly back to Connecticut, and we felt it our responsibility to somehow advise her family how to treat her. Just as we had decided to confront her that afternoon, we advised that her husband and parents should also be more confrontational. In retrospect, I believe neither of us was thinking with clarity, but instead was responding antagonistically to the unbelievably arrogant personality we had just encountered. In any case, we advised Mrs. Lewis that the family should be more firm with Jersey, requiring that she attend to her children and not providing her with all the pocket money she requested, as they had been doing up until then. Mrs. Lewis understood the rationale for our advice and promised that they would follow it. Terry and I promised to keep in touch. Mrs. Lewis and Jersey then drove me to the airport to catch my flight back east. During the drive we were largely silent, since I remained too confused to make coherent conversation. I had several drinks on the airplane, but they failed to clear my confusion. All I could think about was my need to talk to Malachi Martin, as soon as I possibly could, to tell him what had transpired.

Up until that point, Malachi had always been difficult to reach. As I mentioned, he had a whole series of phone answering services designed to keep people away. But eventually my messages would get through, and he would always get back to me within a week. This time he was back to me within half a day. I told him in full detail about my two days of work with Jersey. When I reached the point where Jersey became so arrogant, proclaiming both her brilliance and sainthood and acknowledging her cooperation with the Lord Josiah, Malachi simply said, "That was when the exorcism should have begun."

"You mean," I asked, "that she was in a demonic state at that point?"

"If not, very close to it. You had pretty much flushed her out."

"We kept asking her whether we were talking to a demon," I said, "but she consistently maintained it was herself, the real Jersey."

"Ahh," Malachi countered, "that was just a lie. That was the demon lying to you. It's what we call the Pretense."

Malachi's assessment rang so utterly true there was now almost no doubt in my mind that Jersey was possessed. I told Malachi so and asked, "What do you want me to do now? How do you want me to turn her over to you?"

"Ooh, auch, I'm afraid that won't be possible," Malachi pronounced.

"What do you mean?" I questioned in dawning horror.

"Weell," Malachi explained, "I've been having this terrible trouble with my eyes, you see. They call it a detached retina. It's all related to stress, and they've told me that I'm to avoid all stress for the next year, so I'm afraid there's no way at all that I could take her on as a case."

"Then give me the name of another exorcist," I retorted with a touch of anger in my voice.

"Auch, I'm afraid I can't do that either," Malachi responded.

"What do you mean you can't? Why can't you?"

"I'm afraid I just don't know any other exorcists," Malachi answered. "At least none who would be able to handle a case such as this. You have to realize exorcists don't just grow on trees, and they work alone. Oh, when they do an exorcism, they assemble a team to help them, but basically they operate alone. There's not exactly a directory of them, you know."

"But what do you want me to do?" I asked.

Malachi answered, "It seems obvious to me that you should take the matter up with that fellow you've been working with, Father O'Connor. After all, he's the diocesan exorcist."

I told Malachi I was quite sure I would be back to him at some point and hung up the phone, not only with annoyance, but also with the beginnings of a knot of fear in my abdomen.

I was starting to get a sense of the game. Although in the five cases of possession in his book *Hostage to the Devil* Malachi had never suggested that he himself was the exorcist, I had essentially known that he was. I was also quite sure that on this afternoon he was lying to me about his eyes. But what an effective lie! I did not feel I could accuse him of lying or demand to speak to his ophthalmologist or even say I doubted he had a detached retina. I also understood why he was lying. It was setup. He was trying to set me up to be the exorcist in the case myself. My fantasy of being a detached observer of a master exorcist at work was rapidly collapsing. It occurred to me that there might be only one master exorcist—Malachi. I was quite sure he was lying about his eyes, but I was equally sure he was telling the truth when he said there was no directory of exorcists. He genuinely had been alone in his work. Given the truth of this, it only made sense that he would want to suck me in—trick me, if you will—into being an exorcist. He desperately needed any exorcist to replace him, if he could find anyone stupid enough to take on the job. Yes, I had begun to realize the lay of the land but I was damned if I was going to be a foil. Surely I could find a way out of the snare that Malachi had set for me.

Indeed, Malachi himself had suggested my obvious first move. That evening I phoned Terry and told him of Malachi's assessment. Terry said that, after reflecting, he had come to the same conclusion as Malachi, and that we had a foursquare case of genuine possession on our hands.

"Probably true," I said, "but she's really more on your hands than mine. You're the exorcist."

"No," Terry replied. "It is true that my title is that of diocesan exorcist, but I have never done an exorcism or dealt before with a case of full-scale possession. Oh, yes, I have done dozens of deliverances, but a deliverance is a gentle procedure with a patient under mild demonic attack. If that. Jersey does not need a deliverance. She needs an exorcism, and I am sorry if my title has made me work under false pretenses with you, Scotty. I will be of whatever help to you I can, but I do not have the skill or knowledge to take Jersey's case further than I already have. And, though I am utterly convinced that she is possessed, I do not feel called to even be part of an exorcism team. Strangely, a gut instinct I trust is telling me that I would be harmed."

Unlike my reaction to Malachi, I did not doubt Terry's honesty. After all, when Jersey had suddenly transformed personalities, he'd been every bit as confused as I. Still, he ought to at least have some connections, shouldn't he?

"Is there any way you can help me find an exorcist in some other diocese? Any diocese? All I need is just one honest-to-God exorcist somewhere!" I begged.

"I don't know of one," Terry said. "The only thing I can do is to write to the archbishop of Connecticut with a request from my bishop to give you every possible assistance."

He continued to agree to serve as a phone consultant on the case, if that would be helpful. "I know you're in a lonely place right now," he added.

As promised, Terry did write to the archbishop of Connecticut in Hartford, stating, "Dr. Peck of your state, an experienced psychiatrist, has diagnosed a case of true possession in our diocese. I have enough experience in such matters to be certain of the diagnosis, but I myself am constitutionally unqualified to conduct a combative exorcism. My bishop joins me in asking that you offer Dr. Peck any possible assistance available to you." He then went on to provide the archbishop with my full name, address, and phone number and annotated the letter with the indication he was sending me a copy.

After I received the copy of Terry's letter, I waited a week to give the archbishop or his staff the time to contact me. When he failed to do so I called the archbishop's office. His secretary told me the archbishop was out and she had no knowledge of the matter. I requested she bring the matter to his attention so that he or someone on his staff could get back to me. I repeated this interaction three times in two weeks with the same result. The secretary repeatedly denied ever seeing Terry's letter. No one got back to me. I knew enough about the way the Catholic church was avoiding any involvement in exorcisms during those years to realize there was no point in trying to press the matter further. As was routine in other dioceses, the matter seemed to be closed, as far as the Catholic church in Connecticut was concerned.

———◆———

Meanwhile, I heard from Jersey's husband that using tough love with her, as Terry and I had suggested, had not succeeded. After two days of not being given the money she asked for, she stole all the money from his wallet and ran away. Peter Babcock sounded quite angry with me, and I could tell he was questioning my competence. He took the time, however, to complete the story. She had called home frequently, asking about him and the children, though no one knew where she had run to. She did not seem bothered in the least that she had left Peter the total responsibility for the children. She sounded quite cheerful and expressed no intent to return home. However, the night before our phone call, she called, sobbing, to say that she had just swallowed a bottle of lye. She gave her address at that point, and an ambulance was dispatched to take her to the emergency room of the hospital Dr. Lieberman used. He admitted her to the hospital's psychiatry service with the diagnosis of schizophrenia.

I called Dr. Lieberman the next day and, as before, he was as cooperative as he could conceivably be. I told him that I was in a rather desperate time crunch. As of yet, I had been unable to find an exorcist. I imagined that it might take me as long as a month to find one, and even then I would need at least a week to prepare Jersey for the exorcism.

Dr. Lieberman told me he was authorized to hold any patient of his in the psychiatry unit for up to two months. Beyond that he would start running into problems with the administration. Like most psychiatry units in general hospitals, it was a more or less open ward. If Jersey became unmanageable, he could, by a process of certification, have Jersey moved to the locked ward of the nearest state psychiatric hospital—an unpleasant option, but an option nonetheless. I asked Dr. Lieberman whether I could fly back and prepare Jersey for exorcism at the hospital, assuming I could find an exorcist within the month, even though I did not have privileges at the hospital. He said that he and other doctors on the staff were free to call in outside consultants whenever they desired—no problem. I thanked him and told him I would be back in touch as soon as I had any more information. Hanging up the phone, I offered a quick prayer of gratitude that Philip Lieberman was such a flexible man and physician.

While Dr. Lieberman was so helpful, the rest of the world was not. In the month that followed, I ran up a four-thousand-dollar phone bill scouring the nation for a suitable exorcist. One of the first people I tried was a monk who was quite famous throughout the country as an exorcist, living just across the border in New York State. He told me, "You know, it's funny. My bishop and his priests refer to me anyone who seems conceivably possessed, yet when the bishop is asked whether the diocese has an exorcist he will say, 'No, we have no exorcist in this diocese.' I have, with the help of others and with the bishop's blessing, performed two real exorcisms over here, but if I asked my bishop I can tell you that there is no way he would allow your patient—who isn't a Catholic anyway—to be moved to this diocese and also no way that he would ever allow me to perform an exorcism in Connecticut, a foreign diocese, so to speak, even though it is just across the state line. I understand your predicament. I have talked with others in the same predicament and I am truly sorry; there is nothing I can do to help you."

Most of my other leads were dead ends. The people were simply not qualified. I contacted a famous Presbyterian minister who assured me that he had performed exorcisms. I drove to see him. He was an obviously competent and charismatic clergyman. After hearing my most condensed version of Jersey's predicament he told me he could set aside an afternoon to come up to Connecticut to perform a four-hour exorcism. He was a good man, but his offer seemed laughable. Terry O'Connor and I had already spent eight hours with Jersey and succeeded only in getting to a place of beginning. I told the good man this and said that I had a rather clear sense from somewhere—perhaps the Holy Spirit—that this exorcism would take not four hours but four days. The man replied quite honestly that he was a "big church" pastor and there was no way that he could devote four days to any case.

It seemed I had my best luck when I contacted an Assembly of God pastor out in Colorado whose name I had uncovered in the process of my search. We talked on the phone for a good hour; having heard my story, he opined that Jersey's possession was unquestionable and then went on with precision to list his credentials and requirements. He was not only an exorcist, but specialized in the exorcism of patients whose possession was related to their membership in New Age organizations or cults. I could tell without any question that this man had performed many exorcisms successfully, and Jersey's case fell squarely into his specialty. My spirits rose and reverberated through my chest. The pastor then stated that one of his prerequisites was that the patient's husband be a major member of the exorcism team. I asked him why and he explained it was because a wife's duty was to obey her husband. Naturally a part of the exorcism should be to clarify and cement her obedience, which could best be done with him present. I felt my spirits shrink inside my chest. Although I did not see it as the cause of her possession at all, my impression of Jersey's husband had been that of a man who was probably overcontrolling. If correct, then it would be a significant dynamic in terms of the management of the exorcism itself and, even more important, Jersey's follow-up. As much as the pastor was experienced, I could not countenance the proposal of Peter Babcock being actually present at his wife's exorcism.

There were others far less suitable whom I contacted, and I grew more desperate by the day. Each week I would call Malachi to tell him I could not find an exorcist and to beg for his help. He kept telling me he knew no one. Then, at the end of the month, he called, having found me an exorcist who had had some slight experience with demonic possession and was a bishop to boot. He served one of the several small denominations that had split from the Episcopal church in protest against the main church's increasing liberalism.

I called Bishop Edward Worthington immediately and we spoke at length. Although much more a conservative or fundamentalist than I am, I liked him. I sensed he had a good heart. He did indeed believe in demonic possession, and while he had never performed an exorcism before, he had witnessed one. He seemed undaunted at the prospect of being an exorcist and volunteered to come to Connecticut at his own expense for as long as it might take. I was struck by his courage and simple faith, but I also gathered that his knowledge of psychology was negligible. I told him that if he didn't mind I would like to think about his generous offer and call him back the next day. That was fine with him.

So began one of the most difficult nights of my life. I had to act quickly. Like all patients facing an exorcism, Jersey was deteriorating as the time grew closer. From Dr. Lieberman's reports I surmised that we had no more than another month's leeway. I felt that Bishop Worthington's simple faith was badly needed, but that he was not smart enough to be the exorcist, the captain of the exorcism team. Who then? My own name kept coming to mind. Was I crazy? Baptized for less than a year with no formal theological training? Yet something kept calling me to be the primary exorcist, even though I felt certain that Bishop Worthington was being called as well. As the night progressed I began seriously to consider taking on the role of the exorcist with Bishop Worthington as my assistant. Was this a calling from the Holy Spirit or my own arrogance? I did not know. Where did I, a baby Christian, come off in asking a bishop to play second fiddle to me? Finally, however, I felt it was the path I had to follow, and giving the matter up to God, I managed to fall asleep.

With great trepidation I phoned the bishop the next morning. I told him straight out that the demonic in Jersey was very clever and I did not think that he had the necessary psychological knowledge to manage the case. I said that I had decided over the night, scared though I was, that I was willing to be the exorcist on the condition that he be my first assistant. To my amazement Bishop Worthington immediately replied, "Of course. When do you want me to be there?" We began the process of setting the date for approximately a month later.

It was much easier for me to invite the other five members of the team, each of whom were friends with special skills. Much more difficult was to find a place. Given the fact that our children were under foot, my own home was out. I called a convent and two monasteries, but they predictably wanted no part of it. It seemed as if there was no place anywhere willing to offer Jersey sanctuary—even if it was but a single, simple room for healing. Finally, I asked a good Christian lady I knew if we could use her house, although it would mean sending her young son to stay with his grandmother.

"Sure," she answered. "No problem." I broke into tears of relief and gratitude. Additionally I had now gained another valuable member of the exorcism team.

All that was left was to prepare Jersey for the exorcism. As promised, Dr. Lieberman was willing to bring me into his hospital under the guise of consultant. I flew back to the Southwest for a week, to spend three hours a day with Jersey, not only to prepare her for the exorcism, but also to learn more about her. Two things were remarkable about that week.

Within ten minutes of my seeing her again, Jersey demanded an immediate release from the hospital. Dr. Lieberman and I had prepared for such an event. I told Jersey that in both my and Dr. Lieberman's opinion, she was too sick to leave the hospital. I acknowledged that it was a voluntary hospital, but informed her that I had the authority to keep her there until Dr. Lieberman came, at which time he would sign the papers I'd prepared to commit her to the involuntary locked ward of the nearest state hospital.

The same supercilious sneer that I'd seen after the failed deliverance with Father O'Connor appeared on her face, and she began shouting in a penetrating voice that I did not have the right to do this to her. I tried my best to ignore her, but my hands were shaking from her rage as I filled out the commitment forms for Dr. Lieberman. When I finished the forms Jersey grabbed them from me and, halfway through reading them, simply tore them up, throwing the pieces on the floor. I managed to instruct her to go to her room so that I could fill out the papers again, only this time at the nurses' station.

Instead, Jersey screamed obscenities at me for another two

minutes before trouncing out of the office. It felt more like two hours. As she screamed at me she was also smiling. Grinning. Intellectually, I knew that she was actually enjoying the whole interaction; it was just a game for her. Nonetheless, my guts felt as if they had been twisted and then kicked. It was all I could do to walk to the nurses' station. Never before had I become so upset, almost to the point of incapacity, in response to a patient. Particularly not to one playing a game with me and enjoying it so immensely. I knew by then she was not Jersey but a demon. But the knowledge did nothing to prevent my insides from being raked by its pretended anger. It was a moment of Clash, a phenomenon Malachi's book had warned me about.

Fortunately, our lengthy daily visits together were quite peaceful thereafter. Jersey was incapable of participating in any kind of psychotherapy, but she was quite happy with my attention, whether in the form of questions or teaching. During my next to last day with her, still doing what I could to prepare her, I asked her to tell me about Jesus. In her flaky way, she drew a cross on a piece of paper and proceeded to add three circles to each of the cross's four limbs. With the seeming authority of a theologian, she pointed to these circles and explained, "There are three Jesuses on this part and three Jesuses down at the bottom part and three Jesuses on each side of the crossbar."

Attempting to bring her back to earth, I said, "Cut out that crap, Jersey. How did he die?"

"He was crucified," she correctly answered in a strangely bland way.

Knowing her by then to be a pain-avoider par excellence, something prompted me to inquire, "Did it hurt?"

"Oh, no, not at all," Jersey responded.

"What do you mean it didn't hurt?" I demanded. "With his feet being nailed together and his whole body in spasm?"

"Oh," Jersey informed me, "he was just so advanced in his Christ consciousness that he was able to project himself into his astral body and take off from there."

That night I called Terry O'Connor at his monastery to consult with him, and because it had been such a bizarre New Age type of answer I told Terry about it. No sooner had I finished doing so than Terry said, "Oh, that's Docetism."

"What the hell is Docetism?" I asked.

Terry patiently explained to me that it was one of the early church heresies where a substantial number of Christians believed that Jesus was totally divine and his humanity just an appearance. "So you see," Terry continued, "the Docetists believed that being divine, Jesus had no need to experience any pain and, like Jersey, they believed that His apparent suffering on the cross was nothing but a divine charade and celestial sham. It is a heresy because it obviously undermines the whole notion of sacrifice that is at the center of Christianity."

Until that evening I had never given a serious thought to heresy, believing it was a creation of the Inquisition and an obsolete concept to the modern world. Thanks to Terry, I could see how Jersey's nutty interpretation obviously sabotaged the very essence of Christian doctrine. Still, I gave the notion of heresy no greater heed than recognizing it in this single instance. It would not be long, however, before I realized that Jersey would prove to be a walking textbook of heresies and I would come to understand that the problem of heresy was not something that belonged in the Middle Ages, but rather something that bedeviled almost all of humanity in our postmodern world.

In the afternoons following my sessions with Jersey I spoke to her family, helping them to make their own arrangements to bring Jersey to Connecticut the moment Dr. Lieberman released her. Then I left for Connecticut myself to make the final arrangements with the other six people I had gathered as a team: a psychologist who knew how to videotape, a nun, a retired physician, Bishop Worthington of course, and the gracious woman whose house we would be using. There was also an old friend of the Lewises who would serve as the family representative.

I somehow felt certain that the exorcism would take the seven of us four days to accomplish. While Jersey's husband and mother would accompany her to Connecticut the day before the exorcism, they would not be participants but caretakers during the evenings. After the exorcism, it was planned that Peter Babcock would immediately return home to his work, but Jersey's mother would stay on to play the role of both mother and nurse for three weeks, during which time I would provide Jersey with the most concentrated psychotherapy possible.

During the final two weeks preceding the exorcism, several things are noteworthy. Both Dr. Lieberman and I had advised Jersey to keep quiet about her diagnosis of possession and about the exorcism to come because the other patients and the hospital ward staff were not likely to approve. But that was really too much to ask of Jersey. As would any other human being, the closer the exorcism approached the more Jersey needed to talk about it. For the final week of her hospitalization what was about to happen with Jersey became common knowledge on the ward.

The other thing that occurred was that my mother unexpectedly died right after I got back from the Southwest. She was in the hospital at the time, but scheduled for discharge the next morning. I was actually talking with her on the phone when she suddenly said that she had a terrible toothache and would have to call me back later. As a physician it crossed my mind that jaw pain might be caused by a heart attack. She did not call back, but after thirty minutes my father called to tell me that she had died.

Five days later the phone rang and it was Malachi calling to check up on my spiritual health, knowing that the exorcism was less than a week away. I told him, "I'm doing fine, Malachi. The only thing is that my mother died last week."

"Oooh," said Malachi, "I'm sorry to hear that your mimmy died."

"I'm not sorry," I told him, letting him know that my mother had been ill for many unhappy years, and I was actually glad she had finally gotten her dying over with. "The only thing that bothers me, Malachi," I said to him, "was that she had to die alone. I wish I could have been there with her."

"Oooh, I know how you feel," Malachi responded, "but we never really die alone. There are hundreds there, no, thousands; they come from all oover."

As a scientist, I did not fancy what Malachi had said. After all, he was an Irishman who probably believed in leprechauns and therefore was certainly not above believing in the occurrences of such things at the moment of death. Nonetheless, I found this expression of his Irish mysticism to be strangely consoling.

———◆———

On the first of April (April Fools' Day no less) everyone assembled in Connecticut as planned. Jersey had been discharged by Dr. Lieberman from the hospital the previous afternoon, and with her husband, mother, and stepfather, flew in from the Southwest. They stayed at a nearby hotel, as did Bishop Worthington and the Lewis family friend—both of whom flew in at their own expense. The other members of the team lived in the area. All of us met at the home of the woman who had so freely offered her house for our purposes. The attention was first focused on Jersey and her family as we went over the elaborate permission forms I had prepared for their signatures. I was grateful for my medical training, which included learning about such forms. Although they had a few questions, Jersey and her family seemed to be satisfied with my answers and signed permission for virtually everything. They signed permission for the exorcism to be videotaped. They also gave permission for Jersey to be restrained if necessary during the exorcism; they acknowledged the possibility the exorcism might fail, leaving her no better off than before; that it might even make her worse; indeed that, although unlikely, she could conceivably even die in the process; and they relieved me and the other members of the team of any possible liability for such outcomes.

The form-signing ritual enabled Jersey, her family, and the team members to get acquainted. It also instructed the team about the various conditions of permission. Once the forms were signed, Jersey and her family left early to be well rested for the morning. The rest of us—the team—stayed another hour for discussion, prayer, and team building. But only an hour. We also needed to be well rested, utterly unsure of the depths of the ordeal we would be facing in the course of the next four days. The stage was set. Strangely—blessedly—we all slept well.

CHAPTER 2

EXORCISM

"We don't hate Jesus; we just . . ."

Day 1

Jersey's family dropped her off a few minutes before 9:00 A.M. and returned to their hotel with the arrangement that someone always be available by phone should we need to call. Then, the team and Jersey went quickly to work. We worked in sessions of approximately ninety minutes each. Bishop Worthington began each session by lighting a candle and offering a brief prayer. After that I would address Jersey with a standard set of phrases adopted directly from Malachi's book: "Jersey, child of God, in the name of God who created you and of Jesus Christ who died for you, I order you to hear my voice as the voice of Christ's church and, though I am but a humble and unworthy servant, to obey my commands."

This opening ritual for each session achieved nothing that we could see. In fact the next eleven hours were, to all intents and purposes, a total waste of time. Yes, we prayed a lot, but it certainly did nothing to keep Jersey from talking to us with her customary, unceasingly meaningless chatter, which was somewhere between speech and nonsensical gibberish. This was hardly surprising, since we didn't have the foggiest idea of what we were doing. During those first five ninety-minute sessions we learned only two things. One was that we became ever more certain that we were dealing with the demonic. The other was that Jersey's demons were hiding one way or another behind Jesus. Unlike any account of an exorcism I had read, Jersey would frequently address Bishop Worthington, saying, "Sprinkle me with some more holy water. I want some more holy water. The Jesus in me is thirsty." At first Bishop Worthington obliged her, but soon we understood she was toying with us. Finally, after a brief dinner and having concluded that we had gotten nowhere, in tired desperation to accomplish something, we used the sixth session to run through the entire Roman Catholic rite of exorcism, a rather lengthy affair of many pages. It read like a holy and most powerful rite, but during it Jersey simply zoned out into some private place. I don't believe she heard a word. Anyway, it didn't work. We phoned for her to be taken back to her hotel.

When Jersey left we met as a team, acknowledging our failure. We were obviously doing something wrong or else nothing right. Day 1 clearly belonged to Jersey and her demons. Perhaps by the Holy Spirit's doing, we decided to begin the next day with a different approach. Or maybe we were so tired of her gibberish that we could no longer listen to it. Instead, we decided to speak only with demons on the one hand or a healthy Jersey who made sense on the other. Thereafter we disbanded, having no awareness of the brilliance of the change we had decided upon.

Day 2

Jersey spent the entire morning in a rage when she realized the new rules we had set for the game. She swore at us with language so filthy that it upset the good bishop, but we knew that it was Jersey using such language, and not any obvious demon. The only things we said during the entire morning were to repeat twice a session the fact that we would listen to real demons or only to the true, healthy Jersey, and that we would continue not to listen to anything in between.

After lunch it became clear the strategy had started to work. Now Jersey began increasingly to alternate between periods of speaking like a healthy, even slightly holy adult and periods where she was ever more nasty, vicious, and hateful. One of the other team members, the nun, made it clear to me that we were on the right track. She identified what was happening in Jersey—and what we were encouraging—as an ever-increasing process of separation. We all recognized the truth of this and, tired from the day before, we broke this time before dinner without feeling we needed to attempt more than what we already had.

Day 3

We continued to refuse to listen to or address Jersey's gibberish and to remind her that we would speak only with the healthy part of her or with clear demons. Through the morning the process we identified as separation became ever deeper. Although there had not yet been any great fireworks, we broke for lunch feeling strangely calm about what would happen.

In the first session after lunch Jersey quickly began to speak in a touchingly realistic way about her possession. "I've been possessed for fifteen years now," she said, "and all that time it is as if nothing happened to me, as if I hadn't even lived. I know I'm supposed to be twenty-seven, but the reality is that I am still twelve years old. I have two children but I know nothing about being a mother. I know nothing about being a wife. I'm just twelve years old. How can I be expected to raise my two children or be a wife? Don't you see? It's hopeless."

This was the most real Jersey had yet been, and we told her so. We told her it was not an imaginary problem but the actual position she was in. We said the only way she could make it would be with a great deal of help, and we outlined one by one the specific ways in which she could be supported. I explained again how immediately after the exorcism she would see me for approximately three weeks of intensive psychotherapy—a period when she would not have the responsibility of a wife and mother—and when back home, she could see a psychiatrist of her choice as frequently as she desired. Jersey immediately elected Dr. Lieberman, even though he had failed to help her twice in the past. It was a wise choice I knew, thinking of the man's extraordinary flexibility. We then went through a whole number of other kinds of support she could have and finished by telling her how we would find a small Christian church community for her to work with.

Until that moment her face had been quietly impassive, but now, in an instant, it utterly changed. Her mouth turned into a harsh, malicious grin and her entire face was convulsed in a haughty sneer. The expression was similar to what Father O'Connor and I saw when confronting her the day after the failed deliverance, only now the superciliousness was magnified threefold. The expression could only be called satanic. There was no question whether we were dealing now with the real Jersey. Almost immediately I said, "There seems to be a demon in the room. What is your name?"

It answered in Jersey's own voice without hesitation: "Damien." Jersey had mentioned the names of many of her supposed demons before, but Damien was not among them. We let it talk for a minute. Its words made no sense. I was not about to be drawn back into this meaningless drivel halfway between sanity and insanity. I commented, "You seemed to appear right when we were talking about a Christian church support group for Jersey."

"I don't want her children to go to church and become sissies," it pronounced. "What they need to learn is karate and self-defense."

Now that the demon was speaking in its own language, it did not take us long to realize that it was, in fact, a demon of self-defense. Indeed, it shortly even explained its name to us, saying that the *a* should really be pronounced flatly because the name meant "Dam me in." By "dam" it didn't mean "damn," but a concrete barrier through which no enemy could approach.

After perhaps a quarter of an hour, Bishop Worthington and I arrived at the same conclusion as to the falsity of Damien's teaching, and alternating as a boxer might his left and right fists, we began to bombard it with the truth. We told it that human beings, including Jersey, could not survive behind concrete. They had to be fed and touched and held and loved, and all such things were made impossible by barricades. We granted that a kind of helplessness was inherent in the human condition living without barricades. "There are so many potential dangers," I said. "Humans don't begin to be smart enough to defend ourselves, no matter how much karate we might know. We survive not because of barricades or physical strength, but by the grace of God. Without God, whether we believe in Him or not, we all would have been dead long since. But because we are surrounded by the grace of God, which is our only true armor, most of us get to live out our full life span. In fact," I continued, "the more we are aware of that grace, the more wise we become. Jersey will become very wise when she is rid of you, Damien, with your false preaching—when she no longer has to listen to your lies."

As Bishop Worthington and I went on in this manner—the bishop being far better than I with appropriate biblical quotes—the satanic expression on Jersey's face rapidly turned to confusion and then peace. Damien was gone, no longer in its victim or in the room, and by the end Jersey was actually laughing with pleasure at her relief. Her face, recently so harsh and ugly, was now soft. It was time for a break, the first break that all of us took in joyful celebration, including Jersey.

Though Jersey was glowing with happiness, I noticed that she was frequently clearing her throat and occasionally lightly coughing. I asked her about it. She denied having a cold and had not been aware of her coughing.

After the twenty-minute break, we reassembled in the exorcism room, a sunlit bedroom that gave us all the space we needed. We had moved the bed out of the corner, leaving only its head against the wall so that the entire team could sit around it while Jersey sat back against the headboard. I sat at the foot of the bed and Bishop Worthington to my left, near Jersey's right foot. The only member of the team not ordinarily next to the bed was our psychologist, who furnished us with wise observations while also running the video camera. He had affixed a hanging microphone to the ceiling so that it dangled between the rest of us, several feet above our heads and close to Jersey.

The bishop and I went through our customary rituals and then asked of Jersey, looking ever so serene as she leaned back against the headboard, "Are there any other demons?"

The next second I felt as if someone had managed to insert an eggbeater into my skull and was vigorously whipping my brains into sauce. For a long moment I had no idea where I was—what house or what state or nation—and no awareness of why I was there. One of the other team members later told me that my face had turned beet red during that long moment. I shudder to think what might have happened to me if I had not been a well-trained psychiatrist. For it was my psychiatric training that saved me.

Psychiatrists are taught to examine their own thinking process continually and monitor their behavior from minute to minute, if not second to second. I instinctively asked myself what on earth was scrambling my brains, but I was so overwhelmed that I found it difficult to think at all. After a minute or two, however, I realized that the proper word for my condition was confusion. I was experiencing confusion to a degree that I had never felt before.

Having managed to arrive at this self-diagnosis, I asked myself why. Once again my training came to my aid. Part of that learning was that the emotions we experience do not come from nothing; they come from either our own personality or from the behavior of the person we are dealing with at the time. Knowing this, I had the presence of mind to wonder if Jersey or this newest demon was somehow making me so confused. It dawned on me that I might be dealing with a demon of confusion.

Continuing to rely on my training, I knew that the best way to deal with confusion was to put as much distance as possible between myself and the confusing entity so as to regain my objectivity—indeed, to summon the greatest objectivity possible.

At this point I told the team of my confusion and my consequent need for distance. They took over the exorcism, while I sat in a chair outside the circle around Jersey and the bed. From my briefcase I took out a pen and a yellow legal pad. I sat aside with the pad on my knee and simply concentrated on writing down everything that the demon was saying. As I did this I became quite calm and coldly analytical. I rapidly realized that we were, in fact, in the presence of a demon of confusion.

The confusion even extended to the demon's name. It referred to itself as either Tyrona or Tiarona. Tyrona, it explained, was male, while Tiarona was female.

This hermaphroditic entity seemed to have a particular interest in physics. It explained to us how the world was filled with negative energy and positive energy, and the things of the world were either manifestations of positive energy or negative energy just as they were either male or female. It went on to instruct us that the amount of negative energy and positive energy in the world were precisely equal. It then giggled slightly as it explained how if you added up all the positive energy in the world with all the negative, the sum became zero. It found this prospect of nothingness to be not only funny, but also strangely pleasing.

From my chair of objectivity I realized that what I was hearing was the voice of nihilism—a demonic voice present in virtually every recorded exorcism throughout history. This voice of nihilism does not just teach a physics of nothingness, but also a theology of meaninglessness. Not only things but also people add up to zero.

But how to attack this most cynical of philosophies? Some instinct told me that the attack would fail unless it could discern the roots of Jersey's nihilism and demonstrate each of them to be fallacious. My mind became like a scalpel, cutting through this nihilistic hogwash to the truth.

I moved back into the circle and led the attack. I was soon aided by Bishop Worthington, who, with his training in theology, quickly perceived where I was heading. We pointed out that the demon's classification of everything in the world as negative or positive had no basis in science. Granted that physics does deal with negatively charged and positively charged particles, it still cannot explain the reality of a human being, an iris, or even a loaf of bread in terms of negative and positive energy. Indeed, we noted how modern subatomic physics was awash with all manner of uncharged and often unexplainable particles. Even we, utterly untrained in such matters, recognized the demon's physics to be more than a century out of date. The reality, we told it, is that no one is so brilliant that he or she can explain the essence of all the beautiful things in the world. Despite the triumphs of modern science, at the most basic level the world remains utterly mysterious, just as God, its creator, is mysterious.

We pointed out to the demon that by attempting to explain everything in terms of negative and positive energy it was attempting to explain away all mystery. Its explanation represented falsity, whereas mystery represented truth. And the reality was that it was a demon of confusion precisely because it attempted to do away with the reality of mystery. Human beings were not created to have all the answers. We informed Jersey of how, when he was a young man, Einstein had attempted to arrive at something he called a unified field theory, whereby everything would become explainable and there would no longer be any need for a god. We finished the story by recounting how Einstein never did discover the theory and how, despite the atheistic leanings of his youth, in his old age he exclaimed with joy, "Subtle is the Lord."

As had happened earlier with Damien, once we fully demonstrated the fallacy—the lie—of this demon's cosmology, the sneering satanic expression left Jersey's face. The demon was gone and Jersey was back to normal. No, better than normal: she seemed to glow slightly.

It was five o'clock in the evening and, although there was but one day to go, we all felt as if we had come a long way—such a long way that it was a cause for celebration, so we had cocktails. We asked Jersey if she wanted to join us, but she preferred to be alone in another corner of the living room. From time to time I looked over at her. She continued to glow, but I noted once again that she was frequently clearing her throat and coughing lightly. Suddenly, I recollected reading accounts by charismatic Christians of deliverances in which they noted that the patient would be encouraged to cough so as to cough up the demons. The possibility occurred to me that unconsciously Jersey might be coughing up demons or, more likely, ridding herself of some of the demonic influence under which she had lived for so many years.

Conscious that the next day was our last, I suspected we would need every bit of it and asked everyone to reassemble at seven o'clock the next morning instead of nine. Then we broke for the night. Driving home I was fully aware that we were somewhere in the midst of an exorcism and had no reason to believe that it would be concluded in only one more day. Yet I felt strangely calm. It was unlike me; I am a born worrier. I think God must have somehow been in the car seat next to me.

Day 4

We wasted no time, beginning at seven o'clock sharp the next morning. Bishop Worthington lit the candle and offered his customary opening prayer, and I addressed Jersey with my customary, "Jersey, child of God, in the name of God who created you and Jesus Christ who died for you, I order you to hear my voice as the voice of Christ's church and, though I am but a humble and unworthy servant, to obey my commands."

Then I simply asked, "Jersey, are there any demons left?"

"Yes," she answered, "there's one who very much wants to talk. Well, maybe two. The strong one is the Lord Josiah, but there's also a weak one, Jim, who tends to follow him around."

"Let Josiah speak," I directed.

Instantly Jersey's face was again distorted into the satanic mask we had by now become accustomed to. Josiah's name was the only one Jersey had mentioned prior to the exorcism, and it rapidly became clear he was the demon to which Jersey was the most attached in many ways, including sexually. It described itself as the spirit of love and gentleness. To confuse things a bit, the demon Jim from time to time would interrupt. It described itself as a spirit of war and fun. It was as if Jim were Josiah's shadow side. Addressing Jersey, I simply noted that I was not surprised she should also have a demon of fun, because I had a feeling that throughout her life she had never been able to have the kind of fun that most children or young adults have.

But it was Josiah who spoke the most. Primarily it spoke gibberish, but it was more or less clear that the essence of love and gentleness was either a thought or a feeling. With the gibberish, it took an hour of passive attention before I knew its weak spot, and the strategy of my attack.

We all took a short break during which I discussed the strategy with Bishop Worthington. He heartily concurred, and when we reconvened, after our customary rituals, the bishop and I began. We started by declaring Josiah to be not a spirit of love and gentleness, but in fact a spirit of insanity. We explained that all truth was rooted in reality and that insanity was not so rooted; rather, it was rooted in some kind of lie or unreality. I acknowledged that demons could sometimes speak the truth, but it was always in the form of a half-truth. Indeed, half-truths were the devil's most common weapons.

I gave examples from my clinical practice of how love was not wholly a thought or feeling. I told of how that very evening there would be some man sitting at the bar in the local village, crying into his beer and sputtering to the bartender how much he loved his wife and children while at the same time he was wasting his family's money and depriving them of his attention. We recounted how this man was thinking love and feeling love—were they not real tears in his eyes?—but he was not in truth behaving with love. Bishop Worthington joined me with examples from his own ministry. We proclaimed that love was primarily an action, and unless thoughts and feelings of love were translated into action they were so much chaff. The old proverb "Handsome is as handsome does" was the truth, we explained, and behavior was the test of love. Any "love" that was not reflected by behavior was not rooted in reality; rather, it was rooted in unreality and hence insanity.

Josiah apparently did not like being identified as a demon of insanity. For it was at this point Jersey (or the demon), for the first time, started to argue back with all manner of obfuscation. We told it to shut up. It demanded to be treated with respect. We snapped back that demons were not worthy of respect and commanded it to listen. At that point Jersey got off the bed, proclaiming that she wanted a cigarette—maybe even a joint—and was leaving the room for that purpose. Gently but firmly, all of us on the team took hold of her arms and ankles and placed her back on the bed. It was the first time in more than three days that she had to be restrained. The team even joked about it. We felt it was no accident that Jersey had to be restrained only when the spirit of love and gentleness was present, since, of course, all the business about its love and gentleness was a lie.

We had to restrain her for merely an hour. Occasionally she struggled, particularly at first, but then she almost seemed to enjoy the strength of our hands upon her wrists and ankles. We began to believe that Josiah might indeed be linked with the seldom-mentioned Jim, who had described himself as a demon of war and fun. For throughout the hour, Jersey was clearly having a great deal of fun. And was funny. At times we had to work to keep straight faces. Earlier I had told her I thought she had difficulty in having fun for some kind of psychoanalytic reason. Now it was as if our use of restraint had somehow liberated her to be the raucous little girl she had never allowed herself to be. She continually waved to the camera, saying boisterously, "Hi Mom, hi Dad" as if she were on TV. Repeatedly she asked if the camera was still running.

Although earlier she had rather prissily complained about the team's bad language, now her speech was filled with obscenities. Every time she struggled sufficiently that we had to tighten our grip, she commented, "Watch out how you handle the merchandise." She flirted outrageously with Bishop Worthington, looking for his wedding ring and when she couldn't see it, proposing that they should become much better friends. The performance would have seemed quite human as well as humorous were it not for its shameless quality.

Each time she renewed her struggle it was with the excuse that she wanted a cigarette or a joint, something I soon used to bring her back to the idea that had been such an anathema to the demon Josiah: namely, that love was an action rather than a pure emotion, thought, or desire. She knew how much I liked my cigarettes, so it seemed to have real meaning to her when I said, "I want a cigarette too, Jersey. I'm dying for one, and I am much more hooked than you. But it is not yet time to end this session.

I'm not going to smoke as I normally would. You could say that it is a kind of sacrifice I am making—an action I am making for you because I love you."

This seemed to have a profound effect upon her. By the time I had finished my little speech about sacrifice she had stopped struggling, and for the next quarter hour she lay quietly back on the bed, talking only occasionally but with perfectly good sense. Gradually it dawned on us that the demonic presence seemed to have gone. I asked her, "Is Josiah still there?"

"No," she answered, "he left."

"Good," I said. "Then don't let him back." And that seemed to be all that was required to exorcise the Lord Josiah. We had not been restraining her for some time. It had taken two full sessions—the whole morning—and we were hungry and concluded the session by simply saying, "It's time for lunch."

As was her wont, Jersey did not eat with us but sat in a corner gulping her sandwich. Once again, between gulps, I noticed she was coughing. I called over to her, "Do you have a cold, Jersey?"

She said, "No. Why do you ask?"

"Because of your cough," I replied.

To which she responded, "Was I coughing? I wasn't aware of it."

I thought it possible that Jersey's entire unconscious was engaged in the healing we were attempting.

I was profoundly aware that we had only half a day left, yet still felt strangely calm with a depth of faith I had never been privileged to have before. But I made sure that our lunch was brief, and we soon reconvened in the bedroom with Jersey sitting at the head of the bed in her customary lotus position. After the bishop's and my standard ritual phrases I asked her whether there were any demons left. Jersey answered that there was one more who wanted to speak.

"Let him or her speak then."

Instantly the satanic expression came over her face, and she proclaimed herself to be a demon named Emil. Emil told us he was a deposed Tibetan lama who had previously been a leader in "the White Brotherhood" but had, for unspecified reasons, been kicked out of the brotherhood some one hundred and fifty years before. Emil went on to explain how ever since, he had to make an ordinary living and did so as a professor at various universities, volunteering that he taught the subject of science.

"So you are a scientist then, are you?" I inquired.

"Oh, yes," Emil replied with a kind of self-satisfaction.

"How do you define science?" I asked.

Emil's answer was gibberish.

"That is not a definition of science," I declared. "I don't believe you even know the definition of science." I was beginning to sense that Emil was a pushover, which was fortunate given the small amount of time we had left.

To my taunt, Emil answered, "I'm not talking about Western science. I'm a professor of Eastern science."

"Well, you may be a professor of Eastern science," I commented, "but you wouldn't be aware of that supposed 'fact' unless you were aware of a difference between Eastern and Western science. So, I ask now, how do you define Western science?"

Emil fell silent.

I mocked him. "You call yourself a professor! What a joke. Even to be a professor of Eastern science you would have to know the nature of your competitor. You would have a definition of Western science for your students—that is, if you were, in fact, a scientist or a professor. But you're not. You're not a professor at all, and you don't deserve the dignity of the title. In fact, you are a phony. You're a liar. A pretender. A professor of pretend science! A professor who teaches that science is whatever you want to think it is. Hah! Jersey has no need for any more lies. So get out," I almost spat. "Get out now. In the name of Jesus Christ I command you to leave and never again have the slightest thing to do with Jersey, you lying phony!"

And that was it. As I had sensed, Emil was a pushover and his buffoonery was gone from the room. Nonetheless, to acknowledge the fact that we were done with him, we took a very brief break—just long enough for Jersey and me to have a cigarette.

———◆———

When we had reassembled and gone through the standard ritual I asked Jersey whether there were any demons left. She said, "There may be two of them. I'm not even sure that they are demons. If they are, they seem to be very far away. They always work together. If I had to guess I would say that they are demons of lust and hate."

"Let me talk to them," I directed.

Immediately the satanic expression came back to her face and she—or the two demons—began to talk with their usual difficult-to-understand speech that seemed halfway between sense and nonsense. But after no more than fifteen minutes I was able to discern two patterns. The first was that although there were supposedly two of them, they spoke with the same voice, consistently referring to themselves as "we." I took notice of this because in the accounts of exorcisms I had read it was a frequent occurrence for a demon to refer to itself as "we"—almost like the royal "we" sometimes used by a proud monarch referring to him- or herself.

The other pattern in what they (or it?) said was their repeated use of the word "test." They spoke of the psychological tests that Jersey had taken. They said, "We test her with cigarettes," and added another half dozen ways in which they tested Jersey— ways that seemed to have meaning to them, but not to me.

After fifteen minutes I felt that I understood all that I was going to understand, so I butted into the middle of one of their sentences to demand, "What is your name?"

The satanic expression became more pronounced, and with a smirk not only on her face but now in her voice, Jersey or the demons answered me: "Jeesus."

Spontaneously I retorted, "You must really be a demon of hate to use Jesus's name!"

With a calm note of pride they responded: "We don't hate Jesus; we just test him."

My mind must have been working at the speed of light. As a baby Christian I had never once in my life given thought to the Antichrist. Now I did. I instinctively knew that we were in the presence of the Antichrist. I also knew enough to recognize that the term came from the Book of Revelation, where it referred to a human being who, in the final days, would come to power as a false leader or prophet. Not feeling the least bit bound by the Book of Revelation, however, I somehow knew that the being talking to us was not any human Antichrist but was Satan itself. No more than a few seconds transpired before I turned to Bishop Worthington, noting, "It looks as if we have the true Antichrist here now, by which I mean Satan itself. I think we have come to the end."

Although the bishop had corrected me on my theology several times during the exorcism, he was now silent in agreement. "I need to take a short break," I added. "I need to make a phone call. I should be back in just a few minutes."

Out in the living room I dialed Malachi's number, never expecting him to answer, anticipating that I would get one of his usual innumerable answering services on this Sunday afternoon. But to my amazement, the phone was picked up in the middle of its first ring and there was Malachi himself. "Is that you, Scotty?" he asked.

I was so anxious, all I could do was blurt out my predicament. "In your book you described five exorcisms of demons, but you never said anything about actually encountering Satan. Have you ever in the course of an exorcism run across Satan itself?" I asked.

"Oh, yes," Malachi replied. "It does happen."

"Well, that's where I am now," I almost screamed. "What the hell am I supposed to do?"

"Have you got authority?" Malachi asked.

Knowing from his book what he meant, I answered, "Yes. I'm amazed at the amount of authority I have. It took a long while to get there, but for the past day demons have popped up whenever I asked them to and as soon as I named each of them correctly, I ordered them to leave—and you know what? They did."

"Good," Malachi replied. "Just go ahead and cast it out."

I hung up the phone without even thanking him and walked back into the exorcism room. Jersey's face was still in its demonic mode. Instinctively, I changed my tactics. As far as I was concerned we had indeed come to the end and no more questions needed to be asked. We knew what we were dealing with. Yes, it might be fascinating to ask it questions of theology and mythology, discover how it came into existence, maybe try to convert it. What grandiosity! What a trap to fall into—arguing with it. "Everyone sit back down," I directed.

I sat down myself, and after a few minutes of silence I began to speak softly. "It seems a strange thing to thank you, Satan," I said, "but I do. I think we all do. You have brought us much new knowledge—more understanding than we ever dreamed of. Because of you we have even grown in love. But now you have done that, your usefulness is at an end. There is no longer any reason for you to be here, and it is time you got out."

After a pause, still operating by instinct, I began the final expulsion. Very quietly I said to it, "Get out. You will leave now. I order this in the name of Christ. You will get out now. You will take every last filthy tentacle off Jersey and leave. In the name of Christ I order this. You have infested Jersey for fifteen years but she no longer belongs to you. She does not want you any longer. She will not listen to you. She belongs to Christ now, and not to you. Every tentacle of you must go. Now. I order this in the name of Jesus Christ. You will go. Get out now. Go. Leave her alone forever."

I continued speaking these words over and over again, hypnotically. Occasionally I whispered to Jersey, "This is the time we spoke of—the moment of your choice. Choose, Jersey. Choose now. Kick it out." It was a hypnosis. It was also an exorcism.

At first Jersey continued to sit against the headboard in her lotus position. After a few minutes the satanic expression gradually faded from her face. It was gone for all of thirty seconds, and then it returned in full force. I kept repeating my incantation quietly but steadily and without mercy.

Once more the malevolent smirking grin faded slowly away. This time it was almost a minute before it returned. I took from the table a crucifix that had been given to me years before. I placed it in Jersey's hands. She tried to push it back, but I held it in her hands as I kept repeating my hypnotic mantra. Again the hideous satanic expression faded away, and for the next minute and a half Jersey, with a seeming hint of astonishment, began to lovingly play with the metal corpus of Christ on the crucifix as it lay on her lap. When the satanic expression returned she stopped fingering the body of Christ, but to my relief she did not thrust the crucifix away from her or throw it at me. Meanwhile, I kept repeating the same words over and over as the satanic expression continued to come and go, but each time go a little longer and come back for a slightly shorter time.

It took close to two hours. Toward the end, as if exhausted, Jersey left her sitting position and lay down on the bed with her head on a pillow and the crucifix clutched to her chest. I continued ordering Satan to leave in the name of Jesus Christ until the satanic expression no longer returned at all. It was a distinct moment. It wasn't simply that the satanic expression was not returning; we on the team also felt with a kind of suddenness that it was gone, that Satan had left and there was no longer anything of the demonic in the room.

I stopped my words of exorcism, of commanding expulsion, and we simply sat in quiet prayer. Then I said to her, "It's gone now, Jersey. Do you want to sit up?"

Jersey shook her head and whispered, "Not yet."

Still clutching the crucifix to her chest Jersey lay there, word-less, almost as if dead, and I suppose in a way she had died. But physically she was quite alive. To reassure myself I watched her slow, regular breathing. Her face was in repose. I had no idea what was going through her mind. She had, I suspected, already made her choice. I imagined that now she might be cementing that choice. During the long silence we prayed silently for her continued safety.

After a wordless half hour Jersey suddenly sat up, swung her legs over the side of the bed, handed the crucifix to me, and cheerfully said, "I'm all right now."

She was indeed cheerful—full of good cheer—and more than all right. She radiated happiness and embraced each of us, say-ing, "Thank you," over and over again. The glow of her face filled the room.

We were all more than ready for a little break, after which I told her we would go through the Roman Ritual of Exorcism once more, not to expel the demonic, because she had already expelled it, but just as a ritual to seal that expulsion. Following that the bishop would baptize her. Bishop Worthington and I said we were aware that she had been baptized by her father, which, under ordinary circumstances, would allow for a simple repetition of her baptismal vows, but since we were not sure about the authority of that baptism, we felt we should go through the original rite as if she were being baptized for the first time. Jersey agreed to this. Finally, we told her we would celebrate the success of her exorcism and the joy of her baptism with a Eucharist or communion.

And after the break, although it was already dark outside, we did as I had outlined. Bishop Worthington now took over the au-thority from me and I served as his assistant, giving what few re-sponses were required of me. In this lesser role where I was largely free to simply listen, I was impressed by the sheer power of the ancient rite of exorcism yet simultaneously aware that its power entirely depended upon Jersey's will. Three nights before we had gone through the same lengthy ritual but then it was an empty gesture, as Jersey had psychologically isolated herself and her demons from the words and their potential power. Even as we had said those words back then, we knew in our hearts that they were fruitless. This night could not have been more different. Although we made it indelibly clear to her that she had no responsibility in the rite, since she had already chosen against Satan and its minions, thereby expelling them, this time Jersey was obviously alert, peacefully and fully present. Her state endured during her baptism and the communion that followed it, when she did play an active role. She clearly, vocally renounced Satan and all its works during her baptism and she received the communion host with grace.

Then it was all over but the cheering and more hugs all around. Jersey's face was filled with joy. She departed with her mother and stepfather, and then the rest of the team, save for the woman who had offered her home, departed for our own dwellings with the serene knowledge that our four days had been extraordinarily successful. The exorcism had worked!

CHAPTER 3

FOLLOW-UP

"You're wrong. He was too a medical doctor."

The next morning was the worst of my life.

Her mother brought Jersey to my office. I had set aside an hour for her now and a two-hour block of time for later in the afternoon. In the waiting room her mother told me that Jersey had slept well in the small house nearby they had rented for the month. Jersey was not glowing the way she had the night before, but then I had not necessarily expected her to be. I really didn't know what to expect.

The moment I brought Jersey into my office she said, "Dr. Peck, I want to go home. I miss my children, and they need me." Certainly I didn't expect that.

"I understand," I said, "but we need to work intensively together for the next three weeks. Not for more exorcism, but for ordinary psychotherapy, like I told you."

"Well, my plans have changed," Jersey retorted archly. "I told you, I need to go home."

The last thing I felt like doing at that point was fighting, but I had little choice in the matter. "You knew that we would need the next three weeks here," I said. "I can understand that you want to go home, but it's not the right thing for you to do. It's not what you agreed to."

"Fuck the agreement!" Jersey screamed.

Emotionally, I might have been able to handle her anger, had it not been for her face. As I looked at her I saw her face begin to assume the same satanic expression I thought I had expelled the night before. The expression was not as powerful as it had been then, but it was definitely there, and seemed more definite by the second. I shut my eyes and hung my head in total dejection. "Oh, Christ," was all that I could say, not knowing whether it was a curse or a prayer.

"Well, are you going to let me go home?" Jersey demanded.

I kept my eyes closed and prayed, mumbling, "Jesus, help me. Jesus, help me. Jesus, help me," over and over again.

"What's wrong with you?" Jersey asked. Her voice was sharp and harsh.

I still could not look at her. I opened my eyes to look down at the rug. "What's wrong?" I retorted with helpless anger. "It's no different than it was a month ago when you were demanding that I let you leave the hospital. We're right back where we were, as if the exorcism never happened. What's wrong? The whole exorcism was a failure, that's what's wrong."

Finally, I lifted my head and looked at her again. The satanic look on her face had faded into a ghost of an expression, and as I continued to look at her I watched it rapidly fade away altogether.

"All right," Jersey said. "I'll stay."

I hadn't expected this response; I did not know what that meant. I felt numb with exhaustion and despair and for the first time in my career I broke off a session before it was even half over. "I'll see you at four then," I told her blankly, adding, "I'm just too tired to do any more this morning."

I ushered her out to her mother in the living room. They left. I retreated back into my office, swearing repeatedly under my breath. As far as I could see, it was obvious that the exorcism had been a total failure. All four days wasted. The time of the whole team wasted. Everything wasted.

———◆———

I was wrong. Although there were to be ups and downs, within fifteen minutes of starting our late-afternoon session it was equally obvious to me that the exorcism was indeed a success.

At the beginning of the session I was disappointed to realize that Jersey's mind was still full of the same garbage as before, the same complexes. By the end of the session, however, it had become wonderfully clear to me that the energy had gone out of these complexes. The result was that she was now responsive to psychotherapy, that we could talk about her ideas or complexes and through our talk she was able to modify or even discard them.

For example, as if her rebellion of the morning had never happened, Jersey began by recounting a dream of the night before in which she had been flying over the local countryside looking for her mother and the house that had been rented for their stay together during her postexorcism psychotherapy. It was a brief and simple dream, ending with her finding the correct little house. But Jersey seemed excited by it. I asked her what her thoughts were about the dream. She quickly exclaimed with pleasure, "It's the first time I've ever been able to fly all by myself! I mean, without a plane or anything. I can fly!"

Something about her excitement caused me to pause. "You mean you could fly in your dream," I said.

And she repeated, "I mean I can fly. On my own."

"In your dream, that is," I added, acting on an intuition that she literally needed to be brought back to earth.

"What difference does it make whether it was in a dream?" Jersey asked. "The point is I can fly."

The depth of her innocence suddenly dawned on me. "Isn't there a difference between flying in a dream and flying when you are awake?" I asked.

Jersey looked at me as if I were a little bit crazy. "Of course not," she said. "Why should there be a difference?"

"If I hear you correctly," I answered slowly and carefully, "you seem to believe that your dream was real—as if there is no difference in the reality of your experience when you are dreaming and when you are awake."

"Well, I suppose there is a little difference," Jersey started to explain, almost as if I were the child and the innocent one. "When we dream, we are in a state of astral projection. If I can astrally project myself to fly over your house, then I *am* flying over your house."

I wanted to be as gentle as possible. "I'm afraid I don't understand astral projection, Jersey. Could you explain it to me?"

Jersey began to look slightly uncertain. But she gave it a good try. "Astral projection is when you leave your body behind while the real you is projected someplace else," she tried to teach me. "When I flew over our house last night, it was without my body. If I flew over our house right now when I'm awake, I would be in my body. That's the only difference."

"Let me see if I understand. You think that what happens to you when you are in a dream or in your astral-projection is just as real as what happens when you're awake. It's really the same when you're dreaming as when you're awake."

Jersey nodded vigorously.

"But are you aware that's not the way that most people think?" I asked, speaking softly as if I could somehow lessen the blow. "Most people think that the reality of our dreams is very different—almost entirely different—from the reality of our waking experiences. In fact, most people don't believe in astral projection." Hoping it might comfort her, I added, "Although there are an increasing number of people who believe in something like astral projection during near-death experiences."

"But that's not what they taught me at the Neo-Spiritualist Society!" Jersey protested.

"I'm sure that's true," I acknowledged. "I'm sure you're correct that's what you were taught at the Society. But most people don't believe what the Society teaches. Do you know that?" I persisted. "Most people think that the Society's teachings are weird."

"Well, the members of the Society are more advanced than most people," Jersey countered.

"How do you know that?" I asked.

"They say that they're the most advanced."

"But why do you believe them? Do you believe what everybody says? Why do you trust them so much? Do you trust them more than me? Or Bishop Worthington?"

Jersey now started to look downright confused.

"It must be hard sometimes to not know what to believe," I commented. "Do you ever doubt the people at the Society?"

"I try not to," Jersey answered.

"Why not?" I inquired. "It sounds as if you think there is something bad about doubting." Watching waves of doubt pass over Jersey's face, I knew that I was on the right track. "Certainly, it's painful to doubt," I continued. "It's painful to feel confused, which is the way we feel when we're doubting. But that doesn't make it bad. In fact, in most situations it's good to doubt. It's our capacity to doubt that makes us free. If you believe everything they say at the Society without question, without doubting it, then it is almost like they own you. I want you to be free, Jersey, I want you to be free to think for yourself. I want you to be free to doubt them, and I want you to be free to doubt me.

"In a sense, that's what the exorcism was all about. In my way of thinking, it's also what true Christianity is all about. But I'm not going to try and make you believe that. All I want you to believe for the moment is that it is good to doubt.

"That's sort of why Malachi referred you to me. You see, we got to know each other because he read a book I had written, and then I read several books that he had written. One of the things I said in my book is 'The path to holiness lies through questioning everything.' "

I knew that Jersey had come to believe that Malachi—this important person behind the scenes who she'd never seen—was a very holy man, and I was not above invoking his authority. Certainly it or something was having an impact; Jersey looked truly pensive for the first time since I had known her. "What are you thinking?" I asked her.

"It's too early for me to put it into words," Jersey answered. "It's all about doubting. I've never really thought about doubting before."

"I'm glad you're thinking about it now," I said. "That's the most I could want of you. Will you keep thinking about it?"

Jersey promised that she would.

———◆———

I said that within fifteen minutes of starting this session I knew that the exorcism had been a success. Although it had seemed like an eternity, this entire exchange took only about fifteen minutes. A fifteen-minute revolution that fundamentally changed the way we interacted. In the long moment that followed, I analyzed what was so different. Jersey could now listen. I knew she could hear me before. Several times during the exorcism she had recounted very exactly things I had said to her. But this was the first time, other than during the exorcism itself, that she seemed to be affected by what I said and give it enough credence to think about it. It was a change of such magnitude as to signify the exorcism's success.

Jersey was quick to confirm this, but she broke the silence by first confusing the issue, saying, "I still hear the demons talking to me."

I felt as if my heart had skipped a beat. This hardly sounded like the result of a successful exorcism.

"Only now it's all different," Jersey continued.

"How so?"

"Here, let me show you." In her old way Jersey grabbed a pad of paper and a pencil from the table and seemed to be drawing something. After a minute she got up and, like a proud little girl, showed me her drawing. It was unmistakably that of a womb with a tiny fetus in its middle completely surrounded by a much larger mass of amniotic fluid. "Before the exorcism," she explained, "I was like this fetus. The demons were like the fluid. They totally surrounded me. None of me was visible. No one could hear me through what they were saying."

As she stood next to my chair she proceeded to draw some arrows within the fluid pointing at the fetus. "These arrows represent the voices of the demons. Before the exorcism, I was captive to their voices. I couldn't really separate their voices from my own. Often I wanted to scream out, 'Hey, it's me in here,' but nobody, including you, could have heard me. I was in the demons' control. I was powerless."

Then Jersey drew some more arrows still pointing at the fetus, but this time outside the womb. "This is what their voices are like now," she elaborated. "You see, they are outside of me now. They can't get at me. I can hear them, but they're not as distinct as before. Even more important, I don't have any trouble today distinguishing between them and me, between their voice and my voice. Do you understand?"

I breathed a great sigh of relief. "It's a very good illustration," I complimented her. "It shows exactly how there really has been a change. Congratulations."

"For what?" Jersey asked.

"For being exorcised," I answered.

"But you were the one who did that," Jersey said.

"No," I told her firmly. "You were the one who did it. I only assisted, sort of like a midwife at a delivery. You did all the pushing. You were the real exorcist. The exorcism succeeded because you chose to succeed. You chose the truth over lies. You chose God over the devil."

By the end of our two-hour session there was only one thing

that worried me. Jersey accepted the fact that she was the one who had been the real exorcist, but she seemed reluctant to review in any depth the choices she had made. She didn't even want to discuss the exorcism further. She was quite explicit about this. "I don't want to think about it," she pronounced. "It's over. It's over and done with. It was very unpleasant, but it's all in the past. It's unimportant now."

I realized what was happening. Although she was not schizophrenic, Jersey was behaving just like young schizophrenics I had treated who had had what psychiatrists call a psychotic break. With medicines, they recovered, usually in the hospital. But as soon as they were well, they not only wanted to get out of the hospital but to act as if the whole thing had never happened. They wanted to deny that they could ever have gone "crazy"; they wanted to forget about the whole incident just as quickly as they could. As a psychiatrist, it was my duty to try to combat this denial and keep them from forgetting such an important event. They needed to remain aware of it so they could learn from it. Usually, however, their need to deny was stronger than any therapeutic technique I had to encourage them to remember and grow from what had happened.

I felt no need to compel Jersey to remember exactly all the things she had done wrong before the exorcism or every detail of what we had gone through in the preceding four days. But I was determined that she should not forget it entirely.

I got up from my chair and pulled a medium-sized cardboard box out from under the table. "You're not going to like this," I said to her. "As we agreed, I'm going to see you for sessions like we've had today for the next two to three weeks. That leaves you with a lot of free time. What's in this box are the videotapes of the exorcism. There are eight of them, each four hours long. That means it will take you thirty-two hours to watch them all, but it won't require any more than two hours a day. Starting tomorrow I want you and your mother to rent a VCR and spend two hours each day looking at the tapes from beginning to end. You don't have to remember everything that happens on them. Sometimes I think they will be quite boring. But I do want you to remember the whole thirty-two hours in general, and not forget about them. If you forget about them, you won't have learned anything for the future. Will you do that for me?"

"It's a stupid little house," Jersey answered. "I don't want to spend any more time in it than I have to. I want to go driving around with Mom. It's quite pretty around here. I want to see the sights and I want us to go shopping."

I half expected to see that horrible face again, but it did not show itself. Still, Jersey obviously had some fight left in her—and a little bit of arrogance. "You'll have time to do those things," I said, "but you can also let us treat you a bit like a child for a couple more weeks. It's not only something I think you need to do, but something I'm going to put in your mother's hands. Your mother wants to be your mother, you know. She's been awfully good to you for quite a long time. I'm going to make it her responsibility to watch the tapes together with you."

Without giving her any more opportunity to object, I carried the box of tapes out of the office. Jersey followed me obediently into the waiting room, where I gave the box to her mother and told her what I wanted. I told her where she could rent a VCR and wrote down two appointments for Jersey the next day.

Then they left, with Jersey looking decidedly sulky. Maybe the next few weeks were going to be a rough ride. I crossed my fingers.

But when she returned in the morning, Jersey was cheerful and, with but one exception, our work together for the next eighteen days was peaceful. I did not intend to psychoanalyze her, but simply to prepare her for psychoanalysis. She would need to see Dr. Lieberman quite extensively, and I reminded her that he had been unsuccessful in engaging her in psychotherapy in the past. She acknowledged this to be true, but reminded me, "That was when I was possessed, and I'm not possessed anymore. Besides," she added, "I trust him. He was nice to me when I was in the hospital, and you've told me that he was helpful to you. And he's not religious. I've had enough religion this past week."

I agreed that there had been a lot of religion in the exorcism, adding, however, that I thought she could do with a number of smaller doses, and I wanted to arrange for her to also see a Christian counselor once a week when she got back home. Jersey started to balk, but then seemed to decide to go along with it. I asked her whether she would prefer a man or a woman. "A woman," she answered, "but only if I like her."

"I guess that seems fair," I responded, trusting to luck.

With these plans in place, I spent our sessions looking for little areas where she wasn't thinking correctly. Each of the four demons we encountered during the exorcism before we got to Satan itself represented a lie of sorts or a false pattern of thinking. We had already uncovered another dramatic falsity the first evening: her remarkable misconception that the reality of her waking and the reality of her dreams were the same.

We were, in fact, able to discover half a dozen similar such misconceptions. Jersey, I learned, had virtually no understanding of the difference between a hypothesis, a theory, and truth or proven fact. I described the scientific method to her in detail. Indeed, much of my effort went to teaching her how to be something of a scientist—in the Western sense of the word. Generally, she was a willing pupil. I said that our time together in this postexorcism period of psychotherapy was peaceful, with one exception. It was a very large exception. So large that, without the grace of God, it could have blown everything to pieces.

I recollected her mother telling me how around the age of twelve Jersey had devoured the works of Edgar Cayce. Cayce was a turn-of-the-century American who became quite famous for his ability to enter trances and dictate "channeled material" that often suggested the validity of reincarnation and other more traditionally Eastern theories. It struck me as a most unusual fascination for a girl of twelve to have. Indeed, it was sufficiently unusual to compel me to read up on Cayce during the six months between the time I first met Jersey and the time of her exorcism. He was a fascinating and ambiguous figure.

In his ordinary waking state, Cayce had apparently been a truly devout and quite ordinary Christian from a middle-class Appalachian background, but in his trances he spoke knowledgeably of concepts someone of his background would not have been expected to know much about. Many of the concepts, such as reincarnation, were either non-Christian or very much at the fringes of Christianity. Scattered pieces of evidence suggested that Cayce may have been duped—that he might himself have been possessed from his youth for the entirety of his remaining life. I did not tell Jersey about my research save to comment on the fact I had heard she had been an avid reader of Cayce around the age of twelve. Jersey confirmed the truth of this. It was a week after the conclusion of the exorcism when I inquired, "I wonder what else was going on with you at the age of twelve." She herself had identified it as the age her possession had begun.

"Nothing much," Jersey responded. "I mean, I was just an ordinary junior high school kid. Oh, there was one thing. That was the year I got appendicitis."

"Tell me about it," I asked her with interest.

"It was no big deal. Well, maybe I should take that back. The pain was a big deal. All of a sudden, one afternoon, out of the blue, I started having this incredible stomachache. I mean, did it hurt! It was the worst pain I have ever had. Far worse than my labor with the kids. Mom and Dad took me to the emergency room of the hospital. They seemed to know what was wrong almost immediately, and they rushed me to surgery. It was the first time I ever had surgery, and I think I might have been scared if it weren't for the fact that the pain was so bad. Anyway, they operated on me that evening, just in time before it burst. Thank God for surgeons. The minute I woke up from anesthesia I knew that that horrible pain was gone."

"No complications?"

"No," Jersey replied, "I was out of the hospital within three days. There was no problem with my recovery back home. My father checked me every evening to make sure that everything was okay."

"Your father checked you," I replied. "I'm not sure what you mean."

Jersey blushed. It was the first time I had ever seen her blush. "Well, you know how they do it. In the evening, after dinner, my father would come into my bedroom and put his finger in my vagina and wiggle it around. I guess he was looking for a tender spot. Anyway, after a bit he would pull out his finger and pronounce me to be okay."

"How long did that checking go on?" I asked.

"I guess a couple of weeks. That was all."

"How did you feel about it?" I enquired.

"Since no tender spots developed," Jersey told me, "I felt fine about it. It didn't hurt."

Jersey was calm. Her blush was gone, but the hackles had begun to rise on the back of my neck. "Didn't it seem strange that your father was checking you with his finger in your vagina?" I asked.

"No, why should it have?"

"Because he wasn't a doctor," I answered.

"You're wrong," Jersey said emphatically. "He was a doctor. I told you that."

"You're right in a way," I explained. "I think he had what is called a doctorate in psychology. I believe he had a Ph.D. degree; Ph.D. is the abbreviation for a doctoral degree in philosophy, and that would include psychology. But he wasn't a medical doctor."

"Yes, he was!" Jersey exclaimed with passion.

"No, he wasn't," I countered. "He was a psychologist with a Ph.D. degree. But he did not have an M.D. degree. He was not a doctor of medicine, and he did not have any right to check you that way."

"But you're wrong," Jersey pronounced again. "He was too a medical doctor. I know. He had his office in our house. Everyone called him Doctor. He always wore a long white coat. Beautifully white, and well starched. I used to iron it for him sometimes."

It was quite usual for a psychologist who was a psychotherapist to have his office in his home. It was even usual for him to be called Doctor by his patients. It was distinctly weird, however, for a psychotherapist to wear a long white coat, which is almost always the symbol of a physician. Had I somehow gotten the details wrong when, months ago, Jersey's mother had given me a brief family history? I didn't think so. "Maybe I'm off base, Jersey," I said, hesitant now, "but I'm quite certain your father was not a medical doctor, not a physician."

"Yes, he was!" Jersey retorted, becoming obviously upset, her voice starting to rise to a scream.

"How about asking your mother in here?" I asked. "I believe that she's just sitting in the waiting room, and if anyone can clear the matter up, I'm sure she can."

Jersey could not have been more threatened. Her eyes were wide, like those of a cornered and very frightened animal. She did not answer me at first.

"How about it?" I repeated.

"All right," she answered with the tone of a prisoner helplessly being escorted to a firing squad.

Jersey's mother was very good at waiting. I had told her she did not have to stay in the waiting room during my sessions with Jersey, but she had stayed there twice a day from the beginning, almost as if she had an intimation that she would be needed. And now she was needed indeed. She accompanied me back into my office. "I think Jersey may really need for you to be close to her right now," I said. She moved to Jersey, resting her hand on Jersey's shoulder. She could have sat down on the arm of Jersey's chair, but it was best that she stand, and I appreciated her sensitivity without even being informed that this was a moment of crisis.

In two sentences I described Jersey's account of being checked by her father. Knowing that molestation was at issue, Mrs. Lewis, with dignity and authority as well as deep sorrow and tenderness, said, "Your father was in many ways a good man, Jersey, but he was not perfect. I wish I had known about this earlier. Dr. Peck is correct. He was a doctor of psychology only. He was not a medical doctor. He did not have the right to touch you that way. I am so sorry."

Jersey howled. Never before or since have I heard a cry of such anguish. Only when her lungs were exhausted did she, in a voice of utter dejection ask, "Are you sure, Mom?"

"Yes, I'm sure. I wish I didn't have to be."

Jersey leapt up from her chair. "I can't stay here any longer!" she screamed, running out the office door.

Much as I would have liked to have been able to help, I understood how Jersey felt. She needed to be alone. "Go after her," I instructed Mrs. Lewis. "Better you at this kind of time than me. She doesn't need my attentions now nearly as much as she needs yours. Don't talk about the issue unless she wants to. I hope everything will be all right. Thank you for what you've done. It had to be done. I will be praying for the both of you. Please bring her back in the morning as scheduled."

I had said that I would be praying. That was an understatement. So also would it be for me to say dryly that it was a critical moment in Jersey's treatment, an essential part of an exorcism that had looked as if it had succeeded, but was now very much in doubt again. The clinician in me estimated the odds were approximately three-to-one that Jersey would not return in the morning, that she would leave with or without her mother, and that during the night she would choose to be repossessed rather than to face the truth with which she had just been confronted. I doubted she could handle it. It seemed to me that the stakes for her psyche were just too high. I doubted that I would ever see her again. Oh yes, I prayed. I prayed harder than I had ever prayed in my life.

———◆———

But in the morning Jersey was back in my office, smiling. "Hi, Dr. Peck," she said gaily.

"And a hi back to you," I responded. "But you act as if nothing had happened, Jersey. You were in enormous pain last night. I wasn't sure that you'd be back here this morning. How on earth was your night?"

I was prepared for Jersey's denial. I was not prepared for her extraordinary resilience. "I'm sorry I contradicted you last night, Dr. Peck," she said. "It was childish of me. Even at the time I knew you were right."

"You're really okay?" I asked dumbly.

"Of course I'm okay."

I still suspected massive denial. "But are you aware of the significance of what happened last night?"

"Yes."

"Are you aware that you were, in fact, sexually molested by your father back then when you were twelve?"

"I don't like that word," Jersey responded, "but I guess there's no other one."

"But how do you feel about the fact?"

"I'm angry at it. I'm angry at him," Jersey said. "He deceived me. But there is nothing I can do about it. He died. He's dead now. It's all in the past."

I scanned her face for the reappearance of that dreadful satanic expression, but there was not a hint of it. "You're very strong, Jersey," I praised her. "But are you aware of how you also deceived yourself?"

"What do you mean?" Jersey asked, looking slightly less happy. "He is the one who deceived me. He had everyone calling him Doctor. He wore a medical doctor's coat. And he kept telling me, as he fingered me, that it was all right because he was a doctor."

"And you believed him?"

"Of course. He was my father, wasn't he?"

"You're correct, Jersey; he did deceive you, but why were you such a pushover for his deception? Didn't you have any doubts?"

She thought that I was accusing her of wanting to have sex with her father, as some psychiatrists might have done. "I didn't want him to be sexual with me." Jersey was quick. "I was innocent."

"This is the tough part, Jersey," I said, "but it's crucial. Do you remember the other night how I was telling you that it was good to doubt under most circumstances? How you got in trouble with all the ideas the spiritualist groups were feeding you? You simply believed them, no questions asked. Do you remember us talking about that?"

"Yeah, I remember. So?"

"So you were naive," I pressed forward, as gently as I could. "You bought it all without really thinking about it. Way back after that day I first met you, I wrote in my notes that you were naive. Naive is very close to innocence, but it's not quite the same thing. When we say that somebody is naive, we generally mean it as a criticism of sorts. We mean that the naive person is more innocent than she should be. It is something that's age-related. It's normal for a six-year-old to be naive and innocent. But when an eighteen-year-old is just as naive as she was when she was six, then something has gone seriously wrong. You were twelve at the time your father molested you, halfway between age six and age eighteen. What I'm saying is, that by age twelve, you shouldn't have believed your father so easily, so unquestioningly. By twelve you should have been a little bit more skeptical. Do you follow me?"

"I think so," Jersey answered, "but I feel that you're trying to get at something. What are you trying to get at?"

"Excellent!" I exclaimed. "You're already starting to become less innocent. You're wondering what's behind what I'm asking. You're quite correct, I am trying to get at something."

Bolstered by my little bit of encouragement, Jersey seemed quite calm and open. "What I'm trying to get at," I continued, "is whether you *chose* to believe your father when he told you that what he was doing was all right because he was a doctor. Despite his white coat, I think on some level you knew that he wasn't a medical doctor, but a psychologist, not someone who was trained or privileged to explore your body. By the age of twelve, I think you should already have known the difference between a psychologist and a medical doctor. But I suspect you chose not to think about what you already knew."

I knew Jersey was with me by the very fact that she started to get angry. "I was innocent, I told you," she said. "I was only twelve. What other choice did I have but to believe him?"

"Precious little! You're catching on," I encouraged her. "But I want to talk about that precious little, tiny piece of choice. While I believe you had a tiny bit of awareness that your father was not a medical doctor, you were in an almost impossible bind. Theoretically, you could have confronted your father. But it's not easy to confront your father about such a thing, is it? You also could have gone to your mother and asked her back then whether he was a medical doctor. Or you could have told her what he was doing and how uneasy you felt about it. But again, it's not easy for a twelve-year-old girl to tell her mother such things, even when there is a good relationship between them. No, it would have been very difficult indeed—and very painful—to exercise that precious little bit of choice you had. That's why you chose to believe your father's lie. It was so much easier and seemed so much less painful than holding on to the truth.

"I'm making such a big deal of this, Jersey, because I suspect that was the moment when your possession first began. The moment when you chose to believe a lie even though you knew it was a lie. I cannot blame you for making that choice. Nobody could. No court of law would ever blame you. Your father was the criminal and you were the victim. So I do not blame you. God doesn't blame you. But the fact is that at the time you still, natural though it was, turned your back on what you knew was true and chose to believe what you knew was a lie."

Jersey was silent. I joined her in the silence; I thought we both needed it. I had no idea what she was thinking. I used the silence to pray that she was thinking clearly.

After five minutes I had prayed all that I could pray, and I almost desperately needed Jersey to check in with me. "How are you doing?" I asked.

"I'm confused," she answered. "You want me to question what people tell me? All right, I question what you're saying. I find it hard to believe that such a little thing could have been the beginning of my possession. And if I do believe it, then I find it hard to believe that you or God or life could be so unfair."

"It was unfair, Jersey," I answered her. "But it wasn't God or life that was so unfair; it was the devil. You've noticed how I always call the devil 'it'?"

Jersey nodded.

"That's because I hate the son of a bitch so much!" Jersey laughed like a child hearing her parents swear for the first time. "Of course, a son of a bitch is male," I continued, "so it's not the right term. Satan is neither male nor female. There's nothing male or female about it. Nothing sexual. Sexuality has to do with creation. The devil doesn't create anything; it only destroys. It loves to destroy, and that's why it's not fair. Yes, you had precious little choice. It was natural for you to believe the lie. But in doing that, by not exercising your precious little choice, you left a tiny little crack where the devil could get in.

"Now let me tell you something else," I went on. "Something that's very important but that also has nothing to do with fairness. There are people walking around not only believing but telling all sorts of lies, people who have cracks in their armor, their personality far, far bigger than your tiny little crack ever was, and yet the devil never gets into them. I don't know why that is. Nobody does. But it sure as hell isn't fair."

That was the gist of it. Jersey had survived one of the worst things a psychiatrist can throw at anyone. During the twelve days that followed we were to go over her father's sexual molestation several times, elaborating on the unfairness of it as well as the unfairness that the devil had taken advantage of such a tiny and pardonable wrong choice. But I also emphasized during those times that it had been, in fact, a wrong choice on her part. Continuing a theme from the exorcism proper, I repeatedly told her that God is truth, and truth is what is real. The choice to believe her father's lie because it was the less painful alternative was a choice to believe unreality. And unreality belonged to the devil. "Unreality is darkness, confusion. Truth is light." It was no accident, I explained, that for at least two thousand years the devil has been called either the Father of Lies or the Prince of Darkness.

———◆———

As much as Jersey continued to dislike spending two hours a day watching the videotapes of her exorcism, she did so, and I could not restrain myself from making particular note of Emil, her last demon before Satan itself. I thought it might not be an accident that Emil, the phony scientist, was the last before Satan.

Over and over again I instructed Jersey that the truth was holy and that real science—not phony science—was probably the most lucid way of approaching the truth, I joyfully acknowledged that the world was full of mystery. I explained how mystery is something we can never fully grasp, which we can only approach. Nonetheless, the light of truth—as painstakingly approached through science—was usually the best beacon that we human beings can have.

But I wasn't just delivering great moral homilies from on high. Just as the exorcism was not ordinary or even acceptable psychiatry, so also I did not regard our time together as ordinary psychotherapy. Consequently, I spent a fair amount of that time talking about myself. I told her about how, in the sixth grade, I had been caught drawing dirty pictures and lied to my parents about it, how my parents had caught me in that lie, and how they had begun to teach me my great respect for the truth. I told her about the little bits of scientific research I had engaged in during college and medical school. I told her about my curiosity for the truth, that curiosity that had driven me to seek out Malachi Martin and finally Jersey herself, so that I might know the truth about the devil. I explained how Malachi made the distinction between cases of what he called imperfect possession, such as her own, and perfect possession, which was his term for those people who were thoroughly evil. I told her how people with incomplete possession courageously managed to keep their souls intact even though they had been totally surrounded by the demonic, just like the picture she had drawn for me. I praised her for her courage and humbly thanked her—I too felt closer to the truth.

Just before she and her mother left for their home in the Southwest, we hugged good-bye. I promised that I would see her again sometime, although not soon. I wished her well. When she was gone I prayed that she would be able to have smooth sailing despite all the rocks and shoals and hidden sandbars of marriage, parenting, and life in general that she would have to navigate. It was a selfish prayer. Although I was turning Jersey's care over to Dr. Lieberman and others, a total psychoanalytic termination did not seem appropriate. I knew that to a small extent Jersey would continue to be my case for a little while yet. And I was aware that in praying for her smooth sailing, I was also praying for my own.

———•———

By and large it was smooth sailing for the both of us. Remarkably so, minus two things that happened over the next month.

Somehow I had the erroneous idea, perhaps fed by Malachi's book and the fact that we had baptized her, that the exorcism would not be a success unless Jersey ended up a card-carrying Christian. This was a major reason I arranged through Father O'Connor for her to see an experienced Christian counselor once a week—a woman Terry particularly recommended. About three weeks after she returned, Jersey called to inform me that she did not wish to continue seeing the counselor, feeling that her weekly visits to Dr. Lieberman were all that she wanted. In response to my questioning she told me that the particular counselor was not the problem—in fact, Jersey rather liked her—but that, with caring for her children, all she had time for was Dr. Lieberman. I asked Jersey to not make her decision final until I had at least talked to the counselor. Jersey reluctantly agreed.

When I phoned, the counselor told me that Jersey had expressed no interest in attending church or learning about Christian theology. I wondered whether this wasn't a great mistake, especially given Jersey's involvement with just about every other theology through her attendance at the spiritualist and other New Age centers in her city. Wasn't there some magical trick I could use to change Jersey's mind? The counselor informed me that as far as she could tell, Jersey was currently disinclined to pay attention to any sort of religion whatsoever, and this struck her as a proper outcome of the exorcism. It was not, however, the outcome I had expected, and I shared my disappointment with the woman. "As far as I can tell, Scotty," she said to me, "the exorcism was extremely successful. Maybe you should trust that. At this point I sense you are trying to get her to fit a mold. I think you need to let her go."

Though I was still uneasy, something about the woman's recommendation sounded right on the mark. I continued my relationship with Jersey, but I did let go of my need for her to become overtly Christian, even though it felt I was no longer going by the book.

The other discomforting instance occurred a month after the exorcism when I went down to New York City to meet with Malachi to tell him all the details. I concluded the report with my lingering worry the exorcism had not resulted in Jersey becoming an overt Christian. Completely unbothered, Malachi asked, "Has she become more humble?" Thinking about how Jersey had summarily terminated the relationship I had established with the Christian counselor and how the essential feistiness of Jersey's soul had in no way been lost, I answered, "Well, no. She has clearly become better behaved, and her mother reports that she has gone back to being a very good mother to the children. But I can't really say that she has become more humble."

"Weel, she's going to have to have another exorcism, then," Malachi responded. Bluntly. I felt devastated.

"The one infallible sign of the success of an exorcism," Malachi explained, "is that the victim—or as you refer to her, the patient—becomes obviously more humble. The humility is too dramatic to miss. You are very discerning, Scotty. If you haven't seen that glaring humility, then the exorcism was incomplete."

Malachi's proclamation was so certain that in order to recover from my devastation, I began to doubt his wisdom. Until that moment, as far as I was concerned, Malachi had batted a thousand. His advice to me had been infallible, but I was certain the exorcism had been a full success and left his apartment thinking that Malachi had made his first mistake. His batting average had declined in my mind to about .950. Still superhuman, but not flawless.

As it turned out, we were both right. I was soon vindicated, and Malachi's batting average returned to perfect.

Jersey did not like to write letters, but she began to deluge me with audiotapes. About a week after visiting Malachi, her second taped "letter" arrived, and that evening I sat down to listen to it. Barely into it, I heard her say, "I've got something very exciting to tell you about, Dr. Peck—at least, it's very exciting to me, but it may not seem that way to you."

Today I cannot remember what it was that was so exciting to Jersey, but I remember as if it were yesterday how excited I was. She had qualified her exclamation with the acknowledgment that it might not be a universal assessment. I couldn't remember her doing such a thing before. I listened carefully as she continued on. A few minutes later she said something else that struck me in the same way. In regard to another insight she had had, she noted, "I think that it's true, but I use the word 'think,' because I really don't *know* it's true. Somebody else might think differently." Again, this was not the sort of statement Jersey would have made a month before.

As soon as I sat back to think about the difference, I realized the essence was, in fact, humility. She had not only become able to doubt what others might tell her, but also to doubt herself. She had become more intellectually humble than I had imagined she ever would. Malachi had been dead-on in pinpointing the essence of the resulting change; I simply had never taken note of it until now. I now had overt corroborating evidence to confirm my deep feeling that the exorcism had been more than a partial success. By virtue of Jersey's growing intellectual humility, I realized that even if the exorcism had failed to turn her into an outspoken Christian, it had succeeded in turning her into an emotional scientist. I had not before understood the fact that humility is the very basis of the scientific method.

———◆———

So we were back to smooth sailing. Six months after the exorcism, I flew to the Southwest specifically to see Jersey for follow-up. My initial visit with her at her home was brief. Mainly I used it simply to observe her interacting with her children, one a very young toddler and one about to graduate into a preschooler. She was remarkably patient and loving with them.

The rest of the first day I spent with Dr. Lieberman, in a pre-arranged two-hour visit. He was older than I had expected, a genial man in his late fifties, a good dozen years older than myself. My visit to his office began with my asking him about his religious faith. "As you might gather from my name," he answered me openly, "I come from a Jewish background, and I think of myself as a Jew. But I also would have to be labeled a secular Jew. I do not have any personal relationship with the god of the Jews any more than I have with a Christian sort of god. It is not that I deny the possibility of God's existence. I am not an atheist. But since I cannot affirm God's existence either, I suppose I would fall into the category of agnostic."

As far as I was concerned, agnostic was good, and I said so. Indeed, I believe that the state of not knowing, of being an agnostic, is potentially holy. "But I am a bit concerned about how the details of Jersey's exorcism might affect you, since it was, by and large, such an overtly religious event—and specifically such a Christian one."

"I'm very interested to hear about it," Dr. Lieberman assured me, "but I am not a terribly deep thinker—and I rather like being that way, so don't misinterpret that as lack of interest. Jersey doesn't seem to remember much about it, unlike the way she remembers your postexorcism work, including your excellent work regarding her molestation by her father, all of which she remembers with great clarity. But I doubt that your account of the exorcism will affect me very much. I've not had any experience with such a thing. I do not think that I will tune it out, so to speak, but I also don't expect to tune into it very much. It's sort of my way with things."

So I went ahead and told him. I had gotten Jersey's permission to do so. At the conclusion of my tale, Dr. Lieberman's response was carefully measured.

"I'm not going to tell you anything about my own work with Jersey," he said. "This may seem unusual to you, but it's another example of the way that I deliberately stay neutral. I will only tell you what I imagine you already know, and that is that Jersey is highly ambivalent about the exorcism. On the one hand, she is very grateful to you. Simultaneously, she feels that it was violating—necessarily so, without doubt—but, like a rape, she has no desire to relive it. As for myself, as I suggested, I also have no desire to learn about it more deeply. I don't understand it, and I will put what you have told me into that realm of things I prefer not to think much about. Yet I will say this: without understanding it in the least, I can state that whatever in the world it was that you did, I have no doubt whatsoever that it was extraordinarily helpful to her. Before it I twice had the experience of being unable to engage her in psychotherapy. When she returned from your care, I did not have the slightest difficulty in so engaging her."

I thanked him for all that he had done, noting his flexibility in arranging for Jersey's psychological testing, treating her during her quite lengthy hospitalization, and allowing me to see her professionally during that hospitalization. And that was it. Instinctively I liked the man. I could imagine how healing his cheerful neutrality would be for almost anyone, but it was certainly different from my own much more passionate style. And though I both liked and appreciated him, I don't think I understood Dr. Lieberman any better than he understood me.

Save for a brief pause to accept the gratitude of her mother and stepfather, I spent most of the next day with Jersey. Only in the early afternoon did one distinctly weird thing occur. She was telling me how she continued to be "bothered," meaning that she continued to hear voices, but she added "Of course, as I've told you, it's not at all like it was before."

"Still, you have no question that they continue to be demonic voices?" I inquired.

"Oh," she answered, "they're demons, all right. A large number of them."

Ambivalent, I decided to delve a bit more deeply. "Is there one of those demons that particularly stands out?" I asked.

"No," she replied. "As I told you, it's not like it was before—not like it was with the Lord Josiah. He doesn't seem to be hanging around anymore. They come and go so rapidly, I can't really identify any of them. Certainly I don't know their names."

"Can I talk to one of them?" I asked.

"Oh, I don't think so," she told me with a note of determination in her voice. I guessed that her determination was born of fear: that by my talking with even one of them, it would be like the exorcism. And that she did not want to go through that again. I promised her it would not be like the exorcism. I reminded her of the first time we met six months before the exorcism, and how I had talked to a couple of her demons under hypnosis. Feeling very much like I was wandering toward Alice's Wonderland again, I asked, "How would you feel if I hypnotized you like I did back then and just briefly talked to one of them?"

Jersey was amenable. I suspected this was because she felt relieved of any responsibility for what she might say under hypnosis, and that she somehow enjoyed being hypnotized.

As she had during that very first visit, she entered a deep trance very quickly. "Let whichever one wants to step forward," I said.

There was a full minute of silence. I was almost at the point of thinking that nothing would happen when, in Jersey's voice, I heard: "Hello, Dr. Peck. I've never met a real author before."

"Are you a man or a woman?" I inquired of it.

"Just a woman, a very ordinary woman," it answered me in a flat, slightly depressed tone.

Not wanting it to be an exorcism of any kind, my instinct was not to ask its name. Instead, I asked, "What do you do?"

"I'm just a secretary," it said. "The lowest of the low."

"The lowest of the low where?"

"In an office. Actually, I'm lower than a secretary. I'm really a clerk."

It did not seem eager to divulge much about itself. "What kind of an office is it that you work in?" I asked.

"I'm a clerk in the office of a construction company."

Feeling almost as stupid as it seemed to feel, I inquired, "Whereabouts? Where is the construction company?"

The one word answer it (or the woman) gave was "Anaheim."

Since I didn't have the least idea what I was doing, I felt it was time to retreat. I brought Jersey back out of hypnosis, and we talked a little about her parents and siblings. I didn't want to pry or do anything that would interfere with Dr. Lieberman's therapy. I called a cab. While waiting for it, I watched Jersey feed her children. The cab arrived and I left.

I took a night flight back. I had some writing I could do, but put it aside to ponder the visit. The strangest part of it, of course, had been the brief hypnotic session that afternoon. Jersey remained consistent about her voices being different from those she had when she was possessed, saying as before, "They're outside of me now." But how could they be outside of her, I wondered, if I could talk to even just one of them when she was under hypnosis? Assuming it was a demonic voice I had been talking to, didn't it have to be inside of her? Try as I might, I could come up with no metaphysical explanation. No answer.

I did, however, arrive at a possible insight regarding the little the demon had told me. "A clerk in the office of a construction company" lacked specificity, in contrast to the location of Anaheim. Quite specific. What meaning might it have? Why might Jersey (or the demon) come up with Anaheim? Anaheim where? I knew of only one Anaheim, namely the area of Southern California in which Disneyland is located. Could the two be related? Certainly Disneyland had been constructed. Its buildings were real. Yet they had also been constructed to represent the unreal or a complex of fantasies. Here, there was a faint glimmer of light. It somehow seemed fitting to me that a minor demon should work in a company engaged in the construction of unreality. If I knew anything about Satan by that time, it was that it was in the business of marketing unreality. Yes, it fit, but there was no place further to go with it.

Save for the voices, Jersey seemed well, and Dr. Lieberman acknowledged that even in his secular understanding, the end result of the exorcism had been successful. For the next six months, on those rare occasions when I would speak of the exorcism to the most highly selected of my professional friends, I made no great claims for it. Summing the event up for them, I would conclude, "At most, what the exorcism did was to transform a severe untreatable borderline personality into a severe treatable one."

Time, however, seemed to prove my modest assessment to be excessively so. Every six weeks Jersey would continue to send me a tape, which I faithfully listened to. The tapes usually contained nothing more than her talking fondly about how well her children were growing. But then some fourteen months after the exorcism, a tape arrived in which Jersey informed me that she had terminated therapy with Dr. Lieberman. I knew that she had been seeing Dr. Lieberman only once a week, although he had suggested more frequent visits. Yet on the tape she now told me that Dr. Lieberman had agreed to the termination of their relatively minimal work together.

Patients with borderline personalities do not get well in the course of a single year, even with the most intensive psychotherapy. Certainly not with once-a-week therapy. It just doesn't happen. I was sufficiently alarmed about it to call Dr. Lieberman. He had indeed agreed to the termination, he told me, saying, "I had no reason to keep on seeing her. She's really completely well, you know. There's nothing to treat her for. She's as healthy as any young woman I know."

"But what about her voices?" I insisted. "Certainly they mean something is still wrong, don't they?"

"I'm not so sure about that," he replied. "Oh, I'm aware that almost every other psychiatrist in the country would think that something is still terribly wrong. But I'm damned if I can find out what it is. I can't explain them to you, Scotty. All I can tell you is that although I have been in this business for quite a long time, I don't pretend to understand her voices. But I can tell you that every instinct I have as an old psychiatrist is that they do not signify a presence of any psychiatric disease. There's no question that she was, in my mind, psychiatrically ill when she first came to see me. You remember I told you that I don't think about things too deeply, and you can blame it on that if you want to, but I just don't think there is any psychiatric disease there anymore. As far as I'm concerned, she's well."

And I could not claim differently. Four months after my conversation with Dr. Lieberman, I returned to the Southwest for a second and final formal follow-up evaluation of Jersey. Yes, her voices continued, she told me, but she kept insisting that only occasionally did they really bother her. As far as her husband and parents were concerned, she was completely healed. Moreover, there were signs that she was maturing psychologically as well as, if not better than, any other woman her age. Her oldest child was now in preschool. Her husband had been quite successful in business. There was plenty of money for baby-sitters, and Jersey had already begun to move out beyond the confines of the home. She was taking courses to become a laboratory technician. In response to my questions, it rapidly became clear that she already knew far more about the details of blood and tissue analysis than I did. Indeed, with her simple pride, she joyfully told me that thus far she was at the top of her class. She liked the science of it.

She was not the least bit interested in religion, but she took pains to tell me that she also had no interest in esoteric things anymore. She acknowledged that every so often she did have the beginnings of a desire to return to the spiritualist center or one of the other psychic healing centers in the city, but she believed these desires to be nothing more than demonic temptations that she was able to shove out of her mind with ease. "Before I first saw you," she elaborated, "I had gotten pretty hooked on a lot of those New Age spiritual ideas, but I wasn't mature enough then to handle them. And I'm still not. Besides, as you taught me, they're just hypotheses at best. Maybe when I'm a good deal older I will be mature enough to handle such things. But somehow I imagine when I become that mature, I will probably just look into the ordinary old-fashioned religions. Maybe Judaism. You know, we have several friends who are Jews, and they really seem to have fun during their holidays. They send their children to Hebrew school. Someday I think that I might just like to go to school—not a child's school or a technical school but an adult one, a university, to study Hebrew. Probably you think that's pretty funny, Dr. Peck. You know, because it's not Christian. But something about studying Hebrew someday attracts me."

"I don't think it's funny at all, Jersey," I said. "I wouldn't mind doing it myself."

———◆———

That was my last formal assessment of Jersey. I did see her twice more when I happened to come to her city to lecture. Each time I called her up and asked if I could take her out to dinner, and she was delighted. The last time was just over six years after the exorcism. We went out to a Mexican restaurant, and I very much enjoyed the evening eating outside on the restaurant patio underneath the summer sky. We lingered a little bit after dinner because we were having fun, and without my thinking about it, Jersey had moved from being my patient to being a pleasant and interesting companion. I was struck by her intelligence and suspected that the old IQ test I had gotten on her no longer represented the reality of who she was.

But one thing had not changed, at least not completely. After I had asked the waitress for the check, Jersey took pains to tell me, "I'm still bothered, you know." Meaning, of course, that she still heard voices. "They don't bother me nearly as often as they used to," she went on, "although I must admit that they were really acting up this morning."

"Why do you think that was, Jersey?" I asked.

"I think it was because they knew that you were coming to town, Dr. Peck." She still called me Dr. Peck, although I had given her permission to call me Scotty. "I think they were really annoyed that we were going to have dinner together tonight."

"What were they saying?" I asked.

"They're so dull!" Jersey exclaimed. "They just kept repeating, over and over again, 'We're a closed system, you know; we're a closed system, you know, we're a closed system.' "

I looked at her intently, the issue of her intelligence still at the back of my mind. "And what did you think about that?" I asked.

"It seems so long ago," she mused, "back when we first met. You know, back before the exorcism. I know I was not a totally innocent victim, that I had bought into them—and it still seems like them, not Satan—but way back then they had made me into a closed system. So I know about the kind of closed systems they believe in. But I don't believe in them. I don't believe in any kind of a closed system. In fact I don't think anything ought to be a closed system. I think everything ought to be open to fresh input—to new information. So I just told them, 'Shut the fuck up and get the fuck out.' That was quite early this morning, and they haven't bothered me since."

CHAPTER 4

COMMENTARY

———◆———

Jersey's case was naturally dramatic. So as not to lose any of its dramatic tension, I chose to leave certain complex intellectual questions unanswered. But the questions are valid and important, deserving meaningful answers whenever possible. Consequently, I now address them in the form of a commentary upon the case.

One of the goals of the commentary is to highlight the mystery of evil by clarifying areas where we are still in the dark. I believe that, through more scientific exploration, we will be able to further shed light on the subject. I doubt, however, that it will ever be completely illuminated. In other words, when confronted with evil, I hope that the healers of the future will know better what they are doing than I did, but I suspect that to a considerable extent they will always need to act out of the emptiness of not knowing.*

The commentary will follow the story sequence, proceeding from the questions or issues raised at the story's opening, through its middle, to its conclusion. The commentary will be

---

* A phrase originated by the poet John Keats, which I have elaborated upon at length in a number of my previous works.

divided into four sections, entitled in order Diagnosis, Exorcism, Follow-up, and Further Considerations—the last covering issues that do not neatly fit into one of the three time-bound categories of Jersey's treatment.

Diagnosis

In *Hostage to the Devil,* Malachi wrote that it was rare for people who are possessed to seek treatment themselves. Most commonly, he reported, it is the possessed person's friends or relatives who first bring the problem to the attention of medical or religious professionals. That has been my own experience with the letters I have received from the public who wrote after reading the chapter "Possession and Exorcism" in my book about the broader subject of evil in general, *People of the Lie.* A few dozen such letters were from individuals who thought they might be possessed, but many hundreds were from parents who thought one of their children might be possessed; from husbands and wives who thought their spouse might be possessed; and from those who were worried about a particular friend.

Although the way that Jersey presented herself to Dr. Lieberman was relatively unusual, it highlights one of the most important things the public needs to know about possession. *Possessed people are not evil.* There are evil people aplenty in the world, and they were the primary subject of *People of the Lie.* I consider possession to be a rare condition in which the victims have a relationship with radical evil but have not been totally taken over by it. In *Hostage to the Devil,* Malachi suggested that those persons I called people of the lie and identified as being thoroughly evil were what he called "perfectly possessed." He made it clear that such people are not in any state of internal conflict and hence appear to be superficially well put together. Similarly, I noted in *People of the Lie* that the truly evil are notably self-satisfied, and hence the last people who would seek any kind of treatment for themselves.

The fact that Jersey sought treatment from Dr. Lieberman on her own was a profound indication of the reality that she considered her possession to be ego-alien.* In other words, she believed herself to be sick. To put it yet another way, she was in a state of conflict between her true soul and her afflictions. Malachi's perfectly possessed and my people of the lie have no such internal conflict.

Although there were ways Jersey seemed to fight against the efforts to help her, the essence of her story is that of a person desperately trying to preserve the core of her personality—her soul actually—against the encroachments of the evil surrounding her. Rather than being evil, Jersey was waging a heroic war against evil, and by story's end, her heroism became obvious.

———◆———

Thorazine was the first of a group of drugs called the phenothiazines, the earliest medications to have a clear antipsychotic effect. Dr. Lieberman attempted to prescribe it for Jersey because he suspected she was psychotic based on her self-diagnosis. Almost all psychiatrists in the United States do not believe that demonic possession is a real condition. It was typical, therefore, that Dr. Lieberman (despite the quite extraordinary flexibility he was to demonstrate) should have immediately assumed that Jersey's possession was a psychotic delusion, and he responded accordingly.

———◆———

Although initially I met Jersey with the assumption that her possession was imaginary and her case would be additional proof that the devil or the demonic did not exist, it is no accident I first began to question my assumption when she said she felt sorry for her demons. Physicians are taught that the best way to make

---

* An almost obsolete psychiatric term for symptoms that patients do not want and that are perceived as unnecessary hindrances to the lives they desire.

diagnoses is usually through a process of exclusion. If it was clear that Jersey was suffering from a standard, well-recognized psychiatric illness, then I would be able to exclude the possibility of demonic possession. Her description of her demons as weak and pathetic did not fit with any standard psychiatric diagnosis I had in mind. Consequently, it was then that I first began to include the possibility of possession as a correct diagnosis.

This moment of change on my part also has something telling to say about the demonic. Satan—the ultimate demon—has been called the Father of Lies since the time of Christ. The demonic is evil, and if we know nothing else about Satan, demons, or evil people, it is that they lie. Only as I delved more deeply into the subject of demonology did I learn that in believing her demons to be weak and pathetic, Jersey was the victim of a demonic lie. As I would eventually learn, her demons were in fact quite powerful. They pretended to be weak and pathetic in order to gain Jersey's sympathy, and Jersey had been sucked in by the pretense. But those who have professional experience with the demonic will come to realize that the demonic may actually give itself away by its lies. And that was exactly what happened in this instance, although I was not fully aware of the dynamics at the time. Nonetheless, despite my ignorance, my suspicions were first raised by a lie, and the lie was the first piece that made Jersey's case not fit the standard psychiatric mold.

———◆———

Because its mechanisms are not well understood and because a hypnotist can possess a kind of power easily subject to abuse, I have never felt comfortable using hypnosis as a psychiatrist. Other psychiatrists I have known have used hypnosis extensively to their patients' apparent significant benefit. Unlike them, I had personally never found it a useful tool in treating patients. I had, however, found it upon occasion to be a useful tool for diagnosis. Indeed, by the time I met Jersey, I customarily used it only for diagnosis. So it was for that reason I used it during my first meeting with Jersey. I hypnotized her because I thought that through hypnosis I could potentially obtain a better feel for her purported demons and hence for her diagnosis. But I was not using hypnosis for treatment, and I am glad that I instinctively withdrew when Jersey's demons asked me to treat them while Jersey was hypnotized.

———◆———

In the practice of medicine, we physicians often speak about the differential diagnosis. A differential diagnosis is the broadest possible grouping of different diseases that might account for the patient's complaints and symptoms. Once we have established a differential diagnosis or a list of such possible diseases, then we begin eliminating them one by one through laboratory testing, etc.—i.e., through a process of exclusion.

When we have gotten so far as to consider the possibility of demonic possession as a valid diagnosis, before we can actually make the diagnosis we must differentiate it from the other diseases that might produce a similar picture. The currently recognized disorder that manifests symptoms most like possession is Multiple Personality Disorder, or MPD (currently labeled and diagnosed as Dissociative Identity Disorder). Only in the past few years has MPD itself come under serious question as a valid diagnosis. However, despite its recent discrediting, there are still a substantial number of psychiatrists and other mental health professionals who upon hearing about Jersey's case from a distance would argue that it is a classical case of MPD. Such good men and women will also tell me that they have seen a great many cases of MPD in their practices. I have not.*

---

* There most definitely is such a thing as a dissociative reaction, or as it used to be called, a fugue state. This state is almost never a chronic condition as is MPD but a very acute condition where a person in a position of extraordinary stress will escape that stress by forgetting who he or she is and escaping into

For the present, however, there are some similarities between possession (which most definitely is not a diagnosis accepted by the American Psychiatric Association!) and MPD. I spoke of what an unusually good hypnotic subject Jersey was. People with MPD are also renowned for being easily hypnotized. I will admit that to a believer in MPD, Jersey's diagnosis at this point would certainly seem ambiguous. As the story goes on, however, I think that it will become more and more difficult to sustain a diagnosis of MPD in Jersey's case despite a few more similarities yet to come.

———◆———

Malachi's paragraph in *Hostage to the Devil* about the unusual frequency of people with possession having facial skin that looks strangely stretched, tight, and smooth is an extraordinary observation. Not only did Jersey have such a face; so also did my only other patient with possession, whose case will be recounted in part 2.

The physician in me is particularly intrigued. The phenomenon makes me wonder whether there might be a genetic element in possession to cause such a face. Or might such a face somehow be the result of years of possession? I can only speculate. I have no explanation to offer, but I do offer to the student of demonic possession my sense that this finding of Malachi's— corroborated by my own experience—is important. It is not only a useful factor in diagnosing possession, but also points to a fascinating area for research on the subject.

---

an unreal but more pleasant identity, usually for a very brief period of time. But such acute dissociative reactions are very different from the chronic condition of MPD and, as I said, in more than fifteen years of psychiatric practice before I met Jersey I had never to my knowledge seen a case of MPD. Indeed, my experience is now such that while some clinicians deeply suspect my cases of purported possession are actually cases of MPD, I have come to suspect the possibility that their purported cases of MPD might actually be cases of possession.

———◆———

In retrospect, given the psychologist's observation of lapses in Jersey's presence, it would have been wise of me to have requested that Dr. Lieberman order an electroencephalogram. Although I doubt the test would have demonstrated any evidence of epilepsy, it would still have been an addition to the thoroughness of the diagnostic phase of her case.

———◆———

Just as it is possible to sense the energy level in a conference room, so it is also possible for experienced individuals to sense the presence or absence of demonic energy. This is particularly the case when he or she is praying. Although this capacity can be developed with experience, it is not something a person can be trained to have. It is as if some people are born with a nascent capacity to sense the demonic, while others are not. This is why the early Christians referred to the capacity to discern the presence of evil as a gift. It was a gift from God granted to a relative few—and granted for God's own purposes.

———◆———

My sense that throughout this failed deliverance Jersey had been toying with us is a phenomenon of great significance. I was to have that sense numerous times while working with Jersey and again with the case of genuine possession described in part 2. That sense alone should be a sign for psychiatrists to begin to entertain the possibility of possession. As I acquired more experience with this phenomenon, I concluded that it occurred when the demonic was in ascendancy, shoving aside my patient's true personality or ego. In other words, if you feel that your patient is toying with you, it is possibly not your patient but your patient's demon that is speaking.

———◆———

The Roman Catholic church's traditional and formal guidelines for permitting an exorcism to take place require that an almost incontrovertible diagnosis of demonic possession first be made. Preeminent among its criteria for such a diagnosis is the presence of obvious and dramatic supernatural or distinctly paranormal signs in the patient's behavior—such as levitation, psychokinesis, an inexplicable knowledge of the future, or the ability to fluently speak or comprehend a foreign language the patient has never learned or been exposed to. My own firm belief, based on experience, is that these criteria are so unrealistically strict that they would deny an exorcism to the majority of victims genuinely possessed by the demonic.

While these criteria do, in my mind, have validity, I believe they should be enlarged to include more soft signs of the paranormal. I spoke of how the diagnosis of possession required the exclusion of standard psychiatric pathology. In making this exclusion I was in a very real sense using paranormal signs, by which I mean signs that did not fit normal pictures of psychiatric disease. The signs I used, however, were much more soft or subtle than those suggested in the church's criteria.

Jersey's feeling of sympathy for her demons was the first sign that did not fit with standard psychopathology, but it was so soft I would not classify it as supernatural or paranormal. However, her extremely brief episode of apparently severe schizophrenia while we were confronting her was. There are only two explanations I have been able to imagine that could have accounted for this momentary behavior. One would be classified as normal in that it falls within our traditional understanding of schizophrenic pathology. The only other explanation is a paranormal one.

First to the normal explanation. There is a phenomenon known to at least some psychiatrists as "the schizophrenic solution." By this term we mean that a patient who has at least a predisposition to schizophrenia may, at enormously stressful times, suddenly flip out into a state of schizophrenic insanity as a solution whereby he or she can escape from the stress. Occasionally, it is possible for the psychiatrist or psychotherapist to offer such a patient a different solution to the stress that doesn't require a state of unreality or psychosis. When offered such a solution it is not uncommon for the patient to flip back suddenly from the schizophrenic episode into reality once again. In other words, a schizophrenic state can represent a solution of sorts to the patient, but when offered a better solution, the patient may quickly take it.

Nonetheless, I have never heard of such a schizophrenic episode that was anywhere near as brief as Jersey's. Usually psychiatrists are talking of an episode lasting thirty minutes or more. Jersey's episode lasted no more than three minutes. Furthermore, while her episode may have been precipitated by the stress of learning she did not have a superior IQ, it did not end because she was offered a better solution. It ended because she was ordered to stop her behavior. Lastly, when she responded to this command, she did not return to her premorbid or normal state, as would have happened in a case of schizophrenic solution. Instead, she entered a dramatically different state—one quite consistent with demonic possession. Because of these anomalies, I am uncomfortable with the explanation of a schizophrenic solution for Jersey's fascinating behavior that afternoon.

The only other explanation I have for her almost instantaneous entrance into and departure from a state of classical schizophrenia was that she (or the demonic) was faking it. Faking is not necessarily paranormal behavior. But it seems to me that faking a somewhat unusual, even esoteric, form of behavior by a person who had no history of ever being previously exposed to such behavior is as paranormal as fluently speaking a foreign language one has never learned. And Jersey's imitation of severe, acute schizophrenic behavior was indeed fluent; it was flawless. Consequently, while I am willing to entertain the schizophrenic solution hypothesis, I am more inclined to accept the hypothesis that Jersey (or rather, the demonic) was brilliantly faking schizophrenia in a distinctly paranormal manner.

———◆———

Malachi was, to my knowledge, the only author ever to clearly outline and name the different stages of an exorcism. He used the term "Pretense" to describe the initial phase of an exorcism when a demon is present and speaking, but pretending to be the patient. The phase varies in duration from exorcism to exorcism. It is the first, and perhaps the greatest, task of the exorcist to break down or otherwise penetrate this Pretense, so as to expose the presence of the undisguised demonic.

At the point when both Terry and I kept asking Jersey whether it was she or the demonic who was speaking and it kept answering, "I'm Jersey," we were so ignorant that we could not fully diagnose the Pretense and hence we were unable to combat it effectively and break through it, even though we were close to doing so. As I look back at that afternoon with the knowledge I later gained under Malachi's tutelage, I am amazed at how dense Terry and I were.

———◆———

My visceral overreaction to Jersey's demonic rage is a commonly reported phenomenon during exorcisms or the evaluation of cases of genuine possession. To most it would probably not seem to be a paranormal phenomenon. Nonetheless, to the person who ever experiences it, the phenomenon feels not only irrational but also inexplicable. A well-written drama played by great actors in film or theater can evoke profound, powerful emotions in the audience. My literal gut reaction to Jersey's smiling rage that day in the hospital was ten times more powerful than any emotion I have ever experienced watching a play or movie. I would therefore classify it as another possible sign of true possession.

———◆———

By postmodern world, I am referring to our current time in which so many have lost not only their premodern faith in religion but also their modern faith in science. Consequently, many of us today lack the kind of anchors and stabilizing standards of behavior with which our ancestors were blessed. The term postmodernism refers to a recent mindset in which all values are relative—where one person's standards and judgments are just as valid as any other person's, no matter how different they might be.

In "A Brief Handbook of Exorcism," Malachi's brilliant introduction to *Hostage to the Devil,* he noted the role of the zeitgeist, or spirit of the times, in all of his cases when he wrote "evil moves cunningly along the lines of contemporary fads and interests, and within the usual bounds of experiences of ordinary men and women. No such fourteenth—or fifteenth—or sixteenth century case, for all its possible romantic appeal, would have any relevancy for us today. On the contrary it would remain a simple matter for us to dismiss such cases as fables made up to suit the fears or fancies of 'more ignorant' people of 'less sophisticated' times."

———◆———

Shortly after Dr. Lieberman discharged Jersey for her trip to Connecticut, he was called to meet with the chief of psychiatry and the other most senior psychiatrists of the hospital, to receive proper punishment for his unorthodox medical behavior. The staff took particular issue with the fact that Dr. Lieberman had admitted Jersey with the diagnosis of schizophrenia when the real diagnosis was that of possession. Dr. Lieberman asked his prosecutors what would have happened had he admitted her with a diagnosis of possession. The senior staff conceded that they then would have refused to admit her, despite knowing that she did need inpatient care. Although the senior staff were confused by it all, they recognized they had put Dr. Lieberman in a Catch-22 position; thankfully, their slap on his wrist was a very light one.

Exorcism

Each of the cases Malachi described in *Hostage to the Devil* taught me that the exorcist should never function alone. Only one of the reasons for having a team is to provide restraint for the patient when it is needed. I believe all five patients Malachi described did need restraint at one time or another during the exorcism. It may also be recalled that despite his title of diocesan exorcist, Father O'Connor excused himself from Jersey's case on the basis that he was not constitutionally equipped to conduct a combative exorcism. My experience with two cases would suggest that the exorcism of anyone with genuine demonic possession will probably be a combative one in which the patient will need restraint at some point.

But restraint is not the sole purpose for which a team is required. A most important purpose, I believe, is to serve as witnesses. Some years ago I was requested by a psychiatrist in a distant state to provide him with a phone consultation about a patient he thought might be possessed. Among the thousands of cases that came to my attention one way or another, his was one of the very few I quickly and seriously suspected of being genuine possession. I so informed the psychiatrist, and, in no uncertain terms, told him that he should become involved in an exorcism of the case only with a team of at least three, and preferably more, other people. Unfortunately, this psychiatrist proceeded to attempt to exorcise his patient without a team. Several years later, the man called me to say that he was in serious legal difficulty because the patient in question was suing him for everything he had. During that phone call he acknowledged the advice I had given him and obviously repented his failure to take it. I did not inquire about any other details, but I imagine that the man's legal difficulties could likely have been completely prevented had he a team of witnesses.

There are other reasons for a team. One, which Malachi clearly pointed out, was so that there would be an assistant exorcist who could take over if the exorcist became disabled or unfit. I also believe that a well-selected team greatly benefits the exorcist by providing advice when appropriate, although, as Malachi made clear, the exorcist must have the ultimate authority. Providing witnesses to an exorcism is so important that one of my team in Jersey's case suggested that the entire exorcism should be videotaped. I asked Malachi about this suggestion and he heartily agreed.

One thing I did as a result of my medical experience and familiarity with malpractice, which looms over every physician, was to develop meticulous consent forms for Jersey and her family to sign. This process was not mentioned in *Hostage to the Devil,* and I don't know whether Malachi used it with his cases. His cases were so dramatic, it is possible that several of the victims were not even in good enough shape to give informed consent to the exorcism procedures, including not only restraint but also the possibility of severe physical and emotional stress, and even death. In my cases, however, I found it extremely helpful to use permission forms, not only for my own legal protection and sense of security, but also as a helpful vehicle to thoroughly inform the patient and the patient's family of the risks.

Finally, there is a reason for a team that may be more powerful than all the other reasons rolled together. It is that, by God's grace and the exorcist's leadership, the team will often become a true community. Such a community is too mystical a subject to be explained briefly (it is the entire subject of my book *The Different Drum*). Suffice it to say that such a community is inherently healing and may thereby contribute more than the exorcist to the exorcism's success.

———•———

After telling Malachi about how Jersey simply "phased out" during the formal Roman Catholic ritual of exorcism we conducted at the conclusion of the first day, and how the ritual had therefore been useless, I said to Malachi, "There is no magic, is there?" Malachi answered, "No, there is no magic."

———•———

I suggested that when the team and I decided, very late in the first evening, that we would no longer listen to Jersey's gibberish but would instead "speak only with demons on the one hand, or a healthy Jersey who made sense on the other," we were doing something unwittingly brilliant. This approach was, I believe, the key to the success of the exorcism, specifically because it initiated the separation process, thereby unlocking the otherwise unopenable gate of her Pretense and revealing the demonic presence (another phase of exorcism). I was to use the same technique in the second exorcism with which I was later involved, so that the Pretense was abolished by the end of the first morning.

Although Malachi did not mention its use in his five cases, I particularly want to emphasize this approach or technique so that it at least is considered by any reader of this work who might be involved in some future exorcism. There is a reason beyond my own experience for doing so. I suspect the technique might have proved successful in the only case of genuine possession in twentieth-century America, other than mine and Malachi's, I have read about.

That account is contained in a book by Thomas B. Allen entitled *Possessed: The True Story of an Exorcism.* Allen, a reporter, became interested in whether Blatty's famous book, *The Exorcist,* and the resulting film were based on a real case. It was not difficult to learn that they were, but Allen had considerably more trouble obtaining an accurate account of the case and the exorcism. Blatty had disguised the case, at the request of the exorcist, by making it that of a thirteen-year-old girl who was exorcised in Washington, D.C. The real victim was a thirteen-year-old boy who was exorcised primarily in St. Louis, Missouri, in the spring of 1949. The real exorcism took thirty-three days. The primary exorcist, Father Bowdern, a middle-aged Jesuit priest, behaved bravely and brilliantly. Had he known about this simple technique of encouraging separation, however, I believe it possible he could have reduced the time required from thirty-three days to three.

———◆———

Despite the fact that Jersey's demons hid behind Jesus, I suspect it is no accident that the Pretense finally collapsed and the demonic totally revealed itself for the first time when the issue of the Christian church was raised.

As I said previously, *Hostage to the Devil* was the first book ever, to my knowledge, to outline and define the different stages of real exorcisms. These stages Malachi listed as Presence, Pretense, Break Point, Voice, Clash, and Expulsion. In doing so, Malachi was the first to offer exorcists a map. Although this was a great contribution, I believe the map can be confusing, because Malachi's stages do not always occur in the order he listed them, or two stages may so closely blend together as to be indistinguishable. I myself would choose to simplify the map by deleting Break Point and Voice and reversing the order of Presence and Pretense, resulting in only four stages, ordered Pretense, Presence, Clash, and Expulsion.

I would agree with Malachi that the presence of the demonic can be felt before an exorcism. For instance, Father O'Connor and I had a definite feeling of a demonic Presence within Jersey during her failed deliverance and the day of confrontation that followed it. In my experience, however, this feeling of Presence is quite intuitive and subjective, constituting at best an educated guess. The full reality of the demonic Presence is still, to a considerable degree, hidden behind the Pretense. Thus Father O'Connor and I were uncertain whether it was Jersey or the demonic speaking to us, still being at least partially deceived by the Pretense.

In the chapter on possession and exorcism in *People of the Lie* I compared an exorcism to brain surgery. Physicians do not perform such surgery unless they are approximately 95 percent sure of what they will find when they penetrate the skull and expose the brain to inspection. But there is no absolute certainty until the actual surgery. For instance, they may expect to find a tumor within the brain, but may instead find an abscess—or vice versa. It is only during the process of exorcism that the Pretense is completely shattered and the demonic Presence is fully exposed.

Malachi is correct that the exorcist's first task in an exorcism is to break down the Pretense. He is also correct that this is often the most difficult and time-consuming stage of an exorcism. During Jersey's exorcism, it took us two and a half of the four days to break through the Pretense, and we were able to do so only because we had hit upon the technique for encouraging separation.

The moment when the Pretense is finally penetrated is what Malachi called Break Point. I do not believe it should be designated as a stage because, in my experience, it is so instantaneous. I have said that in Jersey's case the Pretense was shattered the moment Damien appeared and at that moment removed any uncertainty about the Presence of the demonic. It was present.

By Clash, Malachi meant a clash of wills between the demonic and the exorcist. I believe this to be a feature of every exorcism, although there are ambiguities that I shall discuss shortly. What Malachi called Voice is not, in my experience, a phenomenon of every exorcism. For instance, we never heard anything other than Jersey's typical voice during her exorcism.

Her demons did not adopt any different or paranormal voice, nor did we ever hear the "babble of multiple demonic voices" that *Hostage to the Devil* described. I trust Malachi so much as to believe that the phenomenon he called Voice occurs during many exorcisms, but it did not occur in either of my two cases, and I therefore do not think it should be considered an inevitable stage of exorcisms in general.

As for the stage of Expulsion, as the word implies, it occurs at the conclusion of every successful exorcism. Malachi suggested that it is ultimately the free will of the patient that chooses to expel the demonic, but he was not as forceful on this point as I would be. Consequently, he often made it seem as if it were the exorcist himself who expelled the demonic, while to my way of thinking, the most the exorcist can do is assist—perhaps even enlist—the patient in exercising his or her free will by choosing to sever relations with the demonic completely. It may be a very brief moment, as in the exorcism detailed in part 2, or a prolonged period as it was in Jersey's exorcism, but the moment that choice is made is the moment of Expulsion.

———◆———

Malachi also said that in each of his five cases, the "one basic note of possession is confusion." The fact that here we were dealing with a specific demon of confusion should not be taken to mean that Jersey's confusion was confined to this particular demon. It was generalized. She was confused about many, many things.

As described, however, this particular demon almost managed to discombobulate me when it first appeared. In talking about it, however, one team member told me that during the minute or two I was dealing with my confusion she saw my face turn beet red and was genuinely concerned I might have a stroke. She suggested that that was the moment of the Clash between me and the demonic. She may well have been right.

However, my personal subjective experience of discomfort during those two minutes or so was less than my discomfort when, before the exorcism, Jersey screamed at me because I had refused to allow her to leave the hospital. As I recounted, even though I was aware that Jersey—or the demonic—was taking pleasure in her rage, I was helpless to prevent the intense feeling that the entirety of my intestines were being twisted and stomped upon. What I am saying is that possibly there were two separate Clashes, one during the exorcism and one before it, and I simply note that I experienced the earlier one as the greater.

———◆———

I have told how the Presence of the demonic was made most dramatic to me by the sudden—really instantaneous—paranormal appearance of an expression on Jersey's face that I can only describe as blatantly satanic. Jersey and her mother watched the videotapes during the two and a half weeks following the exorcism, returning them just before traveling home. It was years before I looked at them, even though I occasionally wondered whether the camera had captured that ghastly paranormal expression that appeared whenever a new demon presented itself during the exorcism.

It was only in preparation for writing this book that I reviewed the videotapes for the first time, almost two decades after the fact. The results were surprising, to say the least. With but one exception, I could discern no significant change in Jersey's facial expression when each demon presented itself. In the videotape, she appeared essentially like the ordinary Jersey at these times, save for the fact that she tended to twist her mouth in a slightly strange way. However, after Lord Josiah, "the spirit of love and gentleness," made itself manifest and just before she had to be restrained, Jersey turned away from the camera so that her face was in profile for no more then ten seconds—probably less. During those few seconds her face did undergo a transformation, even more dramatic and inexplicable—and horrible—than what I had experienced. For that ever-so-brief period, her expression was not only blatantly satanic; it was as if her very physiology had undergone an inhuman shift. The skin of her face, normally unusually taut and smooth, became deeply creased and wrinkled. In addition to being a satanic face, it was also the face of an old woman—an ancient gnarled witch. It was no subjective experience of mine. It is on the film, and the dramatic shift in facial expression was recently verified by one of the original team members.

As soon as she turned her face back to the camera, the expression was gone, and it looked as if Jersey had instantly grown a hundred years younger. The camera and its film never captured the phenomenon again. Yet the presence of Satan would continue to register itself on my retinas whenever the demonic reappeared for the remainder of the exorcism.

What to make of this? I do not know. For the moment it feels correct to leave the mystery of the matter where it is. Later I will touch upon it in a certain respect, but not in such a way as to explain it scientifically. The mystery will stay unsolved.

———◆———

It is no accident, I suspect, that the demon Josiah did not go away as we spoke about its basic fallacy (i.e., love is whatever you want to call it and does not require any translation into action). It went away only after the fallacy was exposed to Jersey in the here and now, specifically when I wanted a cigarette every bit as much as she but was not going to break to have one because getting rid of Josiah was more important. In a sense I gave Jersey a very minor but still living example of sacrifice (or love) in action, and Josiah vanished so rapidly thereafter we didn't even realize right away that it was gone.

———◆———

Watching the videotape I was struck by the fact that dealing with Emil was the only time during the entire exorcism that I raised my voice and shouted at one of Jersey's demons. It was not inappropriate that I displayed anger at and disdain for these demons and the lies they represented. Such a response to the demonic is even recommended in the Roman Ritual. Still, it was dramatic how vigorously and loudly I displayed my anger. It became clear to me how precious—in fact "holy"—science and the scientific method are to me. So it is that I found this demon of pretend science to be personally even more offensive than the demon of pretend love. Partly, I think, this is because people pretend love all the time and usually are not penalized for it. But when a white-coated professional fakes science, he gets defrocked.

———◆———

It is notable that when dealing with Satan I suddenly changed my entire approach. As for the preceding lesser demons, after identifying the particular falsehood each was professing, the team and I proceeded to demonstrate intellectually why it was a falsehood, making it look ridiculous. But having identified Satan, I did nothing to discern its falseness or try to demolish the lie by argument. Indeed, I even expressed our gratitude toward it and then, without more ado, began to order it quietly to be gone for no other reason than "your usefulness is at an end." Why this change in strategy?

I don't know really. I was, I think, in a kind of hyperalert state and operating on an extraordinarily intuitive level at the time. I did not think out my new strategy; it simply felt like the right way to proceed. And I suspect it was. While it was all right for me to argue with the lesser demons, I think I knew there was no point in arguing with Satan. The only point was to get rid of it. It may have been no accident that the process by which I ordered it out was a kind of hypnotic one. Certainly I knew what an unusually good hypnotic subject Jersey was, and I may instinctively have used her ability in this regard to her benefit. It should be noted, however, that I did not induce a hypnotic state in Jersey, nor did I do anything to bring her out of such a state. It is therefore quite possible that hypnosis had nothing to do with the expulsion.

And then I cannot be entirely sure I didn't change my strategy simply because it was the end of the last day and we had so little time left. I didn't feel there was time to argue with Satan.

Follow-up

Since it seemed as if I (or Jersey) had effectively driven Satan out during the long hypnotic period of expulsion the night before, I cannot explain with any certainty why the satanic expression partially and briefly returned to her face. It was obviously associated with the return of Jersey's belligerent behavior and posturing. But the fact is that while we scientists have a physiology of the body, we do not have a physiology of spirit or spirits. We don't know the mechanics involved. Nor do I know why the expression of Satan so quickly vanished, never again to appear in my presence. The only thing I can say worthy of note is that Jersey and the demonic had been keeping company for fifteen years. The phenomenon will become even more dramatic and clear in the case described in part 2. No matter how much Jersey disliked her demonic company (remember our story began with her asking for help) and no matter how much she came to despise it during the exorcism, I doubt it is possible for us to keep company with anything for so long without experiencing at least some degree of emptiness and longing when it departs. In that respect, it does not surprise me that Jersey might have invited it back ever so briefly. Actually, I find it more difficult to explain why she apparently never invited it back after that.

Jersey's recollection of being sexually molested by her father was the most critical event of her psychotherapy. The fact that this event occurred at the particular time it did was no accident. Indeed, the timing is illustrative of several major principles concerning the nature of psychotherapy and the nature of possession—such major principles that we should stop for a while to consider them.

During the course of successful psychotherapy, the patient's entire mind and soul are cooperating with the therapist and the therapeutic process. It is therefore common—routine—for the patient at this time to recall critical events in his or her life that previously lay in the shadows of awareness.

———◆———

It was both my own experience and that of the very few other exorcists I have known that before we began the exorcisms we had a pretty good idea when our patients' possession had started. Thus, knowing that Jersey had taken to reading the works of Edgar Cayce at age twelve, and from a few other bits of information, I guessed her possession had begun at that time. This guess was corroborated during the course of the exorcism when Jersey, then age twenty-seven, stated, "I've been possessed for fifteen years now. During the last fifteen years I haven't really lived. I'm really just twelve years old."

But while exorcists generally have a good idea before the exorcism when their patients first became possessed, they often have no idea why. The reason they don't know why is because their patients are not cooperating with them before the exorcism. They are too busy cooperating with their demons to cooperative with psychotherapy. This was why Dr. Lieberman had been unable to engage Jersey in psychotherapy and why I was ignorant of the reason for Jersey's possession.

After the exorcism, however, Jersey was able to cooperate with me and the therapeutic process. Before the exorcism I had also asked her, "I wonder what else was going on with you at the age of twelve," but I had not received any meaningful answer. Now, after the exorcism, no longer cooperating with her demons, Jersey was fully engaged and cooperative, so this time when I asked her, "I wonder what else was going on with you at the age of twelve," the facts of her appendicitis and the molestation naturally came out.

I have never had a patient in psychotherapy who recovered a memory he or she had totally forgotten. As in my own therapy, when my patients have recalled an event, it was not something they had forgotten, but simply something they hadn't thought about or given any importance. In therapy these events naturally come to the front of the mind, where they can be ascribed the importance they deserve. So it was with Jersey.

———◆———

I told Jersey there were huge numbers of people with far greater personality defects than hers, but who never became possessed, indicating I did not understand why this should be so and acknowledged to her that it seemed unfair, as well as mysterious.

It was not until I worked with my second case of possession, as recounted in chapter 5, that I began to get an inkling of why such a small few become possessed while most do not. Both that person and Jersey literally glowed upon the completion of their exorcisms, and I have heard of other patients glowing in such a manner. Even Malachi gave passing mention to the phenomenon in several of his cases. I said that glow was literal. Having seen it, I sensed why medieval painters had depicted the saints with a halo. It was, I think, the only way they could capture the light of holiness.

I would not say that either Jersey or my later patient were full-blown saints, but I can say that there was a touch of holiness about them. Christian doctrine holds that the devil was defeated the moment Christ died on the cross and, while it often doesn't seem that way, when we are fighting with the forces of evil it is actually a mop-up operation. According to this doctrine, Satan is basically on the run. Consequently, I surmise, it has only limited energy, just enough to try to put out the fires. I think it is very possible that Satan chose Jersey for attack because of this hint of holiness about her—because she may well have been a saint in the making and hence one of the relative few who represented a particular threat to Satan.

———◆———

To this day I do not understand why Jersey continued to hear demonic voices—voices of demons I could actually communicate with when Jersey was hypnotized—when she was otherwise, by my own assessment and that of Dr. Lieberman, perfectly well and completely restored to mental health. Indeed, the vast majority of psychiatrists would think that anyone who hears voices must have a severe mental illness. It is not, I believe, so much a matter of mental health as it is a matter of the prevailing secularism of modern psychiatrists—many of whom, were they to evaluate St. Joan of Arc, would pass on evaluations that would facilitate her being burned at the stake.

Since working with Jersey I have learned that the charismatic Christians have classified the intervention of the demonic in human lives as falling into four different grades:

Grade 1: Temptation. Not being a charismatic in the ordinary sense, I perceive my temptations as being a natural part of the human condition not requiring any demonic causation. The charismatics, however, are inclined to see the devil behind even the simplest of temptations.

Grade 2: Demonic Attack. Here the individual is either being tempted on many fronts simultaneously or else is experiencing characteristic paranormal phenomena such as inexplicable coldness or bad odors.

Grade 3: Oppression. Here the demonic has obtained a foothold within the person but not yet a presence of sufficient strength to encase the victim's soul totally.

Grade 4: Possession. This was perfectly described by Jersey when she drew the picture of her soul represented by a fetus completely surrounded by demonic fluid to such a degree that the soul could no longer communicate with the outside world—or cooperate in ordinary psychotherapy.

According to this schema, what the exorcism achieved was to move Jersey from the state of possession to the state of demonic attack, where Satan was still hanging around her (because she still represented a threat?) but was not inside her. Now it was where she could routinely assume authority over the attack and over Satan itself. Jersey assumed such authority on the morning of the day I last saw her when she commanded the voices: "Shut the fuck up and get the fuck out."

Jersey was free in her use of the word "fuck," but there was a different quality to her usage after the exorcism and during the exorcism. During the exorcism the word had both a sexual and a shameless sort of quality. Now, however, unpossessed, Jersey used the word to express only her enthusiasm, freedom, and authority.

Further Considerations

There are six matters in Jersey's case that either did not fit into one of the three time periods I focused on or that seemed to me so important as to deserve a different level of consideration. I will deal with these six matters according to their ascending level of importance, beginning with a matter that seemed relatively minor but that is critical nonetheless for anyone involved with an exorcism.

———◆———

The seemingly little matter is that of money. It was fortunate for me that Jersey's husband was relatively wealthy and that a psychiatrist's charges were readily affordable. I am not sure how I would behave were I faced with a case of genuine possession in someone who was poor. What I did in Jersey's case seemed to me an appropriate route to follow. I charged her and her husband my standard hourly fee as a psychiatrist for every hour I spent with Jersey, with members of her family, and with Father O'Connor during the period of my evaluation of the case and during the period of intense psychotherapy and follow-up. I did not charge anything at all, not even for expenses, for the four days of the exorcism, nor did any other team member.

There are several reasons why I did not charge anything for the forty to fifty hours of my time during the exorcism.

One was that during the exorcism I was not operating in the role of a traditional psychiatrist. Mind you, almost every bit of my psychiatric training and experience was called upon. Nonetheless, I was also, although not ordained (except informally by Malachi), operating in the role of priest. This role was dramatically manifested in the litany with which I began each session of the exorcism: "Jersey, child of God, in the name of God who created you and of Jesus Christ who died for you, I order you to hear my voice as the voice of Christ's church, and although I am but a humble and unworthy servant, to obey my commands." Those are hardly the parameters within which psychiatrists are trained to operate.

A second reason was my deep awareness that I was very possibly setting a precedent. I did not feel it was right to set a precedent for mental health professionals to charge for their conduct of or participation in an exorcism.

Most important, I wanted to be totally free not only to respond to Jersey's needs but also to God's will. Money can have a way of being contaminating. I do not believe that by charging for his or her services a psychiatrist of good conscience will be contaminated by such a fee in the course of ordinary psychotherapy. However, an exorcism is not ordinary psychotherapy. Had I charged a fee for my services during the exorcism, I would have needed to continually worry whether my fee was compromising my actions or influencing my thinking. I knew that I would have more than enough to worry about during the exorcism without having to worry about financial issues. Consequently, the most important reason I did not charge was to ensure my own personal freedom. I felt it was vitally important that during the exorcism I should be a totally free agent. I do not mean a free agent in the usual sense of the term; to the contrary, I wanted to be totally free to be an instrument in the service of God.

———◆———

Looking back from a distant vantage point, I am somewhat surprised by my behavior during the follow-up period. The first thing that surprises me is my failure to request that Jersey repeat the psychological testing two to five years after the exorcism. I sensed she had become considerably more intelligent as a result of the exorcism and her liberation from possession. A verification of that surmise would have been not only appropriate but a virtually required part of scientific documentation.

But my failure to do even this minimal piece of research seems to me reflective of a broader kind of failure. There are a thousand questions I could have asked Jersey, now that she was free to answer them, having been delivered of the demonic chains. What happened to her from the time she was molested until the time she first entered Dr. Lieberman's office? Her answers might well have elucidated for me the ongoing process of her possession and provided data for a more scientific understanding of that process. Similarly, there was a great deal I could have asked her about her demons and her relationship to them.

Ordinarily, they were the sorts of questions I should have been dying to ask. Why my remarkable lack of curiosity?

I think there are two reasons. One was my motivation in becoming involved with Jersey in the first place. It had all started with a single question in my mind: Is there such a thing as the devil? The exorcism answered that question to my satisfaction. It converted me from being a skeptic to a believer. Reading my account of the exorcism may not be sufficient to convince a reader of the devil's reality, but actually experiencing the exorcism was sufficient to convince me totally. Having had my big question answered, I did not feel any great urge to pry for smaller answers. In fact, I felt loath to do so. All my instincts told me that one should not play with the devil. Yes, there was more I could have learned to satisfy my scientific curiosity, but I wasn't sure then—and I still am not sure—that it wouldn't have been dangerous to do so. Moreover, obtaining answers to such questions would not likely have provided Jersey with any additional help.

And this brings me to the second reason. When Dr. Lieberman told me that Jersey was ambivalent about the exorcism—she was profoundly grateful for it, but also felt violated by it—I completely understood what he was saying. Even before the exorcism, it had occurred to me that the process could be considered a form of brainwashing—or, more accurately, a variety of deprogramming, which in those days was used to rescue a number of young people from their involvement in cults. Such deprogramming often began by actually kidnapping the youth and routinely required using restraints. It was not a nice or gentle process. The exorcism was an invasive procedure, and I had no difficulty understanding why Jersey had experienced it as a violation. She wanted to forget about it. I thought it necessary to combat her desire to simply forget it by having her review the videotapes of the procedure. I did not think it would necessarily be helpful to confront her further; on the contrary, I thought it might be harmful. I believe this was the other reason I deviated from my identity as scientist in favor of my identity as healer.

———◆———

To this day I remain intrigued by the fact that Jersey continued to be bothered by voices for at least six years after the exorcism. In fact, I imagine she probably still hears them. Still, Dr. Lieberman felt she was healthy and she behaved as if she were healthy. Once someone who abandoned her infant children, she became, as far as I could discern, the very best of mothers. Once a completely muddled thinker, she became a person who could think with penetrating clarity, who routinely submitted herself to the demands of scientific objectivity. I was reminded again and again of Jesus saying, "By their fruits you shall know them." What he meant by this, I am virtually certain, is that the best way to assess people is by their behavior. Mentally healthy people do not behave insanely, and mentally ill people do not behave with consistently good judgment.

The definition of either health or illness by behavior is described within the world of science as an operational definition. That is a fancy term for what the old proverb says more simply: "Handsome is as handsome does." In any case, it became undeniably clear to me that at least one person in this world can hear voices and simultaneously be thoroughly sane. When I last knew her, Jersey was behaving handsomely indeed.

———◆———

In the chapter on possession and exorcism in *People of the Lie*, I took pains to point out that in any successful exorcism there are four different exorcists, and I ranked them in importance. The matter is so significant, I repeat that ranking here:

1. The most important exorcist is the patient. The success of an exorcism depends, more than anything else, upon the

patient's free will and his or her choice to "renounce the devil and all his works" (these are the words used for almost two thousand years by converts to the Christian church during the Rite of Adult Baptism; they were spoken by Jersey when she was baptized after the completion of the exorcism).

2. The second most important exorcist is God. Insofar as I made a great many right decisions during the exorcism, I did so only because I was being informed by God. This was not merely my own perception. Almost all the other members of the team felt the presence of God within that little bedroom.

3. Next in importance comes the team. Earlier I wrote about the medico-legal reasons that essentially require that there be a team. I seriously doubt that any exorcism (with the possible exception of Jesus's exorcisms) has ever been successfully completed without the presence of a team. The fact is that a group of people who are in a true state of community will have a degree of power far greater than that of an individual.

4. Least important, yet still essential, is that man or woman who, by whatever route, is designated as the head of the team and formally named exorcist. While readers may want to glorify the role of the exorcist, I legitimately can ascribe whatever wisdom and courage I found during that process only to God. If this sounds too humble and readers continue to labor under the illusion of my virtue, they will be liberated from that illusion by the time they finish reading the case of Beccah in part 2.

———◆———

Being herself the primary exorcist, why was it that Jersey ultimately chose to renounce the devil and all his works? On the surface it might have looked as if I had hypnotized her into doing so. But that would be a most superficial assessment. When at the end I was hypnotically ordering Satan to depart, Jersey was in obvious conflict, bouncing back and forth between the decision to keep her old friend and the decision to keep her own soul. I believe she ultimately chose against the devil because of all the work we had done leading up to that moment, wherein we not only elicited lesser demons, but also demonstrated their extraordinary foolishness. I think the reason that Jersey finally decided to renounce the devil was because she had concluded the devil was wrong; that in fact, it was outrageously stupid. And she no longer wanted to be burdened by such stupidity.

But I have been talking about why I think Jersey may have chosen to expel Satan. It is pure conjecture because I do not know. And I do not know because I never asked her. Again, I am somewhat astonished by my lack of scientific curiosity. She might well have told me something that could enhance the budding science of demonology or even our understanding of human nature. But I didn't even ask. Why?

Most of our decisions arise out of our intellect and contemplation or else in response to our emotions or possibly as the result of advice. But this was a decision that Jersey made in her soul. Our soul is the very core of us, far more deep inside us than our mere brain, so deep that I'm not at all sure that Jersey could have told me why she made her choice. I chose not to ask her because the place of the soul is so deep that it is the most private part of a human, the most private of our private parts, and I believe it should be kept a private place, a place where only God may enter. While I felt it my duty to cast out her demons, I also felt it my duty to respect and almost worshipfully honor the mystery, the secrecy, and privacy of Jersey's soul. To do otherwise would have been treading on holy ground uninvited.

———◆———

Finally, I am left wondering about the reality of those demons who were named Damien, Tyrona, Josiah, and Emil.

Each of them represented a specific fallacy. After being introduced to the heresy of Docetism by Father O'Connor, I discovered Jersey to be a walking textbook of heresies. "An idea that seriously undermines the essence of Christian belief" is the narrowest of possible definitions of heresy. I have addressed the subject more deeply in *The Different Drum.** Religions other than Christianity have their heresies. There are heresies shared among different religions. And there are some heresies that are purely secular. In its broadest definition, a heresy can be defined as any fallacious way of thinking.

The heresy of Damien was the belief that our safety as human beings is solely determined by our own personal cleverness and strength without any outside assistance whatsoever.

The heresy of Tyrona was that all of existence can be explained by a simplistic formula so that there is no mystery left in the world.

The heresy of Josiah was that love is whatever you choose to call it and that there is no requirement for love to have any operational definition—that love need not be manifested in behavior or judged by its fruits.

The heresy of Emil was a similar lack of requirement of any operational definition, only this time in relation to science instead of love. Emil's thesis was that science was whatever you want to call science and need not be subject to any external verification.

Each of Jersey's four lesser demons was a fallacy or heresy given a particular name and the suggestion of a personality. I doubt seriously that Jersey herself could have invented particular names or shadowy personalities for the separate fallacies in her own thinking. One of the team members happened to be an atheist. Following Jersey's exorcism, he concluded that these demons "were nothing more than the creations of a little girl's

---

* Pages 241–245.

imagination." Beyond stating that conclusion, however, he was unwilling and obviously uncomfortable about discussing the exorcism any further. Jersey *was* a little girl at the time, in reality more of a twelve-year-old than a twenty-seven-year-old, but I find it difficult to believe that a little girl could create such entities—and to what end?

So it is my belief—not wholly scientific—that these demons did have a kind of existence of their own, independent of Jersey's imagination. What I am less certain about was whether they had any existence of their own independent of Satan. Were they true demons in their own right or were they four separate reflections of the One we found behind them, the One who has been called the Father of Lies? I do not know the answer. Demonologists through the centuries have made special note of the fact that demons seem to exist within a very tightly organized hierarchy and hence seem to have remarkably little individual freedom of action or independence.

Most cases of demonic possession reported in the literature are not reported as cases of satanic possession. Indeed, I had to ask Malachi whether he had ever encountered Satan in the course of an exorcism. His answer was that indeed he had, but that was not the way he had written it. Was Malachi playing with the truth? I never debated the issue with him, but I continue to wonder whether there is such a thing as a case of genuine demonic possession where Satan is not present, calling the shots, if only from offstage. Could it be that all cases of demonic possession are in essence cases of satanic possession? I repeat, I do not know. But my experience with Jersey and with the case to follow has left me with a distinct suspicion that in reality Satan is, at the very least, the director of the drama.

PART II

Beccah

CHAPTER 5

DIAGNOSIS

———◆———

"Does the name Judas mean anything?"

I did not have to search out my second case of genuine possession. I stumbled upon it in my own office in a patient whom I had been treating with traditional psychoanalytic psychotherapy for over a year.

Beccah Armitage had sought out my services because Dr. Gooden, the New York City psychiatrist who had been treating her depression for twenty years, had died six months previously, and Beccah felt she could no longer go it alone.

She was forty-five, with a seventeen-year-old daughter, when we met. She could remember as far back as when she was three. Except for her junior year in college when she studied abroad in Italy, Beccah told me she had been depressed every day of her life. She did not think that Dr. Gooden had helped her depression one iota, but he had been a caring man, and she imagined she would have long since killed herself had it not been for his support.

One time early in their relationship, Dr. Gooden had hospitalized her, and Beccah had never forgiven him. During our first session she demanded I promise never to hospitalize her. I told her that I could not possibly make such a commitment. Despite my refusal to accede to her demand, she decided to continue seeing me for psychotherapy, and we had regular appointments twice a week thereafter.

There was no doubt Beccah was depressed. She felt depressed; she looked depressed; she thought constantly of suicide; her appetite was poor; she was dramatically underweight and had severe difficulty sleeping. Dr. Gooden had prescribed every antidepressant medication to no avail, so I did not even bother to go that route until much, much later.

Despite the intensity and duration with which we worked together, there is a huge amount I never learned about Beccah. To this day I am not sure why. It is unclear to what degree her memory was impaired by her depression or to what degree she was evasive—or both. If her memory was shallow, it was not for lack of intelligence. Beccah was one of the most intelligent people I ever treated. She was also one of the most severely depressed.

From the beginning until the end of our relationship there were two human villains in her life: her mother and her husband. Beccah could never describe her mother to me. Given the kind of psychotherapist I was, I would have insisted upon meeting the woman, only her mother died from an unexpected heart attack after Beccah's second session with me. Beccah was the co-executor of her mother's estate, and most of the little I learned about her mother came as I listened to Beccah's tribulations in that role. I wish her mother had lived just a while longer so that I could have met her myself, and could have begun Beccah's story with more than shadows.

Yet perhaps this is an illusion. It is quite possible that if we had met, I too would have found her mother to be strangely but a shadow. In any case, I begin with Beccah's shadowy childhood. This will not be a happy story. The significance of some early details will become clearer much later, but only some. In the end we may painfully conclude that Beccah was a human being who somehow belonged more in the shadows than she did in the light.

People are remarkably different. There is no type of person yet identified who is immune to possession. Consequently, possession can be uncovered in people of every personality type and psychiatric diagnosis. The only commonality among them is that their behavior has differed in a few subtle ways from the traditional diagnoses—ways that cannot quite be explained by the science of psychiatry.

So every case of possession is unique. And no two patients can better demonstrate that uniqueness than Jersey Babcock and Beccah Armitage.

Although Jersey had an essential secret that was not revealed until after her exorcism, there was nothing shadowy about her. She loved to talk. Rather than being depressed, she tended to be exuberant. Multiple family members were available to provide history and confirm crucial facts. The description of her diagnosis, treatment, and follow-up was both orderly and straightforward. It was for this reason that I kept my commentary entirely separate from her case description. Had it been interspersed with that description, the extraordinary dramatic tension of her story would have been lost.

Conversely, Beccah's story was seldom clear, with details frequently obscured by the shadows. Thus I will mix my commentary and text in order to provide places of clarity in order to highlight the drama. Beccah's story is a different kind of drama, more twisted, confusing, and consistently dreary, and therefore requires little interstices where the sun can break through the clouds.

———◆———

Beccah was born Rebecca Weintraub, the younger of two daughters of Aaron and Elena Weintraub. Her sister, Rachel, was three years older. Her parents were both the children of German Jewish immigrants who came to New York City's Lower East Side in 1899. By the time Aaron was born in 1908, his parents had succeeded in establishing a minuscule garment business. When Aaron inherited the business in the midst of the Great Depression, it was still struggling. Yet he and Elena soon had their daughters, and by the beginning of World War II the business began to thrive. When Beccah was nine months old, the family moved out of their tenement to a brownstone on the Upper East Side. Beccah's first memories were of a certain amount of wealth, and she was never allowed to forget it.

Certainly her parents seemed to remember the fact as they worked and worked and worked. They made no time for friendship or community activities. Except for one day a week, Aaron spent fifteen hours a day in their growing stable of sweatshops in the Garment District. Elena was the bookkeeper; she did the hiring and firing and supervised the clerical staff. In deference to motherhood, she worked only twelve-hour days. Beccah's two predominant memories of childhood were of being left alone and of not being allowed to go to the movies.

Beccah had only one pleasant memory of her childhood. It was of her father on the Sabbath, the only day he was home. The family did not go to temple, but Aaron prayed and studied the Talmud the entire day in his bedroom. In addition to his yarmulke, he wore a prayer shawl, or *tallis*. White with blue stripes, it was made of the softest silk. He allowed only Beccah (not Rachel or his wife) into the bedroom when he prayed, and she remembered the prayer shawl with unending delight. Her father did not talk to her during his prayer or the almost unceasing rocking back and forth while studying, but with what seemed like infinite fondness, he permitted Beccah to finger the fringes of his shawl all day long. Each Sabbath he also rested once from study for ten minutes, and during that time he always taught Beccah one new word of Hebrew.

Beccah had no memory whatsoever of her mother on the Sabbath. It was all her father: his praying and one beautiful white and blue shawl. During the other six days of the week when he was at work, Aaron kept the *tallis* neatly folded in his top bureau drawer. Almost daily Beccah would sneak into the bedroom and open the drawer merely to gaze at it and run her fingers through its fringes once again. She never unfolded it or tried to wear it herself. Beccah loved her father very much.

Beccah must have talked to her mother, but there was nothing as memorable as her father's shawl. Beccah could recall only one childhood conversation with her mother, taking place, she guessed, when she was about six years of age and Rachel nine. Rachel screamed and screamed and screamed when her mother locked her in the broom closet for some misdeed. Beccah did not like Rachel, but her sister's punishment horrified her. Beccah clearly remembered her mother telling her that the larger reason Rachel was locked in the closet was so that it would serve as an example for Beccah. Beccah was never put in the closet. She was a remarkably obedient child.

From the beginning of our work together, Beccah calmly labeled her mother as evil. But besides the closet story she could offer no other details to fill in the shadows.

There were only two additional, superficially insignificant things Beccah was able to tell me about her childhood. One was that as soon as she entered kindergarten in the public school—already knowing how to read at age five, and for the first time having access to a library—she became fascinated with the story of Jesus. A passing interest in Christ was not unusual for a Jewish child, but Beccah continued to devour everything she could find about the Christian messiah year after year.

The other thing, even more strange, was a thin book of black and white woodblock prints that simply seemed to appear in her parents' tiny bookshelf when Beccah was six years old. The book was entitled *Gods' Man.* It had no more than a few written sentences, but the succession of prints vividly described a story. It was that of an artist who signed an agreement with a mysterious hooded figure, labeled a fiend, who guaranteed the artist fame. In return, the artist promised to do a painting of the hooded figure at a time and place of the figure's choosing. One day after the artist had indeed become famous, the hooded figure appeared and led the painter, carrying his paints and easel, to a cliff overlooking the sea. Once the artist was ready to paint, the figure opened his hood, revealing nothing but a skull. The artist was so horrified by the skull that he stepped backward in fear and fell off the cliff to his death. The final print in the book was that of the skull laughing.

Beccah's fascination with this book was at least as great as her fascination with Jesus. She remembered carrying the book around with her at every possible opportunity, clutching it the way a toddler might clutch some worn-out blanket or particularly beloved toy. Although she had no trouble identifying the hooded figure in the book as the devil and as the spirit of death—they both seemed the same to her—Beccah could not remember ever thinking there was anything unusual about her fascination. Indeed, she was careful to keep the book among her own possessions until well after she herself had become a mother.

Psychiatrists refer to such precious possessions of young children as transitional objects. They are called such because they seem to ease a child's transition from infancy into mature childhood. To my knowledge, this book that Beccah carried everywhere was the most bizarre and pathological transitional object ever described in the professional psychiatric literature.

Because Beccah's account of her relationship with her father during those Sabbath days struck me as possibly unusual, I checked it out with friends well versed in Jewish culture. I was informed that, in fact, it was not uncommon for a favored daughter to be allowed in the room when her father was praying or studying; furthermore, it was common practice for the father to allow his daughter to play with the fringes of his *tallis.*

What is quite uncommon for any patient, Jewish, Christian, or otherwise, is to outright label their mother as evil. But as her story would evolve, I eventually concluded that Beccah's designation was probably accurate.

Formidably intelligent, Beccah entered Hunter College in New York City at the age of sixteen and majored in art history. The only happy year of her life was her junior year in Hunter's overseas study program when she was eighteen and nineteen. It was the only year she did not live at home with her mother (or later with her husband). There was one other reason for her happiness. The tiny Italian college she attended was near the coast, and Beccah often talked to me about the light—particularly the light of the Mediterranean Sea. She loved that light and loved to sunbathe in it.

During the middle of her senior year, after she returned from Italy, her father died. Beccah grieved. Her mother could not understand why Beccah wanted to keep his prayer shawl. As Beccah remembered it, neither her mother nor Rachel grieved over Aaron's death. Her mother immediately took over total management of the now substantial garment company, which continued to thrive.

Twenty-five years later, when Elena Weintraub died, the family money was still primarily tied up in the business. The estate's other executor was a lawyer who had been a friend of Elena's. Beccah disliked him intensely and was convinced he was trying to cheat her in the sale of the business. I could never tell whether her feelings of animosity toward the man were realistic or paranoid. During the entire time I knew her, Beccah was extremely alert to the possibility that people were trying to cheat her financially. In any case, the business sold rapidly, and Beccah and Rachel each inherited two million dollars after taxes from the sale.

I asked Beccah why she, rather than her older sister, had been appointed the co-executor. Her answer was simple: "Because Rachel is stupid." Beccah also lacked affection for her many uncles, aunts, and cousins. She thought they too were all stupid, but I could never elicit specific examples. I asked her once whether she did not harbor anti-Semitic feelings toward her extended family. Beccah denied the possibility. Whatever the reasons, it was dramatically clear that after her father's death, there was not a single soul in her family with whom she felt any emotional kinship. It was also striking to me that throughout the time the estate was being settled, Beccah did not demonstrate the smallest shred of grief at her mother's death. Both before and after that death, Beccah was a person remarkably alone in the world.

———◆———

With the single exception of the incident when her sister had been locked in the broom closet, Beccah's description of her mother's villainy was vague. Not so her description of her husband's. Beccah labeled him as a religious nut during our first session. Much more gradually she would also label him as a crook, providing plentiful documentation.

The religious nut business seemed to bother her more than his crookedness. When Jack Armitage had proposed marriage to her almost twenty-five years before, he insisted that before the wedding she be baptized and confirmed within the Episcopal church. By that time Beccah had already decided she wanted to formalize her conversion to Christianity through baptism, but she had not decided upon a denomination. It made sense to join her husband's denomination, but almost teasingly she pushed him to explain why it was so important to him that she should specifically be Episcopalian. "Because it's good for business," Jack answered her instantly.

Beccah understood Jack's reasoning. Episcopalians tended to be at the top of the social ladder. Being Episcopalian afforded one a kind of invisible status that would, in fact, be good for business. And business was her primary motive for marrying this large, handsome, up-and-coming young real estate agent, so she decided not to fight the issue. Although it might not have been the way Jesus would have advised her to make the decision, Beccah considered it both sensible and sane.

By the sixth year of their marriage, the Episcopal church was in turmoil over a proposal to revise its 1928 Book of Common Prayer, so as to authorize alternate ways of saying the same thing during the Eucharist and other rituals. Beccah quite liked the idea; Jack, however, was so outraged by it that he insisted they fight against this liberalization by joining with a small minority who left the Episcopal church to form a new denomination, the Anglo-Catholic church, which would keep the old prayer book intact and preserve the conservatism of the "true" church. This time Beccah did not understand his motivations. There was some argument, but eventually she capitulated.

Several years later Beccah became pregnant with their daughter, who she wanted to name Elizabeth after an eighty-one-year-old woman with gnarled hands and sparkling eyes who had instructed her for her confirmation. Jack wanted to name their daughter Catherine, after Saint Catherine of Siena. Again they fought, and once again Beccah gave in to Jack's anger, which was frequently irrational and which she had come to fear.

When Catherine was ready for Sunday school, Jack decided she needed a religious upbringing that was rooted in something more ancient than any 1928 prayer book used by the Anglo-Catholic church. Jack now decided that the family should join the Greek Orthodox church, quite a switch given Jack's origins. No matter that she believed the change utterly bizarre, Beccah seemed helplessly stuck in a pattern; again she consented.

Two years before we met, the whole matter became even more personal than one of theology. Beccah would, of course, dress up for church, but she loved jeans and knew she looked good in them. Only now Jack had come to believe that anything other than a skirt on women was of the devil, and that in her jeans Beccah represented the Whore of Babylon. He threatened to whip her if she continued to wear them. Again there seemed to her no option save to submit, but from the moment she started seeing me, Beccah talked incessantly about her husband's religious insanity.

I took Beccah's side against her husband in the matter of her clothing, and with me as her therapeutic ally she started fighting back. Huge and menacing though her husband was, Beccah told Jack she was going to wear jeans whether he liked it or not, and if he laid a hand on her, she'd call the police. This time it was Jack who grudgingly capitulated.

As was my custom with the spouses of my patients, I tried to make an appointment with Jack to come to speak with me for an hour. It was not customary for me to meet with resistance; it took a good two hours of verbal combat over the phone before Jack finally agreed to come. Physically he was formidable: handsome, massive in size, articulate—and distinctly hostile. Because I was the person who had encouraged Beccah to return to wearing jeans in rebellion against him, he was not well disposed toward me. He proclaimed I had no right interfering with the religious life of a family. I responded that his ultraconservative, dictatorial piety was so excessive as to possibly constitute a psychiatric symptom. He threatened that he was seriously thinking about not paying my bills. I countered that he would find the bills of a lawyer to defend him against suit from me in small claims court together with the bills for a divorce lawyer to be an extremely expensive alternative. It was hardly a meeting of the minds.

In my first session with Beccah afterward, I told her that my predominant impression of her husband was that of a congenital bully. I informed her that dealing correctly with bullies was much the same as dealing with blackmailers. If you gave them what they wanted, their demands would only increase. Conversely, the more vigorously she refused him, the more likely he was to shut up. Beccah quickly became a skilled and vigorous opponent.

The jeans issue now settled, at four months into our work together, Beccah gradually began letting me know about the nature of Jack's business. He was a genius of sorts. Originally a real estate agent, he had become fascinated by REITs—real estate investment trusts—in the very early days of their creation. Over the years he had become familiar with virtually all the managers of these trusts across the country. He was very good at drawing people out and spent more than half his time on the phone in seemingly idle conversation with them about their children and their golf scores. Jack was able to obtain massive amounts of inside information about their companies from those at the uppermost echelons. A few of his multiple acquaintances seemed aware of what was going on, but still cooperated. Most of them were probably not aware of how they were being used.

When not on the phone, Jack was usually writing a monthly newsletter he produced for special clients. Those special clients were investors, and the newsletter consisted of little else than the inside information he had garnered about the REITs. The transmission of such information to investors was blatantly illegal, but his investor clients were doing so well, thanks to the newsletter, that not one of them would ever have informed on Jack. He was the goose who laid their golden eggs. Indeed, they would very carefully interest their best friends in the newsletter. Its subscription list grew inexorably, like a tank rolling forward undisturbed over the trickiest of terrain. So did its price. Beccah told me its fifteen monthly pages had risen to a subscription fee of two thousand dollars a year, and there were at least one thousand subscribers. In other words, the newsletter was grossing at least two million dollars a year with negligible overhead.

Beccah told me these details with a hint of gleefulness. Did they not demonstrate that Jack was a thorough crook and utter religious hypocrite? I agreed even to the point of suggesting that his excessive piety was a cover-up for his criminality.

Next, it emerged that the business was larger than just the newsletter alone. Many of Jack's clients wanted to trade in the various REIT stocks—ordinary and preferred—as well as their bonds. But there were risks to doing such trading on the regulated markets where officials might have guessed about his inside knowledge. Consequently, to oblige his most steadfast and eager clients, Jack had established a miniature stock market of his own.

Now over a half a year in therapy with me, Beccah reluctantly let it be known that she herself played a major role in the company. As I began asking about its employees, only in response to a direct question did she admit that she was the company's bookkeeper, utilizing the skills she had learned from her mother after her father's death.

Beccah let me know that the only other employees of Jack's legally questionable company were a decidedly obtuse secretary and a discreet half-time trader who, for a strikingly large commission, fulfilled the trading orders of the clients. He split half his commissions with Jack.

Ever more slowly, Beccah began to confide to me how a number of clients wanted to trade when the regular trader wasn't there, and that she herself had learned all there was to know about the extremely complicated subject of stock trading. At first I took a position of neutrality. In response, it emerged that Beccah took great pride in her trading ability, and that while most of her commissions were on the high side, a number were astronomical. With a strange joy for someone so depressed, Beccah made no bones about the fact that this kind of trading was particularly vicious. I knew her to be a gentle parent, but she confessed to me that there was something inside her that felt powerfully drawn to the exercise of her brutal talent.

I could never quite understand what made this trading so brutal save that it was unregulated. Patiently she explained to me that the usually recognized markets for stock trading, such as the New York Stock Exchange, were known in the trade as the first market. In addition, I learned that brokers and brokerage houses had other ways of trading, which she called the second market and the third market. It appeared that both of these markets were still somehow regulated, while hers was not. "And you call yours the fourth market?" I inquired.

"No," Beccah answered me, "those of us in the business generally refer to it as the cockroach market."

I commented that many seemed afraid of cockroaches, that they were dirty insects, unusually prone to carry disease. "That's why we call it the cockroach market," Beccah commented calmly, but vocalizing it began to bring out her deeper feelings. Now crying, she spoke of how she too felt dirty and infectious, but somehow couldn't help herself. Seemingly against her will, she was deeply drawn to this dirty, vicious kind of trading that was not quite illegal. On the other hand, she admitted, it was not quite legal either. Slowly her tears dried as she told me that in the whole United States, she did not personally know of any such trader who was as skilled at the game as she.

I told Beccah I was puzzled. On the one hand, she was as sophisticated a Christian as I had ever met. On the other, she seemed to relish this activity that sounded so distinctly unchristian. Did she think it was unchristian?

"Completely," she told me.

"How do you reconcile it all?"

"I don't. Maybe that's why I cut myself," she responded. At this point she proceeded to raise her long sleeves to her elbows and I saw that both her forearms were a mass of two- to three-inch-long straight, narrow scars. I cursed myself for not picking up on the fact that every time I had seen her, no matter how warm or humid it might have been, she had always worn a black long-sleeved blouse or pullover.

For several sessions we explored her self-mutilation. Among other things it was a way of flirting with suicide. Eventually I would come to realize that the spirit of death colored everything Beccah did. However, typical of other cases of self-mutilation, her cutting was a desperate attempt to feel alive. In one respect the mutilation turned out to be highly ritualistic. Beccah did not use ordinary knives to cut herself. Instead, through special catalogs, she obtained from Germany the sharpest knives in existence. At my request she brought in three such knives from her collection of several dozen. More striking to me than the sharpness of their blades was the shining, smooth, somehow frightening blackness of their handles. "I'm no expert in the subject," I noted, "but for some reason these strike me as being distinctly Nazi knives."

Beccah acknowledged that was precisely why she chose them. "They are not advertised that way," she informed me, "but that is how I choose them from the catalog. I choose the ones that look the closest to those that Nazi torturers might have used during the war. I don't know why I have such an attraction to them. I find them both hideous and beautiful at the same time."

"Do you think it has anything to do with the fact that you are Jewish by birth?" I asked.

"I've wondered about that a great deal, Dr. Peck. But frankly I haven't a clue. All I know is I'm attracted to them."

I learned that her self-mutilation was not totally related to her trading or to her marriage. It had begun when she was in college, although only with ordinary knives. The frequency with which she cut herself had gradually increased over the course of her marriage as she became more deeply engaged in the illegal business. She had no doubt that she cut herself when she was feeling particularly ashamed about her love of trading and its vicious-ness. "But it's not only that," she continued. "I also cut myself when I'm trying to be good, when I'm trying to stay away from trading, when I'm trying to live like a Christian. I don't know what it is about trying to be a Christian that makes me want to do it. Maybe it has something to do with feeling bored when I'm working at being good. Trading is so exciting. Being good is not exciting. In fact, it often feels so dull and boring that I hardly feel alive. I think that may have something to do with it. You see, when I cut myself it not only hurts, but also it bleeds. When it hurts—and especially when it bleeds—when I see the blood, I know that I'm alive. I know that I'm not a dead person—at least, not yet."

One might wonder why Beccah so readily capitulated to her husband time after time, but would probably wonder less if he had seen the husband as I had. Jack Armitage was truly a frightening man by virtue of his huge size and possibly psy-chotic anger. I think the more fundamental question to ask is why she had married Jack in the first place, particularly when she was a very keen judge of character. Two possible reasons come to my mind. One is that hers and Jack's shared love of money was a remarkably strong bond. The other is that Beccah married Jack because she was already damaged in some way. Given what we know of her mother, it would seem that both of these explanations were true.

I had commented to Beccah that Jack's excessive piety might be a cover-up for his crookedness. Excessive piety to-gether with criminality is not an unusual combination. I hardly mean to condemn every markedly pious person, but I do admit that excessive and outwardly obvious piety does raise my suspicions. What better way to try to hide your wickedness from the undiscerning world than by adopting a distinctly religious disguise. I have seen the phenomenon among clergy and other religious professionals. I have seen it most frequently, however, among religious volunteers. In a footnote to *People of the Lie,* I wrote: "Since the primary motive of the evil is disguise, one of the places evil people are most likely to be found is within the church. What better way to conceal one's evil from oneself as well as from others than to be a deacon or some other highly visible form of Christian within our culture." I mentioned the above footnote to a friend who was a priest and he responded, "Of course the church is where you're most likely to find evil people. But what better and gentler place could there be for their containment?"

Although self-mutilation is not an extremely rare phenomenon in the victims of possession, it is hardly specific to possession. Indeed, it is a symptom suggesting a truly severe psychiatric disorder, but the disorder may be of many different kinds. I believe that self-mutilation is a more common symptom than the general public is aware. For reasons I do not understand, this serious symptom seems to be far more common among women than men. Two other female self-mutilators I treated in depth were not possessed (although my experience with them predated my recognition of possession as a valid phenomenon). But the dynamic in their cases seemed the same as in Beccah's. They also talked one way or another of internal feelings of deadness and spoke of how both the pain and the blood of their self-mutilation confirmed to them their aliveness.

Since Beccah used very special Nazi knives to mutilate herself, I had raised the possibility of her being anti-Semitic for the second time. That question will be raised again.

One other factor in Beccah's self-mutilation is of note. She stated that she mutilated herself both at times when she had been bad and times when she was trying to be good. One of the times the phenomenon called demonic attack seems most likely to occur is when people are trying to be good. For instance, I have heard that demonic attack is not a rare experience for people who have just converted to Christianity. C. S. Lewis's famous work *The Screwtape Letters* is a bit more than a work of pure fantasy.

It seemed obvious that Beccah's severe depression—it was a depression, wasn't it?—related to her fascination with money and work, at least the work of trading. And that this fascination was somehow rooted in her parents' obsession with money and work. But it was hardly identical to that of her parents. Ten months after I had started seeing her, Beccah announced that during Catherine's spring break in a month, she, Jack, and Catherine would be taking a two-week vacation at a deluxe Caribbean resort. It turned out she and Jack knew how to spend money as well as how to make it. They actually took such vacations frequently, whereas Beccah could not remember her parents ever once taking a vacation of any kind.

When Beccah came in for her first session after that vacation, I gasped. Ordinarily pale, she was now surprisingly dark skinned. "I gather you like to sunbathe," I commented laconically.

"It's my passion," she acknowledged. But before I could probe further, she was off on an unusually sophisticated political and economic analysis of the prevailing poverty in the Caribbean islands. Then she listed with outrage all the ways their resort had been designed to isolate the guests from the poverty just beyond the gates. Most of the guests were not even aware that it existed. "Something's got to be done," she exclaimed, like a Christian missionary social worker.

"I imagine if you looked, you could find something for yourself to do about it. A little something, yes, but something, a start of some kind," I said.

Beccah winced. We both knew the Christian activist part of

her had yet to be born. Her skin color might have changed, but nothing else had. She actually looked like hell. No amount of sunbathing or frequent vacationing was going to cure her condition.

It is customary for psychotherapists to review their cases at anniversary times. Beccah and I had now been seeing each other for close to a year, and a great deal had transpired. I knew her history about as well as I was going to know it, given her vagueness about its shadowy areas. Her mother was not only buried; the estate was settled. She had accomplished all of her duties as co-executor, and with me as her behind-the-scenes ally, she had been able to win all the battles that needed to be won against the family lawyer and difficult relatives. She had dramatically changed the basic nature of her relationship with her husband. Again with therapeutic support, she had moved from a position of resentful subservience to one of considerable autonomy. It was not just that she wore jeans whenever she wanted; she was now calling the shots on all the issues of homemaking and raising Catherine. Most recently she had refused to attend the Greek Orthodox church and had gone back to her original Episcopalian community. Catherine had chosen to join her, and Beccah protected this choice against Jack's rage. We had clarified that his business was actually theirs, and thoroughly crooked.

The path she needed to follow had become starkly clear—not easy, but obvious. She realized that there was absolutely no room for negotiation between her religious beliefs and the conduct of their business. Beccah acknowledged that she needed to leave the business. At the very least, this meant she would have to stop trading. At most it meant she would have to divorce Jack, the prospect of which seemed to please more than worry her.

Yes, a good deal had been accomplished over the year, so much that I would have expected at least some lessening of her depression. But Beccah did not meet that expectation. Instead, she started to move ever more quickly in the opposite direction. Sleep became almost nonexistent; she regarded it as a good night if she got three hours. She lost all appetite. Thin before, she was now gaunt to the point that she was beginning to remind me of a concentration camp victim. Her speech slowed. I became seriously worried about her physical health and the possibility that she might need hospitalization, the one thing she declared she would never accept.

The only thing different was she had begun wearing perfume for our appointments. Lots of perfume. So much perfume that I found it hard to think in her presence. Despite my reticence, I felt this new practice needed to be questioned. She answered me without self-consciousness, as if she assumed I already knew the answer. "I'm wearing perfume because I've started to smell bad."

I commented I had not noticed any odor in our earlier sessions. "You didn't?" she asked with astonishment.

I suggested that she come in for her next appointment without perfume, so that I could tell if she had an odor about her. She refused. She simply proclaimed that the odor was so rotten it would instantly drive me away.

At the same time, she reluctantly confessed she was getting nowhere in her struggle to stop trading. She was trading now more than she ever had, and doing so more desperately. Whenever she awoke from her pittance of sleep, her first thought was of trading, and she was almost beside herself with agitation at the fact she could not trade in the middle of the night. The frequency of her self-mutilation had moved from monthly to weekly. She had also begun to mutilate herself on other parts of her body. Tentatively she had begun to attack her thighs, abdomen, and breasts.

It just didn't fit. Here I had a patient who, by all rights, should have been getting significantly better, but who was deteriorating as if the *hounds of hell* were after her. The picture began to fit only when I dared to think the unthinkable. The moment came when I asked her, for at least the tenth time, why she was continuing to trade. For at least the tenth time, she answered, "I can't help myself."

Whenever someone says, "I can't help myself," I am immediately and instinctively skeptical. Yet, after a year I knew that Beccah was not a weak person. Almost against my will I opened myself to the possibility that she was correct, that she could not, in fact, help herself.

Psychiatrists are rigorously trained to doubt themselves. Was it conceivable that Beccah might not be able to help herself because she was possessed? Everything in my training told me I shouldn't even consider the question. Having recently treated one case of possession—perhaps the rarest of conditions—it was absurd even to imagine that I might now have a second case on my hands. I had to ask myself whether I wasn't imposing upon Beccah some strange need I had to see possession everywhere I looked. Were we in a courtroom, I could imagine the judge concluding it was entirely my problem not hers. The problem, however, was that traditional psychiatric answers didn't fit. Finally, almost choking on my own words, in response to another one of her "I can't help myself"'s, I quietly asked, "Beccah, have you ever thought that you were possessed?"

Beccah's eyes instantly lit up. It had been months since I had seen even a ghost of hope in them. "Yes," she answered, "I've wondered about it almost every day for years. At least since Catherine was born."

The answer was hardly what I had expected. I had anticipated a vigorous denial combined with derogatory laughter. Instead, there was affirmation and hope.

I sat silently, staring at Beccah in wonder. I then noticed for the first time that the skin of her face was unusually smooth, taut and wrinkle-free. It had been that way for the entire time I had been seeing her. How could I have missed it?

I asked her about her fantasies about possession—about

Satan, about demons, about the movie *The Exorcist.* There were no red flags. Beccah was uncertain about every aspect of the subject—and who in their right mind wouldn't have been? I was impressed by this lack of certainty. Her consistently sophisticated, scientific mind made her openness to the diagnosis of possession seem sane.

"Well, why don't we do a deliverance then?" I said.

Of course I had to explain what I meant by a deliverance, and I had to think about the logistics involved. Actually, it was all quite simple. Unlike an exorcism, there was no reason a deliverance couldn't be conducted in my little office. I knew the person I most wanted with me was Wayne Williams. Wayne and I had practiced in the same association for two years. A minister and licensed pastoral counselor, he was a bit of a wild man, apt to do things I never would have predicted, but he had never been wrong. More of his clients seemed to get better than those of any therapist I knew, including myself. And he understood Christian theology in both his head and his heart.

The other person I chose was a friend of mine, Martha, a devout and entirely sensible woman whose primary interest was in her new grandchild. I called them that very evening. Both were willing. We set the date for a Saturday afternoon ten days hence. I told them and Beccah that I doubted it would take any more than four hours, but we set aside five just in case. The only preparation I advised was prayer.

The four of us assembled in my office at one o'clock in the afternoon that Saturday. I had already explained that most of the deliverance would consist of prayer. I began by asking Beccah if she had any unanswered questions. She had none. We then individually prayed out loud in our own words for the success of the deliverance—each, that is, except Beccah, who was notably silent.

For the next two hours we primarily sat in prayerful silence, although from time to time Martha, Wayne, or I would feel moved to pray out loud what was on our minds. But mostly it was silent prayer.

Gradually, over the course of those first two hours, I had an ever-deepening sense that there was a demonic presence in the room. It was as if there were not four, but five people in my office, except that this fifth person was invisible. I did not sense it to be specifically evil, but I somehow just knew it had nothing to do with God. Wayne and Martha also felt this presence, although not as intensely as I. In any case, by three o'clock in the afternoon we were more convinced that Beccah was demonically possessed than we had been when the deliverance began.

After sharing this sense together, the three of us discussed how we should proceed, while Beccah continued to sit without comment on the couch. Between our prayers for God's guidance, we decided to ask Beccah if she was willing to repeat her baptismal vows, knowing that among these vows was "I renounce Satan and all his works." I did not expect Beccah would have any difficulty with the request.

But Beccah did have difficulty. Suddenly verbal, she thought that it was silly, meaningless, unnecessary, formalistic, formulaic, and ridiculous since she already had been baptized when she was engaged to Jack.

By her very resistance, Wayne, Martha, and I became certain we were on the right track and convinced that the issue was crucial to the deliverance. We told Beccah we felt the deliverance would probably succeed if she was willing to repeat her baptismal vows, but we imagined it would surely fail if she was not even willing to take this first step.

Reluctantly, Beccah gave in, and with Wayne assuming his ministerial role while Martha and I prayed, she did repeat her vows.

When she had finished and the brief ceremony was over, there was total silence in the room for five minutes. It was Beccah who finally broke it. "I don't know whether it means any-

lowing Monday afternoon. "Just come in for your regular appointment Monday unless you happen to have some kind of difficulty," I instructed her. "I don't think you will, but if you do, call me."

Beccah left. The three of us spoke gleefully about the seemingly miraculous way in which Judas had been identified by Beccah as her infesting demon. We were joyful, and in our joy we laughed heartily together as we gave God thanks. Then we embraced, and each of us departed to take care of whatever mundane matters might need our attention on that late afternoon.

I was elated. My first experience of a successful deliverance! Dramatically successful. "It was so easy!" I exclaimed to myself. But there was another thought deep underneath my elation—so deep I was barely aware of it and hardly willing to verbalize it. Maybe it was too easy, my unspoken words were saying.

Without considering the matter of follow-up, that Saturday afternoon in my office was an example of deliverance at its very best. No great logistical preparation was required. The team of three was readily available from within the neighborhood. No one even needed to be fed. The process lasted no longer than four hours. During the entire time Beccah never once required any restraint. The time was private, quiet, and dignified. In a tentative way Beccah revealed the name of a common albeit major demon. The known characteristics of this demon fit perfectly with the nature of Beccah's problems. The demon was cast out with absolutely no muss or fuss. Beccah felt extraordinarily relieved. Yes, it was an ideal deliverance—at first glance.

When I went into the waiting room Monday afternoon to get her, Beccah grinned at me, jumped up from the sofa, and almost seemed to glide into my office. Her depression had not simply reverted to its usual chronic state; it was gone entirely. "I haven't felt like this since my junior year in college," Beccah said. "I have no thoughts of suicide. I haven't felt the slightest desire to cut myself. I've been eating like a horse and I slept for twelve hours each of the last two nights."

"Hooray!" I exclaimed. But then I had to add, "It almost sounds too good to be true."

"I've been thinking that also," Beccah reported, "but thinking it hasn't taken it away."

"By it, you mean . . . ? "

"I mean this absence of depression," she answered. "But it's more than an absence. It's the presence of a good feeling. That is, a good feeling when I don't think about it. When I think about it it's more like joy."

"You look joyful," I confirmed. And then we simply sat together for at least two minutes sharing the joy in silence. Then I was overwhelmed with eagerness to see what would come next. "So what happens now?" I asked.

"Well, it's obvious, isn't it?" she answered. "I have to leave Jack. I've already met with a real estate agent this morning to tell her the kind of place I want. I'm meeting her at nine o'clock in the morning tomorrow to start looking at houses she has to rent. And perhaps a few that are for sale. But this is so sudden I think it would be smarter for me to rent until I'm sure that it's not too good to be true. What do you think?"

"I agree. Yes, I think you'd be smart to rent even if you were sure the demon's gone. The sooner you can get yourself out of that house and away from Jack the better."

"You don't have to worry about that," Beccah assured me. "Since I returned Saturday evening I haven't been able to stand the sight of him. I bet you I'll be out of the house within a week."

And she was. When she saw me for her next appointment three days later, she had already signed the rental agreement on a modest house about ten miles away, as opposed to the couple's huge house in Westchester fifty miles distant. "It's a new little house," she informed me. "Everything is clean. Spic and span, really. It's quite deep in the woods with a long drive, but there's a clearing around it, and it must have a dozen skylights. It's a light-filled house!"

"Sounds perfect," I commented.

"It really is, except that I will have a hell of a snowplow bill to pay when winter comes. But who cares?"

"Have you told Jack yet?"

She shook her head. "But I've already arranged for the movers to come on Monday."

"Are you scared about telling him?"

"Yes . . . no . . . I mean yes because he will go into an absolute rage. I don't think he will hit me. I'll kick him in the balls if he tries. And even if he does hit me, I don't care; I'll be so glad to get away from the son of a bitch."

My heart was so full of rejoicing it was impossible for me to settle down to any real psychoanalytical work. Mostly we simply laughed together for the rest of the hour. Just before the end I awkwardly asked her whether she would mind if we prayed together in thanksgiving. It was very rare for me to pray with a patient during a session. I hadn't done it more than twice before, but on this occasion anything else seemed inappropriate.

As for Beccah, she couldn't have been more eager to thank God. "Delivered," she said. "That's exactly what I feel. God has delivered me from hell."

And so together we prayed our gratitude.

Whenever a demonic spirit or the demonic spirits that are responsible for the patient's troubles are successfully cast out, the results, in my experience, are immediate and dramatic. Never in my life have I seen such joy in a person's face than that which Jersey demonstrated that night once Satan was gone. I would literally pay to see that face again.

In only slightly muted form, that same joy was on Beccah's face this afternoon. But the results of successfully casting out a demon or demonic spirit are much greater than some mere feeling; more important, they are very substantial, factual, and perfectly measurable by behavioral indicators. For the first time in years Beccah was eating and sleeping well without any suicidal thoughts. But the effect was still more than that. Her entire manner had changed; she was now a determined woman eager and ready to leave her malignant husband. She had already contacted a real estate agent and made an appointment to look for a new house. And her plans were realistic. All this within less than two days!

It lasted for three wonderful weeks.

During those three weeks Beccah and Catherine moved into their new little house in the woods. Jack, as expected, had a fit and probably would have hit both of them had Beccah not threatened him with the police. She told me she missed nothing about the business. Her first priority was finding a new private school for Catherine and helping her get settled. Then Beccah turned her attention to getting the services of an expensive, top-notch divorce lawyer. The lawyer was in the process of preparing the documents for her to sign so that Jack could be served. But it was to be almost three months before she signed them.

Top-notch lawyers do not cause such delays. Instead, the problem was Beccah, who came in to see me for her regular twice-a-week appointment twenty-three days after the deliverance of Judas. During her previous appointments, her eyes had been sparkling with the joy of her newfound zest for life. But this day I knew something was drastically wrong as soon as I stepped into the waiting room. Her eyes looked dead. On the way to my office her carriage had changed to that of an old woman. I did not have to enquire why. As soon as she took her seat in my office she exclaimed with a mixture of anger and despair, "My depression has come back. Totally. Worse than before."

I was stunned, but I knew she felt far worse. "I can see it," I said. "I'm so very sorry."

"I went back to Westchester this weekend," she informed me, "not to see Jack, but to trade. Our customers seldom trade on weekends, but I was calling them in desperation to see if they wanted to. I had to trade again. And, of course, I cut myself last night. Deeper than ever before."

She pulled up the sleeve of her blouse and showed me a gaping three-inch-long wound deep into the subcutaneous fat.

"What time last night?" I asked, distracting myself with the medical details.

"About nine o'clock."

"Then there is still time to stitch it up," I said, knowing that such a wound should be left open if it was older than twenty-four hours. "We ought to run down to the emergency room, right now."

"No," Beccah responded in a tone of finality. "I want to leave it open. The scar will be bigger that way. I want the scar to be big."

All kinds of purely medical concerns were rushing through my mind. Should I try to force her to the emergency room? Should I bandage the wound right now? Should I prescribe her antibiotics? But within fifteen seconds I knew these were almost ridiculously minor matters that my mind was devising to divert me from the real problem I had to face. "What the hell happened to you?" I blurted out.

"And I've started hearing voices," Beccah said almost dreamily. "You know, I've never heard voices before. All different kinds of voices. Some are quiet, some are loud. Some are male

161

and some are female." The dreamy expression faded from her face to be replaced by one of utter dejection and hopelessness. "It doesn't really matter," she continued. "They're all the same anyway. It's just the same voice in different forms. It's all one voice."

"Whose voice?" I asked.

"You know."

"No, I don't. What voice is it?"

"It's Lucifer," she said.

There is no question that Beccah's deliverance was temporarily successful. Patients with her degree of depression do not simply pop back to normal for three weeks on the basis of some hypnotic suggestion. Something very major had happened down at the level of her soul. Judas had been expelled. Naturally, I was disappointed that the success had been so temporary. But I was not surprised. I had wondered at the time if it wasn't too easy. Nor was I surprised that Judas had now apparently been replaced by the big boy. After all, when Jersey's demons had been expelled we found the big boy behind them in the form of Satan.

What did surprise me, however, was that Beccah referred to it as Lucifer. "Lucifer" is the term for the devil in the Old Testament, but "Satan" is the term in the New Testament. Operating primarily in a New Testament culture, in our discussions (as well as the repetition of her baptismal vows) "Satan" was the term we used. Why the difference? I wondered about it then and I've wondered ever since.

The most obvious reason was that Beccah, as a Jewish girl, had been raised in an Old Testament culture and that Lucifer would have been the name she was first familiar with. I do think that is a part of the answer, but only a part. As Beccah's story goes on I will refer to the other parts, but we will never have them neatly answered. Primarily we will have only more questions.

Intuitively I knew better than to dance to Lucifer's tune, so Beccah and I simply continued with our twice-a-week sessions, only their nature became more exploratory than supportive. Why had Lucifer replaced Judas after three weeks of freedom? The answer seemed clearly to have something to do with the document Beccah needed to sign to initiate divorce proceedings formally. Although she denied it, I strongly felt Beccah had some deep ambivalence about actually divorcing Jack. Neither she nor I, however, understood this ambivalence. It was another area that would remain shadowy.

How did she know it was Lucifer's voice? Upon questioning, Beccah explained that the voice never named itself, but that she somehow just knew. I probably would have seriously doubted her intuition on this matter, except that in the midst of one session she idly mentioned to me that no matter how the voice sounded—commanding or cajoling, male or female—it invariably referred to itself as "we." Furthermore, all of its messages were destructive. It told her that she was needed in the business, that she was only useful to people as a trader, that divorcing Jack would be insanely expensive, that her lawyer was over-charging her. "Why don't you grow up and be realistic?" it asked her. At other times it told her that she should cut herself for one reason or another, but also that she should go further. It accused her of being cowardly, it told her that she really wanted to commit suicide and that she was right to do so. Even her importance as a trader and to the business was only superficial at best; when she got down to it she would realize that her little life was useless, meaningless. Why not just get it over with? There was no meaning to anything anyway.

Unfortunately, Beccah did not seem to represent either a diagnostic or a treatment puzzle. As Jesus had warned, it is quite possible for a person to dispel a demon only to have seven more come to take its place. Or, by inference, a worse one.* This is what appeared to have happened. Assuming such to be the case and that the simple deliverance had been insufficient to take care of the problem permanently, it seemed obvious that the treatment required would be an exorcism. These were assumptions, of course, and I spent the next two weeks with Beccah testing them as best I could. The behavioral indicators that suggested the deliverance had been an initial success now supported the need for an exorcism. Her depression deepened almost daily. Within those two weeks she had lost all the weight she had put on and again was not sleeping. She never knew when the voices (or Voice) would return. She might go as long as two days without hearing anything, and then, for no apparent reason, the Voice would say with impregnable confidence, "We don't have to bother with you very often. You're ours. And you know it. You've been ours almost from the start."

I consulted with Martha, explaining that Beccah was so thin, so depressed, I wasn't sure she could even tolerate a full-scale exorcism. "I have a sense she might die during it," I said.

"She's going to die without it," Martha responded with simple logic.

With that, I set about gathering a team. For no obviously rational reason, I had a profound sense that the exorcism would require no more than three days. I had an equally profound sense that it would be far more difficult than Jersey's and that I would need as large a team as possible. Naturally, Martha and Wayne were my first two candidates. Martha, without my even having to ask, volunteered her tiny isolated house for the three days. Rodger, the quiet counseling psychologist who had so ably man-

---

* Matthew 12:43–45.

aged the videotaping of Jersey's exorcism, was another obvious choice, and he agreed to help once again. There was a middle-aged, highly competent psychiatrist in Ohio, Harvey, who had questioned me about exorcism during one of my speaking engagements. I knew him to not only be interested in the subject but also—unusual for a psychiatrist, particularly in those days—to be a highly sophisticated churchgoer. He promptly agreed when I located him, as did Peter, an older Protestant minister with whom I was quite close and whom I chose as my assistant. Finally, there was Edie, a doctor of psychology, a woman of my age prominent in the field of psychotherapy whose professional judgment I deeply trusted. She would be coming from Chicago (at her own expense, like everyone else). That would make seven of us in total, one more than the team for Jersey, and a number I mistakenly thought would be sufficient.

I also arranged for an eighth member of the team to play a much less visible, but perhaps more noble role. I realized that it would be unwise for Beccah to be alone during the nights of the exorcism and for an indeterminate number of nights thereafter. I was familiar with a late-middle-aged woman in the neighborhood, Mrs. Cowper, a Christian with unusually strong mothering instincts. She was a very proper lady, and I was uncertain about her ability to handle the kind of sacrilege and obscenity likely to occur during an exorcism, but otherwise she was a perfect candidate to take care of Beccah during the nights. She could be firm, if necessary, and had the good sense to call me if she was having trouble. I asked her if she was willing to play this unglamorous nursemaid role. She was clearly disappointed that she would not be present at the exorcism, but thankfully she regarded it as her Christian duty to accept the role of caretaker.

Malachi had recommended that a relative or close family friend should ideally be a member of any team. But Beccah had no friends and no one in her family with whom she was close.

Without even thinking about the matter, I simply assumed

that I would be the exorcist. I was not going to go casting about the whole nation unsuccessfully to find someone with more experience. I had learned that lesson.

Although I had no real evidence, I had a strong enduring intuition that Lucifer would be out to get me during the exorcism, that it was enraged by my success with Jersey and was going to use Beccah to pay me back. I felt that I was on its hit list and it would pull out all the stops. This sense did not frighten me, but warned me to be as cautious as possible. I did not feel any of the excitement I had before Jersey's exorcism. My mood was one of grim determination. It was probably going to be ugly.

As a measure of additional caution, I had Beccah psychologically tested by Ned Greasely. Ned was an unusual psychologist. For one thing, he was a deeply religious man and worked mostly with religious communities. For another, he was getting on in years and no longer cared much about what his colleagues thought of him. As I expected, he was not bothered in the least by Beccah's diagnosis of possession or the fact that she would very shortly undergo a major exorcism. As I also expected, after testing Beccah, he gave me an unusually brief and nontraditional written report that said nothing about what kind of tests he had used, but was exactly the kind of report I needed. It stated that he had tested Rebecca Armitage at my request. He said that he had never seen a genuinely possessed person before, and therefore had no one to compare her to for my purposes. He said that on the basis of his testing alone he could not get up in court and swear to the fact that she was demonically possessed.

However, he did say that he'd be happy to tell the court that she was the single most possessed person he had ever seen in his practice, and that he had no better word for the nature of her relationship with her deceased mother and her husband. He stated that she was utterly possessed by these two in terms of her thinking processes. She therefore demonstrated what he called "the dynamics of possession," and he said he would also have no difficulty telling the court that as an experienced psychologist, he had no reason to question my diagnosis of her being a case of satanic possession.

I kept Beccah informed of every move I was making. She was totally compliant; how could she be otherwise when she was so desperate? The date was set for the exorcism to begin at Martha's house on the second Friday in October, counting on it concluding by that Sunday, the eve of Columbus Day. It was the first possible date it could be done, and I feared for Beccah's life were there to be even a single week's delay.

I had Beccah sign roughly the same forms as Jersey had, only this time there were no forms for the family to sign, because there was no family to speak of. Catherine, thank God, was in boarding school and much too young to be dragged into something like this. Although Beccah had gone back to trading, which meant occasionally returning to the Armitage mansion in Westchester, she was continuing to live alone in her rented house in the woods. Neither she nor I had the slightest desire for Jack to be informed of what was going to occur.

Certainly the papers made Beccah well aware of the seriousness of it all since one of the clauses she agreed to (as had Jersey) was her acknowledgment of the possibility that she might die during the exorcism. Actually, none of the clauses caused any concern to Beccah—even the one that she might die. She was so depressed I don't think she cared whether the outcome would be successful. Most likely she even relished the prospect of dying.

In retrospect I have serious concerns about my judgment during the period of time immediately preceding and during the exorcism. My relationship with Beccah was unusually intense, having seen her for over a year and a half and going through the deliverance with her. I am not sure that this degree of closeness alone shouldn't have been reason to disqualify me from being the exorcist. Admittedly, one must operate largely on the basis of feelings in these matters. For instance, exorcists commonly get a very clear feeling about the likely length of an exorcism, and I do not fault myself in this regard. However, the feeling I had that Lucifer would be specifically out to get me in order to pay me back for my success with Jersey strikes me as a feeling that should have been deeply questioned, and which was probably also sufficient reason to disqualify me as the exorcist. Why did I not think of disqualifying myself? Why did I not, at the very least, request that Malachi be the exorcist? I believe he would have accepted my request, yet I never even thought of calling him. Finally, during this period I was spending a great deal of time away on the lecture circuit, and as such, I was extremely busy—too busy I believe to have assumed primary responsibility for an exorcism. Regardless of whether the exorcism was going to be a success or not, I feel that my judgment was seriously compromised by a combination of excessive good will and definite arrogance.

We met as a team for the first time Thursday night at my house, the night before the exorcism was to begin. Unlike the first team meeting in Jersey's case, this time I had managed to obtain a more or less official blessing from the Episcopal church for the exorcism, and the church had dispatched a priest to our house for that purpose. He prayed with us and for us, and anointed each of us with oil to signify that we would be protected. I knew the priest to be a well-known expert in Jungian psychology. Although this was not true of Jung himself, most Jungians believe the devil to be merely an archetype—an almost universal image within humanity's collective unconscious, but nothing more than an image. A symbol of a possible reality, but nothing real in itself. The priest seemed like a nice enough chap, so before he left I asked whether he had any interest in attending the exorcism and in being part of the team himself. He shook his head. I am not sure I have ever seen a look of such terror on another person's face. As he was walking down our front steps to his car, I realized it may have occurred to him that, for the first time in his life, he might come face to face with a living archetype.

CHAPTER 6

EXORCISM

———◆———

"I have no reason to join your ranks
and be put in the toaster!"

Day 1

To make time to receive the church's blessing on the previous evening, I had not yet told the team about Beccah's case in any depth. Instead, this would be handled first off the next morning. When we all met at Martha's house at 9:00 A.M., the team squeezed into a small room where Beccah sat at the head of the one bed. As promised, I spent the first hour telling the team in detail about her case. Periodically I reminded Beccah that she was free to speak up if she thought I was either leaving something important out or was misstating anything. I had a notion that it might properly be a part of the exorcism for Beccah to hear her own case told in an objective, clinical manner. Whether my notion was correct or not, Beccah never interrupted the case history, but only sat silently: thin, wan, and with her head listlessly hanging down in a posture of utter dejection. It was depressing just to look at her.

After the rendition of her case history we took a brief break, and then began the next session the same way we had begun each session of Jersey's exorcism. Peter, my assistant, started with a brief Bible reading relevant to Jesus's practice of exorcism, followed by a prayer for God's assistance. Then, ritualistically, I said the words that were now so familiar to me: "Beccah, creature of God, in the name of God who created you and Jesus Christ who died for you, I require you to hear my voice as the voice of Christ's church and, although I am but a humble and unworthy servant, to obey my commands." Following this injunction I told Beccah that we were most interested in talking either with her or with Satan, but that we would refuse to speak with some confused mixture of the two.

Over the next hour and a half little was said. Just before the break, Rodger, an insightful psychologist as well as our videotape expert, was the first to note that while Beccah's head was continuing to hang down listlessly, it had slowly started to move back and forth in a strange weaving pattern that looked remarkably like that of a cobra. We had some brief discussion as to whether this phenomenon might somehow be representative of the snake in the Garden of Eden—of the devil in its earliest recorded appearance.

During the break Beccah sat off in one corner, not eating any of the sandwiches Martha had placed out for us, as isolated and dejected as she had been during the session.

When we began the next session, after our customary rituals, Beccah's head continued to weave back and forth as if in tune to a fakir's flute. I asked Beccah whether she felt like a snake. I got no response. I then addressed myself to Satan and asked if it was manifesting its presence as a snake. Again, no response.

I went on getting nowhere until it occurred to me that while I had informed the team of Beccah's practice of self-mutilation, they had not seen the results for themselves. I told Beccah that I thought it would be helpful for the team to see exactly what it was that Satan ordered her to do to herself. I imagined it might be slightly embarrassing for her, but asked her if she would be so kind as to lift the long sleeves of her sweater. She did not respond. I told her that I was going to raise one of her sleeves for her and moved to do so.

At that moment Beccah's curled body sprang toward me, its mouth flared open. Fortunately, the team was extremely alert. Before she could bite into my arm, they grabbed her shoulders and pushed her back toward the head of the bed. Her legs still free, she tried to twist away, but with all seven of us in action, we were able to hold her legs down as well. It was not long, however, before our arms began to become exhausted. Unlike Jersey, who had required virtually no force for restraint, Beccah, seemingly sickly, had close to superhuman strength and fought against us with amazing violence. Knowing that the seven of us unaided were inadequate to restrain her well, it was not long before we employed our medical experience by raiding Martha's linen closet. Soon we had a sheet around each of Beccah's wrists and ankles, with each sheet tied tightly to the bed frame. Later, there would be times when we would even need to use additional sheets around her midriff.

Although we did not know it then, Beccah would require this massive restraint for the entirety of the exorcism—meaning almost all of the next two and a half days in that room.

The extraordinary amount of restraint required was one of the less remarkable features of the exorcism. The most remarkable was the change in the appearance of Beccah's face and body. Except during break times and a few other occasions when Satan would seemingly be replaced by Beccah, she did not appear to be a human being at all. To everyone present, her entire face became like that of a snake. I would have expected it to be the usual kind of poisonous snake with a triangular head, but that was not the case. The head and face of this snake were remarkably round. The only exception to this roundness was its nostrils, which had a distinct snub-nosed look. Most remarkable of all were the eyes. They had become hooded. The lids lazily drooped down so that the snake appeared to be tired, almost asleep. The face was one of pure reptilian torpor—except at certain moments, when suddenly its eyelids would flare open as it thrust out its head to bite any one of us on the team. At such moments the blazing fury in the snake's wide-open eyes was palpable. Despite our constant wariness, two of us on the team were to suffer superficial wounds on our forearms where her front teeth had come close enough to graze the skin and draw a bit of blood.

The snake—Satan or Lucifer, if you will—was remarkably uncommunicative for the rest of this first day, no matter how we tried to address it. Throughout the rest of the first afternoon we learned but one item more about this thing that we had on our hands: it hated not only us but also certain Christian religious symbols. Unlike Jersey, in whom the demonic had hidden behind Jesus, this thing seemed frequently—not always, but frequently—to wince at Jesus's name. Most of the time it winced even more strongly when Peter marked the sign of the cross on its tightly restrained forehead. Often when sprinkled with holy water it seemed to writhe in agony, sometimes shouting with Beccah's voice, "Stop it, you fucking bastards."

Its violent response to being afflicted by Christian symbols was in one instance distinctly paranormal. When she writhed with sufficient vigor against the restraining sheets and our forceful arms, she was able to twist herself around to the point where she was lying on her stomach and her face was buried in the pillow for minutes at a time. At one point, curious as to whether it might soothe her, Peter put a Bible on her back and it had no effect. We used three books on psychology from Martha's library and we used several Bibles. There was no response from Beccah to any of these books. Knowing that Beccah had been baptized an Episcopalian, Peter's experiment inspired me to try another book. Instead of a Bible, I substituted the Episcopal Book of Common Prayer. Rather than soothing her, Beccah or the snake would scream in pain and writhe in fury to escape its touch, even if it meant twisting herself right side up again so she could face us, her torturers. None of the books affected her except the updated Book of Common Prayer, which consistently drove her mad each time. I cannot explain the phenomenon. She couldn't see which book we were using; the books were all approximately the same shape, size, and weight.

As in Jersey's exorcism, the sessions lasted roughly an hour and a half, interspersed with half-hour breaks. Also as in Jersey's exorcism, for the present at least, when we told Beccah that we were ready for a break, she would seem to put aside her demonic personage and no longer needed restraint for that time. Also similar to Jersey, Beccah was well behaved but was also withdrawn, demonstrating no desire to join the team. Unlike Jersey, however, Beccah never coughed.

Mrs. Cowper arrived at Martha's house right on the dot of five as I had requested, and Beccah went home with her. Shortly thereafter the rest of us broke for the day, frustrated we'd not accomplished more.

The single most dramatic part of that day, and the days to come, was the appearance of the monstrous snub-nosed snake with hooded eyes. I use the word "appearance" because I am speaking now strictly as a skeptical, typically materialistic scientist. With the exception of a moment but a few seconds in length, Jersey's satanic appearance was not captured on the videotape. Similarly, this snakelike appearance was also never captured on the videotape—although I might add that with the team constantly having to restrain her it was difficult for the videotape to capture Beccah's face at all. During Jersey's exorcism the team had not taken the time to discuss Jersey's satanic expression. Beccah's snakelike appearance was so commanding that we all perceived it and everyone commented on it. The team's experience of Beccah as a snake was unanimous.

To my knowledge, the Roman Catholic church is the only body to have listed the kinds of paranormal phenomena it believes to be required to make a valid diagnosis of demonic possession. It does not even clearly mention inhuman facial appearances as an example, even though Malachi Martin noted, correctly I believe, that the most striking feature of the Presence is its inhuman nature. When the Pretense is penetrated so that the Presence is revealed, everyone feels the unmistakable presence of something inhuman in the room.

Instead, the church focuses on such paranormal phenomena as objects flying across the room, bureaus shaking, chairs turning over, the patient levitating, and an ability of the patient to speak foreign languages he or she has never studied, etc. As I have mentioned, I believe it is excessive and unrealistic to require such gross paranormal phenomena to make a diagnosis of demonic possession. I do believe there should be at least one paranormal manifestation, but in my experience it is so subtle as to often be overlooked. The more realistic and usually revelatory signs are merely such things like Beccah's depression worsening when it should have been getting better, or the tiny matter of Jersey feeling sorry for her demons.

Nonetheless, Beccah would please the Catholic church by her negative response to such religious symbols as the holy water, the cross, and the reading of certain Bible passages. Certainly it should please the Episcopal church that the most dramatic of such paranormal phenomena was her inexplicable ability to discern the Episcopal Book of Common Prayer from other books of equal size and weight that were laid upon her back, including the Bible. Although I will later delve into it a little more deeply, the phenomenon will remain inexplicable.

Day 2

Everyone had assembled at Martha's well before nine on the morning of the second day. Mrs. Cowper said that Beccah had been peaceful, dignified, and no trouble whatsoever during the night. I thanked her profusely before she drove off, sulking slightly, but promising to return again at 5:00 P.M.

Beccah's transformation into a very dangerous snake had been the primary happening of the day before. As the previous afternoon had worn on, Beccah's thin body seemed to be replaced by an ever larger snake composed of giant coils, each a yard in diameter and weighing tons. Intellectually I knew that we were looking at an emaciated human female body, but in fact our intuitive minds were so powerfully affected that what we *saw* was a snake. My predominant feeling about this snake, except for the moments when it viciously tried to strike us, was one of profound immovability. Its sheer weight seemed oppressive, and I could not envision how we could possibly get rid of its overwhelming hugeness. A miracle would be required. God would have to intervene. But how could we prepare the way for God to enter that little room?

On the small chance that the magic would work, we began that second morning by going through the formal Roman Ritual of Exorcism. The minute we started the ritual, Beccah returned to her snake form, and the restraints were needed again. Even with the knotted sheets, it was all the team could do to hold her down.

Once again I was impressed by the potential power of the words of the ritual, which went back five hundred to a thousand years or more. But, as I had suspected, their power had no effect upon the beast on the bed. It was not as if it actively "phased out" the way Jersey had; rather, it simply lay there, absolutely inert.

After the completion of the ineffective ritual, we untied Beccah, took a quick fifteen-minute break, and immediately reapplied the restraints. We all talked for a few minutes about how each of us perceived Beccah to have a snub-nosed face with hooded snakelike eyes, and how none of us had the slightest doubt that we were in the presence of the inhuman and the subhuman. Not wanting to burden the team with my sense of near despair at the pure weight of the snake, I did not tell them of my plan to violate Malachi's clear teaching by deliberately offering myself up as a possible sacrifice. I felt the only way I might be able to get the snake to move would be to seduce it into attempting to take me in Beccah's stead. Over and over again as the morning went on, I ordered it "to leave Beccah, to come out of her and from behind her so as to deal with me."

I was aware that I was not commanding the snake to deal with Jesus, but rather just me as a mere mortal, and I was aware that I was on shaky ground. But at least it did seem to give me a way of communicating with the beast. When I consulted with Wayne about my dangerous tactic he told me he firmly believed I was on the right track.

During the dialogue it seemed that the Pretense had returned to some degree. Although I could see the snake in front of me, much of the time I did not feel I was speaking with Satan but rather with Beccah. Nonetheless, throughout the dialogue the two—Beccah and the snake—seemed to oscillate back and forth, and there were occasional moments where I did feel it was actually Satan or Lucifer who was answering my questions.

I demanded to know of Satan why it hated Beccah so. Initially the answer was vague, suggesting that it just hated people in general. But with my prodding it warmed up to the subject, saying, "I am against people loving one another. They need to work."

I demanded to know why.

"They need to work," it replied, "so there will be war and prosperity instead of love and all that crap."

"There are times Beccah seems under your sway, compelled

to work at trading," I noted. "But at other times she rebels and stands for love."

"I won't leave her," it answered. "She was meant to be mine. She was given to me."

"Given by whom?" I demanded.

It avoided the question, instead saying, "I attacked her when she was five because she was always alone and couldn't watch the movies. I told her she was better than her friends."

"You will obey my commands," I ordered. "You haven't told me who gave Beccah to you."

Again its answer was indirect, but possibly closer to the point. "Because Beccah's mother gave the orders," it said.

Beccah looked exhausted. For that matter so did the team. I called for a break. During it Satan seemed to go away and Beccah, for the first time, laid her head back against the shoulders of several of the team members and was smiling wanly, even laughing.

Still, I was aware of how tired we all were, just from restraining Beccah if nothing else. I had thought that a team of seven would be more than enough, but I was wrong. I used the break time to call for additional reinforcement from two people I knew I could trust to respond immediately. They both arrived shortly after I began the next session.

After our usual opening rituals I asked Satan what Beccah's mother was like.

"She was filled with wonder and glory. How's that?" It was the most withering piece of sarcasm I had ever heard. I wondered whether Beccah's mother had been possessed. The answer was yes. Using Malachi's terminology, which I don't believe Beccah knew, I asked Satan whether the mother's possession was perfect or imperfect.

Satan answered, "There was a little of her left once but not for long." It was a response that suggested a clear understanding of the distinction between perfect and imperfect possession.

Although I had no reason to believe it to be the case, for the sake of thoroughness I asked it whether Beccah's father had been possessed. Without hesitation the snake answered, "We had no hold on him because he wasn't perfect."

As noted, it was often difficult to impossible to discern whether it was Beccah or Satan/Lucifer who was speaking at any particular time. This had been one of those times. Whoever or whatever was speaking, however, was saying something not only profound, but also from the standpoint of both psychology and religion, something utterly accurate. Evil people and spirits are both characterized by a kind of excessive pride or narcissism that causes them to believe they are without fault. Satan is renowned for speaking the truth in one sentence while lying in the next. "We had no hold on him because he wasn't perfect" could be a priceless example of Satan at its more honest.

"Did you have any hold on Beccah's sister?" I asked. It said yes. I then asked what was the nature of that hold. "She was greedy and self-serving."

"But was she possessed?" For some reason the snake continually refused to answer this question. Feeling blocked, I decided to return to my strategy of attempting to seduce the snake into physically attacking me, demanding that it deal with me directly instead of through Beccah's body. After repeating this demand several times the only response I got was "Get that fucking cross off the bed."

I returned to asking it more questions. I asked about the book Beccah had been so attached to, *Gods' Man*. As I did the body on the bed struggled more fiercely than ever before. It clearly did not like the subject. "What was your involvement in that book?" I demanded.

It screamed, "I will not." Then, fighting the restraints, it screamed, "Just let me at you!"

"You're perfectly free to get at me," I taunted it. "Why don't you just leave Beccah's body right now?"

"Just let me at you!" it repeated.

Finally I began to understand. "You're a spirit. Why do you cringe at the holy water when you're just a spirit, when you have no body? Beccah's body must feel the holy water, but you shouldn't feel it because you have no body."

"NO," it screamed.

Sensing that my simple logic was infuriating it, I continued. "Why are you so upset? I wasn't calling you names or insulting you. I was merely saying the truth: you have no body. Which means you are a No Body."

Still making no sense, it now screamed, "I have no reason to join your ranks and be put in the toaster!"

Wayne intuitively said, "The toaster's no joke. I think it feels it will be put in the toaster if it gives up Beccah's body."

"I think you're right," I said. And then we began to have a discussion. I told the team it was becoming increasingly clear to me that Satan was not about to leave Beccah's body, even to get at me. It was not willing to take the risk: it needed Beccah's body too desperately. Wayne spoke of the several instances in the Gospels where demons pleaded with Jesus not to be cast out of bodies. We wondered about the strange attachment demons had for bodies, and slowly we came to the conclusion that demons were powerless without human bodies—that they could commit evil only through the use of human hands, they could speak evil only through human tongues. Were they to be cast out, they would be in a metaphorical toaster of utter impotence.

During this discussion the body on the bed became increasingly agitated and then began to roar over and over, "She is mine forever, I will never give her up."

As the roaring continued, the team either sang hymns or listened as I repetitively read the first chapter of the Gospel according to John, knowing how much that particular chapter seemed to be an anathema to the demonic.

After what seemed an almost endless time of this, Satan suddenly changed its tune and almost plaintively said, "I need Beccah."

Wayne instantly commented, "That's the first true thing it's said."

At that moment, inexplicably, Satan seemed to be replaced by Beccah. It was an angry Beccah who asked Wayne, "Do you know the direct way to God like Jack thinks he does?"

Wayne did not answer. Before our eyes Beccah's anger seemed to evaporate. Edie exclaimed, "Beccah's back. She's so beautiful." And then to Beccah herself, Edie said, "You're glowing."

Beccah was indeed, and making perfect sense as well. She announced that she wanted to take her wedding ring off, but she needed soap to do it.

The soap was not sufficient. Martha produced a tube of Vaseline, which did the trick. We all clapped when Beccah tossed the ring to Edie, saying, "Here, you keep it."

Now that Beccah was back, I felt moved to address her. "One of the things that bothers me about this exorcism," I said, "is that it's been something like a battle between me and Jack. You have to discern which of us has a direct line to God. I know very well that you have the gift of discernment, Beccah. You know how to distinguish between good fruit and rotten fruit. If money is the good fruit, then you need to side with Jack. But if you think that friendship—the kind of friendship we have here—is the better fruit, then you need to side against Jack as you seem to be doing."

Instantly Beccah was gone and Satan was in her place.

Knowing how much Satan hated Gospel readings and picking up on my use of the word "fruit" in relation to the process of discernment, Wayne proceeded to read the passage in the

Gospels where Jesus laid down the single greatest principle of discernment when he said, "By their fruits you shall know them." *

Predictably this enraged Satan, who furiously asked, "Are you happy now, Dr. Peck?"

Throughout our psychotherapeutic work prior to the exorcism, I had become aware of how Beccah would shrink away from any possibility that I might touch her. Yet earlier this afternoon when Beccah had replaced Satan, she had not only allowed some of the team members to touch her but had seemed to start to enjoy their touching and holding. I raised the issue by saying, "Beccah has always wanted me to keep my distance. It is like she has had that flag with a snake on it and the words 'Don't tread on me.' I'm starting to sense now that it was not Beccah's banner, but yours, snake. And now I'm treading on you, Satan, aren't I?"

The snake on the bed writhed more fiercely than ever, desperately trying to bite anyone.

I raised another issue. I had suspected that in her generalized dislike of her family and in her penchant for Nazi knives, Beccah had been manifesting a hidden anti-Semitism, which she had not been willing to acknowledge. It occurred to me that she hadn't been able to acknowledge it because it wasn't hers. Addressing Satan I said, "You have many names. One is the Prince of Darkness. Today I am sensing a proper name for you I haven't heard before. You are the Prince of Anti-Semites. I believe that Beccah the Christian hates the Prince of Anti-Semites."

The snake tried to twist so that its head was buried. Edie sensed that I had hit upon something and went into action. Motioning to the others to twist the snake's head back without being bitten, she loudly said, "Face this man!"

---

* Matthew 7:16–20

"SHUT UP!" Satan roared.

They went at it for a good five minutes with Edie repeatedly ordering Satan to face me and each time Satan screaming at her to shut up. Finally Edie shrugged her shoulders. "No luck," she pronounced.

"Not for lack of trying," I said.

I noted that it was some minutes after five, and I had heard Mrs. Cowper arrive. I didn't feel that we were on the verge of making any great progress, and I suspected that Satan would be replaced by Beccah as soon as I suggested that we call it quits for the day. And so it was. Within two minutes Beccah was present again and departed peacefully with Mrs. Cowper, as she had done the evening before.

Feeling confused myself, I believed the team needed whatever encouragement I could provide. Giving voice to the optimistic part of myself, small as it was at this time, I told them, "It may seem that we have not made all that much progress today, but we have touched upon a lot of issues in many different ways. Do whatever you feel called to do, but from my experience with the other exorcism, I would suggest that you not worry about the fact that tomorrow is the last day that we have. I myself will be doing a lot of thinking about what has transpired and about tomorrow. I can only tell you that I have a deep faith that tomorrow will be a very different kind of day."

We briefly prayed for ourselves and for the day to come, and I concluded by chanting the petition from Compline, the concluding ritual of the day in monastic life.

Guide us waking, O Lord,
And guard us asleep
That awake we may watch with Christ
And asleep we may rest in You.

My attempt to lure the snake or Satan out of Beccah's body so that it might attack me was made out of a sense of desperation caused by the snake's appearance of utter immobility. My attempt was most ill advised. For one thing it was unsuccessful. Indeed, the next day the team would realize why its lack of success should have been completely predictable.

But what feels even more wrong about my attempt was that there was nothing of Christ in it. I may have thought that I myself was being Christlike by offering myself as a sacrifice, but, as I have thought about it, I had forgotten about Christ in my focus upon myself. As Malachi repeatedly wrote, "The exorcist should act only under the authority of Christ, making Christ the center of all that he says or does." I once again had raised the possibility of Beccah's anti-Semitism, which Beccah had previously denied. This time the snake evaded the issue. At the conclusion we shall return to reexamine the possibility of both her anti-Semitism and her anti-Episcopalianism. Although my executive assistant (one of the two I'd summoned for emergency help) had been present for only two hours, her predominant reaction to the exorcism when she spoke about it with me some days later was notable. "You had told me, Scotty, that evil was essentially boring," she said, "but I never believed you until now. Now there is nothing I believe more. I have never in my life witnessed anything so utterly boring as that ugly snake just lying there doing nothing but hating for all eternity. I told you I had to leave because of my children. That was true. But I could have stayed for another fifteen minutes were it not for the fact that I couldn't tolerate even one more minute of that horrible empty boringness."

Beccah's exorcism could not have been more different from Jersey's. In Jersey's case, my attempt to encourage the separation between her and the demonic succeeded extremely well, to the degree that, by the last day and a half, there was absolutely no difficulty discerning between Jersey and the demonic. Although the same technique of separation may have encouraged the rapid emergence of the snake, Beccah's exorcism thereafter was characterized by the ongoing utter confusion between her and the demonic. This is why I was profoundly struck by that moment when it screamed at me, "I have no reason to join your ranks and be put in the toaster!"

I don't know what kind of being made this bizarre proclamation. Despite all the confusion of the exorcism, I can tell you one thing with clarity. It was not Beccah who said those words. It was nothing she would ever have thought of saying. It was completely out of character for her.

Day 3

As soon as Peter had given his opening reading and prayer and I had addressed her with my ritual words, Beccah, as expected, turned back into the snake that needed restraint.

I quickly commented for the team's benefit as well as Satan's, "As I was thinking last night I realized, Satan, that while I asked you why you hated Beccah so, you never really answered the question. You did give us some useful information about Beccah's mother and father, and her mother's role in your possession of Beccah, but you still didn't tell us why you hate her. I suspect the reason you didn't answer my question was that it was not the right question. I think the basic reason you hate her is because she is a human being. I suspect you particularly hate her because she is a potential spiritual leader, but your genuine enemy is not just Beccah, but the entire human race. I believe the real question is Why do you hate humans? I order you now, in the name of Jesus Christ, to tell me why you hate humans so much. Why it is your guiding motive to do everything you possibly can to prevent humans from achieving their potential destiny."

The snake writhed and writhed as if I had hit upon the ultimate issue. But it would not answer me, and I knew I had no power to make it answer. I felt hopeless and helpless. The very next moment the Holy Spirit—or something—gave me the answer to my own question. It was not an answer in accord with the established Christian theology and worldview, but as I pondered it, I felt it did not meet the criteria for heresy.

"Since you are not going to give us the answer, Satan," I said, "I think that I can say it. Everything I have read in the field of demonology suggests that demons have remarkably little free will, that they are tightly organized like little soldiers in an army under your command. Individually they have very little room to maneuver, to exercise any kind of independent judgment, precious little freedom. And even though you are their commander, from what I have read, about the only thing you are capable of is attempting to carry on with your hopeless mission of trying to subvert God's desire for the human race. There really isn't anything else you can do, is there? It is as if you are damned for eternity to do the same futile thing over and over and over again, as if you lack the capacity to take any other path or move in any other direction.

"So many times I have heard it said that God created us humans in His own image. What does that mean? I've wondered. What I concluded, ultimately with certainty, is that being created in God's image means, above all else, that God created us as creatures with free will—with total free will, the freedom to choose whatever we want, no matter how wise or stupid, the freedom to move in any direction at all. In other words, we are created with a freedom that demons don't begin to have and that you yourself, Satan, can hardly begin to understand. Even though most Christians think of angels as exalted beings, higher than themselves, it finally dawned on me that this common Christian vision is wrong. The reality, I believe, is that by giving us free will God created us higher than the angels, that it is not the angels who are superior to us but we who are more fortunate than them. And that's why you hate us, isn't it, Satan? You hate human beings so much because God decided to create them higher than even you who were once the bearer of light and the chief of all angels. Oh yes, your position was once exalted indeed, and you simply could not stand it when God decided to create creatures even more exalted than you. No, you would not stand for it. You refused to tolerate it. And that is why you rebelled against God, isn't it? And why you have hated the human race from its beginning."

The snake had stopped writhing, intent on looking at me with murderous rage. I knew it would never admit the correctness of what I had just said.

The notion that angels are not only beings of light but that they are more powerful and more important than human beings is one that so pervades our Western Christian culture that it will likely be upsetting for people to entertain a different notion. Nonetheless, mine is hardly an original idea. Were I to research the subject, I suspect I would find that a few other individual Christians have entertained it. Perhaps more to the point, after Beccah's exorcism I happened to discover it to be a standard doctrine of Islam, the world's second largest religion, that human beings were created higher than the angels. In fact, Mohammed himself proclaimed it in the second sura of the Koran.

Despite its unorthodoxy, the team had liked my sermon. Inexplicably, the tone of the sessions then became remarkably different. Although I was still technically the team leader, we began to function primarily as a community. For the most part, we stopped addressing Satan and increasingly addressed one another. Almost gaily we began by reviewing the conclusion we had reached on the previous day that Satan would never risk leaving Beccah's body in an attempt to hurt me because it couldn't hurt anything without use of a human body. "That's why we restrain you, Beccah," Edie said. "We restrain you not only for your sake but also in order that Satan is unable to use your body to murder Dr. Peck."

Harvey then told us that the evening before, he had called a large library in California, where the libraries were still open, and had obtained a full description of the book *Gods' Man*. The librarian knew of the book and told him how famous it had been in its day. She even read to Harvey its very few words, including its label of the hooded figure as fiend with a capital *F.* Between us we then identified the fiend as Satan, who was also the spirit of death.

Rodger suddenly suggested how close the word "fiend" was to that of "friend." Picking up on this, we immediately recognized that, from the age of six on, Beccah in all likelihood had not envisioned Satan as an enemy so much as a friend—indeed, a rather constant companion she could trust, the one thing in which she could believe.

With this input I turned to Beccah, who had been listening to our conversation so intently that she seemed to have forgotten to be Satan. "For the exorcism to succeed," I said, "maybe all that is required is that you stop believing in Satan."

Instantly flipping back into Satan she screamed, "It's not an illusion!"

But we ignored her. Our discussion was much more interesting. "So what we need to exorcise," Harvey said, "is not Satan but Beccah's faith in Satan."

"We're getting close!" Peter exclaimed.

"I agree," I noted, "but I'm not sure it's ours to exorcise. In the end it's going to be Beccah's choice. There was some old bishop in England who once defined faith as the choice of the nobler alternative. Beccah has mostly chosen Satan as her companion. I think we have some sense of the forces that were at work to compel her to make such an ignoble choice. But if she is to become free—as we humans were meant to be—she's going to have to choose a nobler alternative. She's going to have to change her choice."

Becoming ever more active, Edie commented, "I wonder if a whole part of this isn't that Satan has somehow appeared to be noble to Beccah, as if Beccah perceives her bondage to Satan as somehow more noble than her freedom—although God knows why anyone would fall prey to such a delusion."

To which I responded, "Loneliness could be such a reason. Remember how much of her childhood she was left alone by her parents who were always working."

"So could revenge be such a motive? Maybe to get revenge against her parents for leaving her alone. Maybe against her sister, for all I know."

I acknowledged that Beccah had plenty of reason to hate, but added a new conjecture. "I think Beccah has been letting Satan do her hating for her all these years."

On an intuitive roll now, Edie noted, "It takes a deep despair to hand over your hate."

I responded by turning to Beccah, saying, "We can deal with your hate in psychotherapy—the hate that you couldn't deal with as a child."

But Beccah was not there, and it was Satan who responded by shrieking at Edie, "GO BACK TO BOSTON!"

Edie giggled. "It seems that the great Satan has Boston confused with Chicago. I don't think that Boston will like that." The whole team roared with laughter.

When the laughter died down I addressed both Beccah and the team. "We don't have to talk to Satan anymore. Really we should just talk to Beccah about the truth, because it will be Beccah and Christ who will do the exorcism."

I noted that the team had begun to function as a true community. The difference between a community and an ordinary group may seem like a tiny matter, but isn't. For the moment all I need say is that when an ordinary group becomes a community, its members become free to offer their gifts of leadership in an orderly fashion because they have been liberated from their dependence upon a single leader. It is for this reason I once, somewhat facilely, defined a genuine community as a group of all leaders.

Thus you will notice that Edie suddenly assumed a powerful role in the group; Harvey told about how he had researched Beccah's transitional object book, *Gods' Man;* Rodger suggested that there might be a crucial similarity between "fiend" and "friend"; that together we began to arrive at the idea that what we needed to exorcise was not Satan, but Beccah's faith in Satan; and that Peter urged us forward by commenting excitedly, "We're getting close!"

So it was that the team had suddenly become much more productive. The transformation of the team, from a group dependent upon the leadership of the exorcist alone to a true community, will often happen naturally as it did in this case. However, I believe that exorcists should ideally be familiar with group dynamics and community-building skills so that they can facilitate the evolution of the team into a community. It is not simply that a community is more efficient and effective than an exorcist operating alone; it also has an almost mystical healing power that often plays a more important role in a successful exorcism than does the exorcist him- or herself. Thus it would soon be put to Beccah that she had a choice between Satan and the friendship of community.

It had been a long session thus far. Satan had seemed to turn back into Beccah and Beccah now wanted to have a cigarette. Not quite sure we could trust her yet, the two of us who were smokers shared our cigarettes with her in a form of communion without releasing the restraints. In fact, we shared several cigarettes, and this communion went on for more than ten minutes. During that time Beccah seemed to become ever more relaxed and herself, joking gaily with the team. Cigarettes done, she said that she needed to go to the bathroom. Feeling we had nothing to fear at this point, we unleashed her restraints so that Martha could lead her to the bathroom. We told Martha we saw no need for her to go into the bathroom with Beccah, since Beccah seemed so much like her old self.

Within thirty seconds of Beccah entering the bathroom and closing the door, we heard the unmistakable crash of breaking glass. We rushed to the bathroom. Thankfully, Beccah had been unable to lock the door from the inside. When we opened it we discovered that she had put her hand through the bathroom window, had withdrawn it, and was simply standing there with an expression of mild pleasure on her face as blood streamed from her lacerated hand and wrist onto the bathroom floor. She or it had obviously succeeded in pulling one over on us.

We led her back to the bed and reapplied the restraints to her legs and left wrist, leaving the right wrist exposed so that Harvey could practice his medical skills. He asked Martha for tweezers, which he patiently used to pluck small slivers of glass from Beccah's wounds, and then carefully wrapped the wounds in the white gauze Martha provided.

Hoping to prevent further such behavior, Wayne stepped forward to the foot of the bed, saying, "In the name of Christ I bind you Satan. You are henceforth bound so that you will no longer be able to use Beccah's hands for your mischief. You are now bound by the grace of God into the care of Jesus Christ and you are therefore incapable of any further violence."

As I assessed the situation it occurred to me that Beccah, despite the depth of her knowledge of Christian theology, might not have any real sense of the power of God inside her, no awareness that she had a built-in ally with which to fight against Satan. Telling her I was sure she already knew this, I gave her a little lecture about the existence and nature of the Holy Spirit. To emphasize how central the role of the Holy Spirit was in Christian theology, we all proceeded to recite the Nicene Creed. Beccah joined in the recitation without having to look at the words.

As soon as we had finished reciting the creed, Beccah did something very much like what she had done during the deliverance. "I don't know why," she told us, "but ever since you started talking about the Holy Spirit the name of Judith has kept coming to my mind. I wonder if it has any meaning?"

"Well, what do you think?" Peter asked, turning the matter back on her. "Does Judith have any meaning to you?"

"It's the name of one of the books of the Bible," Beccah answered him.

I thumbed through the table of contents of one of the many Bibles in the room and announced to the group I could find no Book of Judith.

Beccah was now so comfortable she was even able to tease. "It's in the Apocrypha, stupid," she said directly to me.

"Does anyone here know the book?" I asked.

None of us on the team did, and Beccah chuckled at the superiority of her knowledge. Gleefully telling us that she knew the book quite well, she asked whether we would care to hear the story. We told her we were eager to hear it. She recited it fully, saying that the book was possibly left out of the orthodox Old Testament by both Christians and Jews because its very powerful hero was a woman, namely Judith.

Judith was a beautiful, wealthy young widow who had worn sackcloth and ashes in the years since her husband's death. Judith lived at the edge of a Jewish hill town that was under siege by the Assyrian army of King Nebuchadnezzar, led by its greatly feared general, Holofernes. Holofernes had cut off the town's water supply. The town leaders debated and decided that there was nothing they could do but wait, and they set a number of days as a way of testing the will of the Lord. If Holofernes gave up the siege within five days, it would obviously be a sign that God looked upon the Israelites with favor. If Holofernes continued the siege beyond five days, then it would be a sign from God that the Israelites should surrender. Judith heard about this decision and gave the leaders hell. How dare they test the Lord God at all, let alone in such a stupid way?

Judith told them they should not surrender, that she would take care of the problem, and they all bowed to the power of her will. Judith waited thirty-six hours, and on the night following, dressed as seductively as possible. She left the town with her maid and walked proudly into the enemy camp demanding to see Holofernes. The general allowed her into his tent. Judith simply told him that she had long wanted to meet such a great man, famed through the world and obviously of greater stature than her own people. Holofernes was naturally flattered. Judith continued in this manner, claiming her allegiance to the Assyrians, until after four days of Judith's company, Holofernes had become completely enamored of her. Trying to bed her, he became so drunk that he fell fast asleep before succeeding. At this point Judith took Holofernes' sharp scimitar from the wall and proceeded with two sure strokes to cut Holofernes' head right off. She then marched out of the tent through the enemy soldiers with her maid carrying their general's head in her bag.

When she got back to her hilltop town, she presented Holofernes' head to the town fathers. Encouraged by Judith's triumph, they vowed to fight to the end. But they did not have to. The huge Assyrian army was totally demoralized when it looked up to see Holofernes' head hanging from one of the ramparts. The siege was abandoned.

The story says nothing further than that Judith never remarried and lived a quiet and respected life until her death at the age of 105.*

At this point Beccah seemed to be in as much control of her situation as Judith had been, and we sensed in her the same kind of power. We prayerfully praised the Holy Spirit for bringing Judith to Beccah's mind. It seemed to us that Judith was obviously a counterpoint to Judas by simple sound, as well as in her leadership and love for God. Judas had needed to be expelled; now what was needed was for Beccah to take into herself the power of Judith so that Judith, not Satan, would be Beccah's new identity. We told Beccah that she was a born leader who was destined, like Judith, to provide our frightened people with her leadership.

Beccah seemed to enjoy this interpretation but also noted she was very hungry. We realized we had totally forgotten about a lunch break. Beccah joined the team and sat joking with us happily while Martha and Rodger prepared sandwiches. By the time we were in the midst of gobbling them up, Beccah had seemed so much a member of the team that we utterly forgot about guarding her. We suddenly became aware that she was no longer sitting with us, and at that moment we heard the front door slam. Peter and I ran after her. By the time we were out the door she had a fifty-yard lead on us. We ran faster than either of us had for years, and it was only just before the road entered the woods that we tackled her, rolling into a leaf-filled ditch. Holding her arms tightly as she struggled, we dragged her back to the house to start the next session.

The first order of business, of course, was to put Beccah back in restraints. The second was to say a good-bye. Harvey Ransome had unexpectedly announced he had to leave after lunch

---

* *The Apocrypha, An American Translation,* Edgar J. Goodspeed, copyright 1938, Vintage Books, New York, 1989, pp. 131–164.

to catch a plane back to Ohio. Everyone hugged. It seemed as if our little community was already fading away.

Certainly, we were well aware that the community was coming to an end. We knew the exorcism had to be completed somehow within the next four hours. We had no idea how to proceed save the certainty we could no longer trust Beccah to be Beccah. Rather than having succeeded in driving Satan out, the days seemed to have melded Satan and Beccah together to the point where they were practically indistinguishable.

I have pondered a great deal about how Satan and Beccah seemed to be flicking back and forth so rapidly toward the very end of the exorcism that we could no longer tell which was which. When the snake vanished and Beccah seemed to return, we had twice in as many hours been deceived by this Beccah on her best behavior.

This indistinguishability between Beccah and Satan did not look at all like the conclusion of an exorcism; rather it seemed that we were back at the beginning, mired in the Pretense. But what about the snake? Much of the time the snake was still with us as the inhuman Presence of Satan. What was going on? At the time I did not know. I was aware of the question but did not have the foggiest idea of the answer.

It was only years later that I arrived at a dark hypothesis. My only possible explanation is that Beccah was far more possessed than Jersey; in fact, a hair's breadth away from being perfectly possessed. I believe that the virtual indistinguishability we were observing was more than an appearance, it was a manifestation of the reality. After forty years of intimacy with Satan, Beccah had, to all intents and purposes, become Satan. But not quite. There was still a germ—but only a germ—of Beccah's own soul left. Still, it was enough of a germ to allow what then happened.

The next hour was a strange one. The Beccah we could no longer trust seemed to be in ascendancy. She taught us more about Judith. She denied having done any research on the subject, but seemed to know even more about that heroine than was in the apocryphal book. Harvey and both extra assistants having left, the team had now dwindled to six and, although I worried whether there would be enough of us to restrain her, we loosened the restraints. I asked the team, however, to be extra alert should Beccah/Satan act up again. She seemed young and playful, often joking with us. Yet even when she was joking we noticed that her head was weaving from time to time.

The ending began a little after three. Edie said to me, "You know, Scotty, we haven't been successful. Maybe we will be. But I think it would be irresponsible of us not to start considering how we're going to deal with Beccah should Satan not depart. I don't think she is in any shape to go home at this point."

Reluctantly, I had to agree with her. Edie was speaking good psychiatry. Unless there was some dramatic change—I couldn't begin even to imagine what it might be—I could not responsibly let Beccah go alone to her little house in the woods or even go home with Mrs. Cowper. Slowly I pushed myself to face the reality that Beccah would need to be hospitalized. There was a private open-door hospital where I had privileges and to which I could admit her, but in her current state she was so untrustworthy and unpredictable she clearly needed to be on a locked ward. Furthermore, that facility was a voluntary hospital into which Beccah would have to sign herself. I doubted she would be willing to do that.

The only locked wards where patients could be certified against their will were in the state psychiatric hospitals, the nearest of which was in Newtown, Connecticut. The procedure for certification was that two of Newtown's psychiatrists would

have to interview Beccah (and me as the referring physician) and agree among themselves that Beccah represented an immediate danger to herself or to others before committing her. I could vividly see the scene in my imagination as I tried to explain to these psychiatrists that Beccah was suffering from satanic possession and we were bringing her to them because our attempt at an exorcism had failed. In my imagination I could also see Beccah sitting there with a slight smile on her face, calm and as logical as Socrates. Until that time I actually had a reputation in the state as being a competent psychiatrist. I could now imagine that the two admitting doctors might well lock me up and let Beccah go. My face was already beginning to turn red with embarrassment at the prospect. Nonetheless, reality had to be faced.

So I answered Edie, "You're right," specifying the details of the law governing psychiatric hospitalization of a patient against her will in Connecticut. I concluded by saying, "I think we need to start praying for a miracle, because I sure as hell don't look forward to taking her down to Newtown. Still, you're correct. Right now that's how we will have to conclude this day."

I was vaguely aware of how intently Beccah had been listening to my recounting of the details of psychiatric commitment, and no sooner had I finished agreeing with Edie than I heard her clear her throat. She started to speak. No, to scream, but every single word was utterly precise and hit me as if it were a perfectly aimed arrow.

"YOU KNOW HOW I FEEL ABOUT BEING PUT IN A PSYCHIATRIC HOSPITAL. I TOLD YOU THAT THE FIRST DAY WE MET. YOU PROMISED ME YOU WOULD NEVER DO IT. YOU HAD ME SIGN ALL YOUR GODDAMN PERMISSIONS. GET THOSE FORMS. GET THEM NOW. DID I EVER SIGN ANYTHING AGREEING TO BE COMMITTED TO A STATE HOSPITAL? DID YOU EVER INFORM ME OF THE POSSIBILITY THAT THIS ATTEMPTED EXORCISM MIGHT LEAVE ME IN WORSE SHAPE THAN BEFORE? IN SUCH SHAPE THAT I WOULD HAVE TO BE HOSPITALIZED AGAINST MY WILL? SHOW ME THE FORM. SHOW ME WHERE YOU INSTRUCTED ME OF WHAT MIGHT HAPPEN. BUT YOU

CAN'T, CAN YOU? YOU DIDN'T PUT IT IN YOUR FUCKING FORM. SO YOU
CAN'T HOSPITALIZE ME. I THOUGHT YOU WERE THE ONE PERSON IN THIS
WORLD I COULD TRUST. BUT NOW I SEE YOU FOR WHO YOU ARE. YOU'RE A
GODDAMNED LIAR. YOU LIED TO ME YOU SON OF A BITCH, YOU LIED, YOU
LIED . . ."

This was the Clash, I knew, and I simultaneously knew I had
lost. I realized I had forgotten to put that sentence in Beccah's
permission forms even though I had made sure it was in Jersey's
forms. I had failed to be thorough. I had failed to be utterly clear
with Beccah. I had not meant to lie to her, but I had. I was incompetent. I was a liar. I was not worthy of being a psychiatrist,
much less an exorcist.

As I was thinking these things I fell to the floor on my knees as
if I had been pushed there by Beccah's power. I was weeping,
and over and again I kept repeating, "I'm so sorry, I'm so sorry." I
was totally incapacitated by self-recrimination, by the guilt of
my blatant incompetence. After saying "I'm sorry" for the twen-
tieth time I realized I could never compensate for my incompetence and there was absolutely nothing I could do except pray to
God for his grace. Through the tears pouring down my face, I
prayed for the grace of His forgiveness of me and I prayed for
Beccah's soul, I prayed that something could exorcise Beccah, I
prayed for God to do His will, I prayed so hard that my eyes were
clenched shut and my body was trembling.

But I could still hear. And suddenly I heard Wayne's voice ad-
dressing Beccah. It sounded like the voice of God. It said: "NO!
NO, YOU HAVE IT WRONG. DR. PECK NEVER LIED TO YOU. I SAW THE FORMS
YOU SIGNED. YOU SIGNED THAT HE HAD MADE YOU AWARE THAT YOU
MIGHT DIE DURING THIS EXORCISM. YOU SIGNED THAT YOU WERE WILLING
TO DIE TO BE RID OF SATAN, AND NOW YOU ARE TRYING TO TELL DR. PECK
THAT HE LIED. NO. DO YOU SEE HOW STUPID IT IS OF YOU, SATAN, TO
PROTEST BEING HOSPITALIZED FOR THE SAFETY OF BECCAH'S BODY,
WHICH YOU INHABIT? WHEN BECCAH SIGNED SHE WAS AWARE SHE MIGHT
DIE, THAT THAT MIGHT BE THE OUTCOME? DR. PECK DIDN'T LIE TO YOU, HE

WAS STRAIGHT WITH YOU ALL THE WAY. YOU'RE THE LIAR. YES, YOU'RE THE LIAR, AND WE ARE FED UP WITH YOUR LIES. GET OUT! IT IS SAID THAT ONCE WHEN JESUS CAST OUT SOME DEMONS HE CAST THEM AT THEIR RE-QUEST INTO SWINE, INTO PIGS. IS THERE ANY ANIMAL YOU WANT TO GO INTO? ANSWER ME! TELL ME IF YOU WANT TO BE IN AN ANIMAL OR WHETHER YOU WANT ME TO SEND YOU TO JESUS FOR JESUS TO DO WITH AS HE SEES FIT. NO, YOU DON'T ANSWER, SATAN. ALL RIGHT, THEN GO TO JESUS IN WHOSE NAME I CAST YOU OUT OF BECCAH, NOW, THIS VERY MO-MENT. GET OUT. GET OUT, YOU LIAR, YOU FATHER OF LIES, GET OUT. GO NOW TO JESUS, GO!"

And then there was silence. I had no idea what it meant. My hands clenched together and my eyes still shut tightly, with tears pouring out from under the lids, I just prayed and prayed and prayed for what seemed a small eternity. I then became aware of someone's arms around my neck. I did not know whose they were or why they were there. I did not know why they should feel so soft and loving and then I heard Wayne say, "It's gone, Scotty, it's gone."

I didn't believe it until Edie chimed in, "Wayne's right, Scotty. Satan is gone. It's been exorcised. Wayne exorcised it. And Beccah is here, the real Beccah. It's over, Scotty. Open your eyes and see. See for yourself."

I opened my eyes and saw Beccah's face inches in front of mine and I realized that it was her arms that were around my neck. I could see that she was crying too. But I could see through her tears as if they were tiny diamonds reflecting light. I could see behind them that Beccah's face was lit with joy so bright I could hardly bear it.

I can't remember much more than that. I remember that Mrs. Cowper came. I remember that Peter put on his stole and that Beccah, Mrs. Cowper, and the other six of us celebrated the Eucharist. I remember giving Beccah a card with an appoint-ment on it for her to see me early the next afternoon. I can re-member thanking Mrs. Cowper for taking care of Beccah that night and bringing her to her appointment with me the next day. I thanked everybody witlessly, I kept thanking all of them over and over. I remember Beccah putting her arms around me once again and kissing my cheek. I remember kissing hers and then I remember getting into my little car, and somehow or other, managing to drive myself home.

I have said that the exorcists at a successful exorcism are in descending order of importance: the patient (Beccah), God, the team, and the exorcist. During the follow-up, Beccah would tell us more about why she chose against Satan. My role and the team's role are relatively clear. But what about God's role?

God is always too mysterious for me to answer such a question fully. But there is an expression among a number of us Christians (and perhaps those of other religions) that God can use our sins.

I don't know about the sins of anyone else there, but I have some familiarity with my own. I have already mentioned that I had allowed myself to become too busy, and I think this is why I left the crucial clause out of the agreement that Beccah signed. I think it is a sin that I tend to overcommit myself. But there is another sin I have—perhaps a kind of arrogance—that I can best describe with a brief little story. Some years ago as a member of a board of directors of a nonprofit organization, I was required to take a psychological test that is widely used in organizations, the Myers-Briggs.* The test classified me as an INTJ, one of the rarer types. Fortunately, the board had a con-

---

* Trademark of Consulting Psychologists Press, Inc., Palo Alto, Calif., copyright 1976, 1987 by Isabel Briggs-Myers. The Myers-Briggs test categorizes people into a number of personality types. Each type has its virtues and its limitations, as the consultant made clear in my case. The letters INTJ signify that I am an *i*ntroverted, *i*ntuitive, *t*hinking, and *j*udgmental sort of person.

sultant to interpret the test results for us. The consultant explained that while INTJ was a rare type, it was common among top executives and other highly successful people. I began to quietly beam inside until he added, "However, if you want to totally demolish an INTJ, all you have to do is to tell him that he's incompetent." He had me.

Just as Beccah had me. With her satanic accuracy she had hit directly at my weak spot, focusing on my incompetence. A weak spot sufficiently sinful that I was indeed demolished, brought to my knees and rendered incapable of further functioning, thereby making room for Wayne, the better exorcist, to take over the leadership.

CHAPTER 7

FOLLOW-UP

"I guess it's always about money, isn't it?"

Mrs. Cowper brought Beccah to her scheduled appointment the next day, right on time as usual. I could immediately see that Beccah had lost her peace and joy overnight. As I escorted her to my office I did not feel that she was depressed so much as dejected. She took her usual chair. I thought I would let her start. It was more than a minute before she spoke, expressing her dejection with sarcasm. "Well, I'm afraid I have to tell you that your beautiful exorcism was a failure."

"How so?" I asked.

"The voices have started again. In just the same way. They're all Lucifer. Nothing has been accomplished."

I rose from my chair, went over to her, and, sitting at her feet, took her hands in mine. "I should have warned you about this," I apologized. "Let me tell you about the other patient I treated who was possessed. The morning after, she too thought that the exorcism had failed because she too was hearing voices again. But as the day went on we realized that while her voices had not changed, she had changed in relation to them. She described them as being more outside of her, more in her control. For the first time in years she could actually order them to shut up."

Her voice still dripping with sarcasm, Beccah commented, "And that was some big deal sort of change, huh?"

"A very big deal," I replied. "The whole balance of power had shifted. Before the exorcism, Satan had been totally in control of her. After the exorcism she was totally in control of Satan. Satan was still hanging around and bothering her, but it was no big threat to her. Yes, it was a very big change."

"Well, I don't feel that I have changed," she insisted, almost petulantly.

"But you have," I retorted. "Just look at how we are together now. Before the exorcism you wouldn't even let me close to you."

"That's true," Beccah acknowledged.

I pressed home what advantage I had, saying, "Yes, I think we can conclude that the exorcism succeeded. What I don't know is why. You see, I was a total wreck at the time and couldn't observe what was happening. Why did you finally decide to push Satan out?"

"Two reasons," Beccah answered. "One was because you were such a wreck. In another circumstance I might have rejoiced at that—that I had brought you to your knees. But at the same time there was Wayne's voice, so loud and clear and it wouldn't leave me alone. I can remember him telling me in no uncertain terms that I was the liar. And I realized he was right, so rather than rejoicing over how I had brought you to your knees, I felt disgusted with myself for being so cruel to you. For distorting things so much. I felt ugly and unclean. It was a horrible feeling. I wanted to do anything to get rid of it. And Wayne, in a way, was telling me how. He was yelling at me. It was as if he had the power, only his power was the truth. So I just gave in to it, and then Lucifer was simply gone."

By this time Beccah had brightened up considerably. She told me she did not think she needed Mrs. Cowper to be her guardian anymore, and that she was actually eager to get home to her little house in the woods. I agreed with this, but gave her some instructions first.

I told her that I could not explain the matter scientifically or rationally, but there was no doubt in my mind that the name of Jesus or Christ, if used correctly, had extraordinary power in the matter of keeping Satan at bay. I was not talking about simply my personal observation, but the personal observation of hundreds of exorcists across the centuries. "I do not mean to imply that this power is magical," I continued. "For instance, there was evidence in the Book of Acts and elsewhere that the name of Christ or Jesus had no power when spoken by people who had no belief whatsoever in Jesus. If you are in jeopardy, try to remember to use Jesus's name, but when you do so, do it with all of your Christian faith."

She understood. I gave her an appointment to see me the very next day, not yet ready to feel certain about the firmness of the ground beneath our feet. Finally, we hugged, something we had never before done at the end of a session.

And I thanked Mrs. Cowper again, now that her job was over. I told her that her role had been so crucial—Christlike actually—precisely because she had been willing to play it out of the limelight.

I spoke about how God had possibly used my sin in orchestrating the conclusion of the exorcism. Now Beccah told me what had caused her to be exorcised, why she had chosen to give up her allegiance to Satan. We are being inexorably led to a point both mystical and extremely profound.

Well before the exorcism I had a sense that Satan would be after me in particular. That sense may have been the result of my imagination or it may have been a true premonition of things to come. In the end Satan—or was it Beccah?—did pounce on me. It or she succeeded in beating me by using possibly supernatural insight into my weaknesses. They had brought me to my knees and incapacitated me. I had described their success in getting me, but now Beccah was telling me that thanks to Wayne, their demonic success had backfired on them. When I had taken on the role of exorcist, I arrogantly thought that I could probably endure their onslaught. I was wrong. I was also aware, however, that I might not succeed and was therefore taking a great risk. On some level, although it was not my intention, I was willing to be beaten if necessary, and the exorcism succeeded through my being beaten. Perhaps Saint Paul would have considered it to be a kind of proof of his great motto "In weakness, strength."

Beccah almost danced into my office the next day, saying that I was right, that she did have a power over Lucifer and his demons that she had not had before. She also told me that she had already made an appointment with her lawyers to sign the papers that would be served to Jack by the sheriff. But then looking a bit perturbed, she recounted how Jack had called her the previous night, demanding to know where the hell she had been for the past week and demanding that he be allowed to visit her little house in the woods to talk to her that very night. Justifiably, she was feeling uncomfortable—no, plain frightened—at the prospect. Adding to her fear was a sense that she was ethically obligated to tell him to his face that she was asking for a divorce. Indeed, by now he might already have been served. He would be white hot with rage.

This raised a problem for me also, one that I had increasingly discussed with Beccah. I was traveling ever more extensively for speaking engagements and would not be as available to Beccah as she deserved. Indeed, I was leaving late that afternoon to catch a plane for an engagement the next day in Chicago. In order to deal with the problem, we had decided that Beccah would use Rodger as a backup therapist when I was away. So we phoned Rodger only to learn that he himself had a compelling engagement that night. I then called Wayne on the off chance that he would be available to be Beccah's guardian. Luckily, he was, and I handed the phone to Beccah to make arrangements for both Wayne and his wife to meet at her house at least a half an hour before Jack's scheduled arrival.

When I got back from Chicago several days later I eagerly phoned Wayne to ask how it had gone. He told me that it had been a stormy meeting, but that Beccah had held up admirably well. He also told me that Jack had been all the more furious to find Beccah not alone but in the company of supportive friends. Then I asked Wayne, "What did you think about Jack as a person, you know, on a gut sort of level?"

Wayne answered me with all the authority of his lengthy career in the ministry. "Jack Armitage," Wayne replied, "is the single most blasphemous human being I have ever met."

Wayne was using the adjective "blasphemous" in its proper sense, a sense we do not often hear. As I traveled the country lecturing for fifteen years I was amazed that the vast majority of Americans did not understand the meaning of blasphemy— the violation of the third commandment. The most common translation of that commandment is "Thou shalt not take the name of the Lord in vain." There are many other translations. Some speak of "in vain" as meaning "irreverently," others to mean swearing, and particularly swearing to a falsehood. What all that has come to mean to the majority of Americans is that thou shalt not swear or use bawdy language.

That is *not* what the third commandment means. It doesn't mean you are blasphemous if you hit your thumb with a hammer and yell "Goddamn." God, like the good parent he is, is quite capable of absorbing that kind of anger and would rather that you be in an angry relationship with Him than none at all.

So the third commandment does not refer to bad language.

On the contrary, it refers to sweet religious language about God, which is used to hide or disguise one's godlessness or wicked behavior. Some of the worst crooks I have ever known were the most pious people, regularly appearing in church solely motivated by the hope their churchgoing would hide their criminality. To take the name of the Lord in vain means to vociferously proclaim your faith in order to hide your faithlessness.

I do not think the order of the Ten Commandments is an accident. The third commandment follows the second commandment not to worship false idols, the disobedience of which is called idolatry. Idolatry one way or another is the basis of all sin. Blasphemy, which comes next, is the sin of sins. It is the lie of lies, the use of God to hide your sins rather than to repair them. I can assure you that if oil were discovered under Jack Armitage's church, he would have had that church demolished within the day.

Beccah seemed to grow stronger each day. Making certain that there was nothing sexual about it, I usually now sat at her feet and often held her hand. In a childlike way rather than a sexual one, she seemed to flourish with our new closeness and the pleasure of being touched.

About ten days after the exorcism, she did something I doubt she would ever have done before. She started offhandedly, as if the matter were of little consequence. "Do you remember how just after I started seeing you I went on a vacation with Jack to the Caribbean, and I came back so deeply suntanned that you commented on it?" I told her I did remember.

She then went on to say, "I am a sun freak. I don't want to be with anyone during those times, particularly Jack. The only thing I want to do is lie in the sun, and I would do it forever if I could. I *need* the sun."

She said the word so powerfully that I inquired, "Is there some reason you're aware of that you wish you could sunbathe forever?"

"Yes, it's the coldness."

"The coldness?" I repeated.

"Yes, for some reason, no matter what the temperature, I always feel cold. I don't mean I shiver or anything like that. This coldness is very deep inside me, as if it were in my soul. Although it never works, I always have the sense that if I could just let the sun sear me as long as possible that it might somehow bake this coldness out of my soul."

"Why are you telling me this now?" I asked.

"It's because I trust you enough to show you something I've never showed anybody. I think that the sun has damaged me. Around the area of my shoulders. I've not wanted to show anybody this before. I am worried about it, I wish you would take a look at my shoulders even though I will have to let my blouse down. Would you?"

"Of course. I am a physician, after all."

So tentatively, shyly, Beccah undid the top two buttons of her blouse and slid it down her shoulders as discreetly as possible. She was right about the damage.

She had three lesions: one was at the very tip of her left shoulder just at the beginning of her upper arm; a second was at the base of her neck overlaying her backbone; the third and largest was over the upper part of her right shoulder blade. All three were similar in configuration. Each had a relatively small pit of gray colored material exactly in the middle surrounded by a distinctly elevated and very firm circular ridge. Having spent two months during my internship working on a dermatology service, I immediately knew what all three lesions were. They were basal cell carcinomas.

Basal cell carcinomas are the most common and least malignant of the three different skin cancers. As I now know, while they can appear in areas where there has been little or no sun exposure, for the most part they occur on areas of the body that have been sunburned, and their incidence tends to relate directly to the amount of sun exposure. Beccah had seriously hurt herself through excessive sunbathing.

A basal cell carcinoma is an unusual type of cancer because it does not metastasize. Nonetheless, it is indeed a cancer because, unlike benign tumors, it is invasive. It does not have a capsule around it that contains it. Rather, the cancer cells will freely reach out like tentacles and will therefore destroy any normal tissue in their way.

I felt each of the three cancers with my fingers as if palpating a small volcano. As expected, the rims of these tumors were not only firm and elevated but also remarkably hard. I could move the two smaller tumors in such a way that suggested they had not invaded structures deeper than the skin itself. The largest of the three cancers, the one on the top of her right shoulder blade, was not moveable, from which I could only surmise that it had already invaded the bone.

I told Beccah I was not a dermatologist, but I recognized she had a serious problem. I encouraged her by explaining that they were the least malignant of skin cancers. However, I did confront her with the reality that she needed the urgent attention of a dermatologist, who I was quite sure would quickly refer her to a surgeon for excision. I tried to prepare her for the fact that these excisions would likely be unusually wide, and revealed my belief that the largest cancer had already invaded her shoulder blade. I suspected it would need particularly extensive surgery.

Beccah cried quietly and I waited until her tears were dry. I was proud of her that she had the courage to show me the tumors and said so. I continued by saying that I imagined that she herself had known for some time that they were cancerous. She nodded. "So showing them to me now," I said, "is another representation of the change in you. It isn't just that you are a little

GLIMPSES OF THE DEVIL

less modest as much as it is that now you very much want to live." Beccah agreed.

I phoned the best dermatologist in the area and we set up an appointment for Beccah. She was almost smiling when she left the office, though I doubt she would have been had she known what I knew about the pain ahead of her. I had no idea, however, that the future for Beccah would contain far more suffering than I could at that time imagine.

Filled with unrelenting hatred, Satan is without a shred of love. It is therefore the coldest being in the universe. Although most commonly associated in people's minds with the fires of hell, there is reason to believe that association is incorrect. Dante probably got it right when he described the very center of hell, the Ninth Circle, to be ice rather than fire. Certainly, when I think of myself having to spend eternity naked at a freezing temperature I can understand Dante's vision.

More than that, however, I have heard tales of observers who, upon entering the room of a possessed person or someone under demonic attack, have felt an inexplicable but extremely uncomfortable coldness in the room.

The dermatologist and then the surgeons handled Beccah with great dispatch. The dermatologist said that he had seldom seen basal cell carcinomas so large and felt that the largest one, growing into her right shoulder blade, represented an emergency. The surgeons agreed, and within ten days Beccah had had her surgery and was out of the hospital and taking large doses of antibiotics.

At our first appointment after she got out of the hospital she said, "Jesus Christ, you had warned me that the surgery on my shoulder blade would be painful, but you didn't tell me it would be agonizing. They are unsure whether I will ever regain full use of my right arm. And I certainly won't have to mutilate myself for years. I will have enough scars on my shoulders for a whole army in retreat."

Although I sympathized with her discomfort I was glad to hear the note of humor she injected into it. It was a real sign of health. In fact, Beccah was doing really well those first months after the exorcism. Her divorce was proceeding slowly. Jack, being Jack, naturally objected to any proposed assignment of their assets. I also noted, however, that Beccah was certainly asking for all she could hope for. During one session, after she moaned for the tenth time, "I don't see why we just can't have an amicable divorce," I answered, "Beccah, there's no such thing as an amicable divorce between two greedy people."

She laughed, agreeing that she was a fighter, and the best defense was a good offense. Like everyone else present at her exorcism, it was obvious to me that Beccah was a fighter; only this time I had admiration for her fighting spirit. She was working with her lawyers continually and doing her damnedest to push the divorce ahead as rapidly as possible. Still, I had a twinge of uneasiness. I had let slide a tiny fact. When I had suggested she too was greedy, she had acknowledged she was a fighter. The words were not the same. I should have pushed her to admit that she was greedy as well as a fighter.

Meanwhile, she was enjoying her privacy in her house in the woods, had no desire whatsoever to return to the business, and in every ordinary way appeared to be a remarkably happy woman.

There was only one fly in the ointment. She would not or could not take communion in an Episcopal church. She loved the celebration of the Eucharist and asked if she couldn't conclude virtually every session with the two of us sharing bread and wine in remembrance of Jesus. Technically, being a layperson, I was not allowed to celebrate the Eucharist. But several years before, a prominent interdenominational group of Protestant leaders had given me a communion chalice in something that felt like an ordination of sorts. I had prayed about the matter, and God did not seem to have any objection. Consequently, upon occasion I had previously celebrated a "rogue communion" when it felt right. And at first it did feel right with Beccah. She seemed starved for the ceremony. But I began to worry when it was obvious she was having difficulty going to an Episcopal church, whether with me or alone. She did not want to join another denomination and would contentedly remain in the pew of the nearby Episcopalian church without going to the altar rail to take communion.

I questioned her reluctance. All she could say was, "Kneeling at the rail together with Jack and receiving the sacrament while our shoulders were actually touching made it sickening for me. I can hardly believe I did it for almost twenty years. Ugh."

In a sense this resistance seemed quite rational, but I felt uneasy. I kept challenging her with the fact that the ceremony was something totally separate from Jack and his blasphemy; that she would never have to take communion alongside him again; that she was living a whole new life now, and in that new life Jesus was all the more eager to share Himself with her.

But my words had no effect. On one occasion I practically forced her to the rail, and she did partake of the sacrament. But the next day when she came in to see me she showed me a fresh cut on her arm, the only time she had mutilated herself in three months.

It had been stupid of me to try to force her, and I did not attempt to do so again. Moreover, I started to wean her from the routine of having communion with me. This angered her, but I was adamant. I did keep trying to explore her resistance on a deeper level, but she could not or would not be any more informative. I felt she was being evasive. It was like trying to pin her down to give me a description of her mother. I knew I was missing a part of the picture, but it was clear that, along with other parts, it too would remain in the shadows.

Meanwhile I remained slightly uneasy, wondering whether there still wasn't a part of Satan that Beccah had not given up during the exorcism.

I did not have the opportunity to accompany Beccah to a Roman Catholic or other eucharistic church for communion, only the Episcopalian church. The fact that she deeply enjoyed communion in my office suggests that she did not have an antipathy to communion so much as to the church and perhaps specifically the Episcopal church.

Throughout my three years of work with Beccah I had a profound sense that, in addition to an antipathy toward the Christian church, she also had a deep antipathy to something about the Jewish faith or culture. But despite almost endless prodding I was never able to get her to acknowledge it. Like so much of Beccah, this too is permanently obscured within her seemingly endless shadows.

Finally, it is my experience with all cases of genuine possession I have encountered, personally or by hearsay, that the victims had been hurt in some subtle or gross way by the church or in its name. They have had conscious or unconscious reason to hate the church. I have not read about it in the available literature on possession, although it seems a most important fact since it may explain something about the victim's behavior during exorcism, as well as the reasons for possession in the first place.

I still did not know precisely when and why Beccah had become possessed. I knew that around age six she had developed an abnormal attraction to a book of woodcuts that told one version of the pact with the devil story. We had learned that the book was popular and had very few words, thereby perhaps making it particularly attractive to a child. During the exorcism we had also learned that the Satan figure was referred to as a fiend. And finally I knew that this fiend was the equivalent of the spirit of death.

My executive assistant located a used copy of the book, and it arrived six weeks after the exorcism. As soon as I unwrapped it, it was no longer an abstraction. It was the darkest, ugliest book I had ever seen. I wondered why the author had created it. There seemed only two possible explanations. Either the author was psychotic or otherwise severely depressed when he had done the book, or he himself was possessed, perfectly or imperfectly, and was acting as an agent of the devil at the time.

There is a nun, six years my senior, who has been my spiritual director for more than twenty-five years. I have phoned her only twice on an emergency basis. Once was after spending a half hour with that book, *Gods' Man*. I called her sobbing with a complex of emotions, including hatred for the author, disgust at the book, rage at its destructiveness, sorrow for all the other young boys and girls who had been the book's victims, and a feeling of deep contamination that I had received just from looking at it. After we spoke, I sent her my newly purchased copy and she called me back to agree that it was the single most destructive thing she had ever seen in her fifty-plus years. Those years had been mostly spent as a missionary of sorts at the front, working in the actual trenches that manage to keep good and evil separate. There was a furnace at the convent, and despite the sum I had just paid for the book, we agreed that would be its new home. It was the only decent disposition.

I have speculated about the motives or the state of the soul of the book's author, but there is one detail of the book about which I cannot even speculate: namely, its title. The hooded figure seems to represent both Satan and the spirit of death and in no way seems to represent God. The artist has made a pact with the fiend and is not portrayed as a godly individual. In any case, neither figure seems to be God's man. The title does not say that they are because of the placement of the apostrophe. "Gods' " would seem to signify not a single god but a number of gods. Was the author trying to make some strange plug for polytheism? God knows.

Jersey was unable to tell me the why of her possession until after her exorcism. Beccah was never able to. But two months after her exorcism she gave me a hint from the shadows. I have been haunted by its tragic power almost daily ever since.

Malachi Martin taught us that the possessed person is not a hapless victim, but to some degree cooperates with the demonic. This cooperation is somewhat like the pact with the devil so often described in literature. As one patient on the verge of becoming possessed put it to me, he would never have made such a pact except under duress. I suspect it is always so, but there are levels of duress, and his was relatively minor. Jersey's was greater. I have heard accounts from colleagues where the duress was greater still.

Beccah, of course, could not remember making a pact, much less being under duress. But in the midst of a postexorcism session she idly told me of a supposedly funny story of an incident from her early childhood she had heard from members of her extended family. It was commonly recited with much laughter and gaiety.

On the surface it was a rather simple incident that apparently occurred when Beccah was a toddler, reportedly eighteen months of age. It was never clear exactly how the incident began, but Beccah was alone one afternoon on the Manhattan street in front of her brownstone home. Unattended, she somehow managed to cross Lexington Avenue on her toddler's legs and then nine other Manhattan streets before strangers worried about her enough to summon the police. Beccah apparently had some kind of identification on her, so that the policeman who arrived had no trouble taking her home. He was a jolly sort of man who might have thought about matters more deeply save for the fact that almost nobody back in those days thought much about such matters. Apparently, all he said to Beccah's family was "This is the first time we've had one that couldn't even talk yet." That was the part of the story that seemed to amuse her family the most.

"What do you suppose the policeman meant?" I asked her.

Beccah suddenly became irritable. "How the hell should I know what he meant?" she retorted.

I ignored her irritation. "The first time we ever had one who couldn't even talk yet," I repeated. "It's an odd sort of thing for him to have said. It must have meaning, and I can't believe you haven't at least wondered about what he said." I took her hand in mine and caressed it for a minute. "What do you think he meant, Beccah?" I asked again.

"I suppose he might have meant that I was a runaway," she answered.

The family tale of Beccah's probable attempt to run away from home at the age of eighteen months may not seem all that horrifying to some. But not so to any psychiatrist, psychologist, or other observer of childhood behavior. Perhaps the most dramatic event in the life of normal infants occurs with exactness at the age of nine months. That occurrence is the first appearance of stranger anxiety. Before that time the infant will play as it usually would in its crib when a stranger enters the room. But suddenly, at nine months, when a stranger enters the room, the infant will start screaming frantically for its mother. The appearance of strangers has now begun to terrify the child. The terror of stranger anxiety persists generally for the next two years or more. Now playing in the living room, the minute the stranger appears the child will throw itself at its mother and clutch at her bosom as if in mortal danger. The age of eighteen months is one when children are naturally terrified of being separated from their parents, and particularly their mother. Hence it is almost inconceivable for a child to run away from home at this age. The only way to imagine the possibility is to conclude that such a child must be the victim of some repetitive form of abuse administered within the family, abuse probably so severe as to constitute torture.

Beccah asked me to meet with her lawyer. He was obviously competent. I told him what I knew of Jack Armitage, although I imagine he himself had figured the man out. "At this point," he said, "I find it hard to imagine that Jack isn't going to fight over every single piece of furniture as well as everything else. I can't stop him from doing this for the present. Eventually, however, I believe he will make such a fool of himself that I will be able to bring a writ to the judge requesting him to bring a halt to the process. Still, it's going to be a very drawn-out affair, I'm afraid. I wish I could make it otherwise, but you might as well settle in for the long haul."

Beccah was hardly happy, but very shortly she had something else to preoccupy her. Three days after I had met with her lawyer, Beccah called me in the middle of the night almost screaming with pain in her shoulder, the one that the basal cell carcinoma had invaded and had required extensive surgery. "Tell me again which hospital it was where you had the surgery?" I asked, hearing the severity of her pain over the phone.

Beccah named the most prestigious hospital in Westchester

County. It was a good distance away. "I want you to call your surgeon and tell him about your pain and that you will meet him in the emergency room." Beccah balked, asking, "What's the big deal? Can't you just prescribe some really strong pain pills for me?"

"I'm afraid it is a big deal," I told her, "and if your surgeon is available, he should be able to explain why. Actually, he did warn you about this risk, but you probably didn't think much about it when you signed permission for the surgery. I think you should pack a bag expecting that they will keep you in the hospital for a while at least. Are you in shape to drive yourself down all that way?"

She hesitated for a moment. "I can arrange for an ambulance, if you like," I said.

"No, I can get myself there. The only good thing about this pain is that it will keep me from falling asleep at the wheel. It's bad, but I'll be able to pay attention."

"Okay, Beccah," I said. "I'll call you at the hospital in the morning."

Not being an orthopedic surgeon I did not know for certain the cause of Beccah's severe pain, but I could make a pretty good guess. It was not a happy one.

The greatest danger of the kind of surgery that Beccah had had is infection, and the sort of infection that is most common is called osteomyelitis, an infection of the bone that is extremely difficult to cure. It often becomes a chronic condition that is frequently extremely painful. The antibiotics to treat it need to be given intravenously over a prolonged period of time, which in turn means a lengthy hospitalization.

When I called her in the morning I learned that my guess was right. I cancelled our regular appointments but made new appointments to visit her somewhat less frequently in the hospital. The hospital was a little more than an hour's drive away, and I knew that my visits were going to be a very tiring, even exhausting burden on me for a long while to come. This meant I would have to devote a good three and a half hours to every hour appointment I had with Beccah while she was in the hospital. Additionally, my lecture schedule was becoming more formidable, and I knew intellectually that something in my own life would soon have to give. Still, in my forties I assumed that I was somehow indestructible, fancying that I could continue to play the iron man indefinitely. I certainly never dreamed that my long-distance visits to that hospital would come close to killing me.

Two weeks before the onset of her osteomyelitis I had started to worry about Beccah. There was nothing I could put my finger on. She was proceeding aggressively with the divorce. She told me that she was sleeping well. She had gained back enough weight that she was a more handsome woman than I had imagined. She had started to joke about dating, and I was gently encouraging her. So why was I feeling worried? There was a subtle sense of emotional distance between us that had not been present since her exorcism. She did not seem to enjoy our appointments particularly anymore. She was smoking twice as much as usual, and her hands were always busy with something. I felt within her a sort of frantic energy that had no place to go. Could she possibly be becoming possessed again? I didn't broach the matter to her. Frankly, I didn't even want to broach it to myself.

Now I was forced to. Certainly Beccah was not doing well. I wondered if her physical condition and her psychological state were deeply related. True, it was not uncommon for patients who had Beccah's kind of bone-penetrating surgery to develop osteomyelitis. But that does not mean that everyone developed it. Most did not. Was it an accident that Beccah had become a member of that unfortunate minority? Most physicians would assume so, but not psychiatrists. We are very much aware of how psychological disturbances, particularly depression, demonstrably affect physical outcomes. Depressed people are far more likely than others to develop infections in the first place, and then their wounds are likely to heal much more slowly. Yes, I was worried.

My first visit to see Beccah in the hospital confirmed that we were on the verge of a crisis. One might think that with two IVs running into her arms she would be somewhat immobilized. But she was on the phone when I arrived, smoking a cigarette and writing notes on two different pads. What immediately popped into my mind was, "My God, is she trading again?" As soon as she hung up the phone, she regarded me without any sign of welcome. Instead the first words she spoke to me were "I'm going to sue that son of a bitch of a surgeon for all he's got."

So I had to get tough with her. I told her she seemed to me to be going downhill mentally faster than she was physically, and I asked her whether she was possessed again.

"Of course not," she answered with a smile that held a hint of seductiveness. "I'm sorry I was busy on the phone when you came in. I was just talking to my lawyer and we were trying to figure out how much alimony Jack ought to pay me. We had to look at it from many vantage points such as how long I had been working for the company, what job level I was at, and so on. Money, money. I guess it's always about money, isn't it?"

I told Beccah that I wanted to just sit there in silence for five minutes to collect my thoughts. After three minutes she broke the silence by saying, "You really are worried about me, aren't you?"

I nodded and continued my thinking. I had to go by my feelings. I felt it was time I took charge. "Beccah," I said, "we are at a point of crisis."

Crises are generally points in our lives where we are faced

with a tough decision, a decision whose outcome will determine how our lives go thereafter, for better or ill.

"I see you surrounded here by activities, and I wonder why. Hospitals are often places where we can get rest—rest that our bodies and our minds need—and I see you as trying to run away from what you need through activity. Why should this idea of rest frighten you?

"Hospitals are not only places of rest but they are also sanctuaries—places where you can be safe from anything that might threaten you. You can be safe here.

"Finally, hospitals are places where you are taken care of. The care isn't always perfect. The food is often poor, a nurse here or there might have an unpleasant disposition, but generally the people in this hospital want to take care of you. During the five minutes of silence it occurred to me that you've never been taken care of, have you, Beccah? Not at home with your parents because they usually weren't there and you were left alone to care for yourself as best as a little child can. And then as you got older there was always work to do, first helping your mother out with the family business and then helping Jack with his business. No, I don't think you've ever been cared for, and I imagine that it might seem almost frightening for you to let yourself be cared for, just as it might seem frightening for you to be quiet and at rest for once in your life. You know, the word 'hospital' comes from the old word 'hospice.' A hospice in the Middle Ages was a monastery that offered ill or weary travelers rest and healing, safety and lots of silence.

"I would like you, Beccah, to think of this hospital as a medieval hospice, as a place that has been designed not only to heal your body but to give you precious silence. There are two ways you can go with this silence. One is to be grateful for it and to use it as monasteries have always meant it to be used, for prayer and meditation, for contemplation and self-examination and for nurturing a relationship between you and God. Or you can run away from God and from the silence by making yourself just as busy as you have always been.

"In other words, Beccah, this hospital offers you a chance to do it new, differently, in such a way that you can move ever closer to God and to having a real center of peace within you. I could not have designed a more perfect place for you at this time, Beccah. Please use it for what it was intended. Please don't throw this opportunity away."

My pretty speech did not work. Each time I saw Beccah in the hospital there were more papers and more phone calls. I asked her whether she had returned to trading. She acted insulted, as if I had misjudged her by even asking such a question. "Of course not," she said. I did not believe her.

In a similar fashion I would ask her whether Satan had returned. Her response again on each occasion was emphatically negative.

And there really wasn't anything else I could do. I prayed for her, of course. I did not try to pray against Satan. My experiences of trying to pray against Satan or other demons had always been the same. The phenomenon was like trying to push your thumb into a well-inflated tennis ball; the harder you push the harder the ball will push back against you until finally your thumb becomes impotent. So instead I prayed only for Beccah and only to Jesus or God on her behalf. I prayed hard for the entire six weeks of her IV antibiotic treatment even though it felt like so much wasted energy.

Physicians will recognize that nowadays Beccah probably would not have needed to be hospitalized for her intravenous antibiotic therapy, since the technology has rapidly evolved. With little difficulty under general anesthesia, a catheter can be placed within one of the largest veins inside the chest. Then the catheter is attached to a bag of antibiotic fluid that flows through a small pump worn at the waist. The pump will then deliver the fluid at a measured pace. This surgery can be performed at an outpatient facility. Thereafter the patient need return to the hospital only for a few minutes each day or every few days to have the bag of antibiotics replaced by a new one. This same arrangement is also employed with cancer patients undergoing long-term intravenous chemotherapy.

The four months after Beccah was discharged were as dull as any time I'd spent with a patient. The scientific literature on psychotherapy quite bluntly refers to the boring patient. Boring patients are a real problem for psychotherapists, and now Beccah had joined their ranks. Rodger, who was continuing to provide her with backup therapy, also found her to be boring. Maddening as it was, we did our best to soldier on. Most boring patients are empty, unsophisticated people. This was hardly Beccah. We knew she was so dull because she was resisting us. We were no longer on the same team.

Beccah was also looking depressed again. There was no joy in her. She seemed to be losing weight. Just as she denied repossession, she also denied being depressed. She did admit, however, to quite severe insomnia with trouble going to sleep and waking up during the middle of the night with agitation—a type of insomnia very common in depression. It was so bothersome that she asked for help, and for the first time I put her on Elavil, one of the first-generation antidepressants that were likely to be most helpful with insomnia. Beccah reported that she was sleeping better with the medicine, but she did not look any less depressed. In treating depression, however, we psychiatrists are often required to be content with even small improvements, so I continued to prescribe the Elavil for her on a monthly basis.

During this time three moments definitely aroused my interest and concern.

The first was that once every three or four sessions I would for no discernible reason have the feeling that Beccah was no longer in my office, that the woman sitting in her chair who looked like Beccah was in fact a complete stranger to me. This new presence seemed to be trying to act like Beccah, but intuitively I knew it was not the woman I knew. The presence seemed to have no personality save for the fact I always felt it was mocking me in a way I could not quite put my finger on. Each time I accused it of being either Satan or one of its representatives. It always denied the reality of my intuition. In one way the strangest thing about this repeated experience was that I could never explain its timing. I reviewed my notes thoroughly and could never perceive that Beccah and I were talking about something particularly meaningful when it appeared. When I asked it why it had appeared at that particular time it would simply repeat that it was not an evil spirit; it was only Beccah.

Twice I had a different, more distinctly paranormal experience. The first occurred when Beccah and I were talking about something seemingly ordinary. For no more than a minute her face suddenly changed so that it did not look like Beccah's face nor, for that matter, any human face. It was not the face of the snake. Instead it struck me as the face of some amphibian creature. Beccah's whole head looked like that of a newt I saw every so often in my basement, a Gollum-like creature that would peer at me from one of the drainpipes. Almost as soon as I would recognize the change in Beccah's face it would be gone. The only other thing I could say about this "newt" was that it seemed like the most primitive creature I had ever seen—more so than the viper at the exorcism.

During another appointment, again for but a minute, Beccah's face appeared to be that of a very dry, thick-skinned, lizardlike creature—possibly an iguana. Definitely a reptile but nothing like a snake. As with the newt face, this one had emerged for no discernible reason and vanished before I could question Beccah about it. I did question her after the fact about these temporary "appearances" but, as expected, she claimed to have no knowledge of them while at the same time seeming to be a bit pleased by my frustration with the phenomena.

I did not try to avoid discussing these instances and was completely frank with Beccah. I had stopped asking her whether she might be possessed again and had started to clearly state my opinion that she was possessed. She did not so much fight my opinions as simply ignore them. Meanwhile, we were getting nowhere.

An early, prepublication reader of Beccah's story wrote: "The postexorcism part dragged for me a bit." I wrote back: "It dragged for you! What do you think it was like for me living it? It *was* a total drag. It damn near dragged me to death."

This response was made off the cuff, instinctively. Afterward, however, I thought about it, wondering if it wasn't literally true. I was soon to have a brush with death. I had already realized Beccah's case might have been a cause thereof. But only now did it occur to me that it could have been deliberate, that Beccah might have wanted to kill me. Or was it Satan? Yes, Satan, or Lucifer, could have been using Beccah to kill me.

My mind flashed back to the period just before Beccah's exorcism, to that time when I had the sense that the devil I would encounter in Beccah was specifically after me, out to get me for the success of Jersey's exorcism. In a sense it had gotten me, reducing me to a blob of guilt and tears, so ineffective that Wayne had had to take over my part. That possibility I had considered. But only now, writing about the case twenty years later, did I consider the possibility that Satan/Lucifer might have continued to be out to get me once the exorcism was over.

Meanwhile, although I denied the fact, I too was not doing well. As described, my speaking schedule was becoming ever more full. I had been exhausted by visiting Beccah in the hospital but never gave myself time to recover. All possible recovery time was consumed by my new lecture business and the endlessly depleting process of dashing to this airport or that. I was also attempting to relinquish my private practice of psychotherapy as best I could. My patients were not happy with me. They recognized that I did not seem to be as deeply present for them as I had been. Many thought I had no right to involve myself in the lecture business when, in their minds, I had an unending commitment to them. Some were very gracious about the problem and were pleased to accept my referral to other good therapists in the area, but the majority were not happy campers. I had not taken a vacation in years. Looking back on the time, I am amazed I coped as well as I did.

Ultimately, it was my body that stopped coping. I caught a mild strain of pneumonia that was floating around. Of course I treated myself, taking an ordinary amount of the appropriate antibiotic and continuing to work. My condition gradually worsened over the course of ten days before I finally asked for help. I was immediately hospitalized, and by that time there were more serious bacteria in my sputum. On the afternoon of my second day in the hospital I could no longer breathe adequately and turned a dramatic shade of blue. I was a very sick man. Looking back on it, I have to agree with the opinions of others that I would not have become so ill had my resistance not been shot.

The morning I entered the hospital I phoned Beccah, and Rodger as well. I had no reason to believe Beccah wouldn't be able to handle the situation. She was sleeping better since I had placed her on Elavil, and she seemed to have a good relationship with Rodger.

By the fifth day of my hospitalization my fever had started to come down slightly, but I was still mildly delirious. At that point one of the most bizarre experiences of my medical career occurred.

Unbeknownst to me, two nights previously Beccah had attempted to kill herself with an overdose of the Elavil I had prescribed. Fortunately, after taking the overdose she called 911 and was taken to the psychiatry ward of the hospital in Westchester. Because the psychiatrists there knew how lengthy and involved my treatment with Beccah had been, before discharging her they sent her all the way up by ambulance to the little hospital where I was lying in delirium. They were concerned about whether Beccah should be maintained on her Elavil and given another prescription. And so it was that Beccah, satanically repossessed, suddenly appeared in my hospital room dressed in her own hospital robes and presented me with a consultation form to fill out.

Fortunately, I was not so delirious that I couldn't get a sense of how bizarre the situation was. I responded appropriately to the question of whether Beccah should receive more Elavil. There are few situations in psychiatry that are as clear as this one. I think my own mental state was sufficiently impaired that I did not give Beccah the attention she probably wanted and needed. But I was able to explain to her—quite kindly if I can remember it—that it was not the custom for psychiatrists to immediately represcribe a medicine to a patient who had just attempted to kill herself with that medicine. I was able to legibly write on the consultation form Rodger's address and phone number, explaining that he was the one to provide her backup care while I was incapacitated. I then added that I would not prescribe any more Elavil at this time and advised the Westchester psychiatrists that they should not either. I finally concluded by saying that the issue of represcription would be under ongoing consideration.

I read all this to Beccah, emphasizing that the reason for my unwillingness to represcribe for her at the moment should be obvious, but I was serious in saying that that matter would be re-

considered by Rodger working in conjunction with another local psychiatrist, and they might well represcribe Elavil, depending upon how her condition developed. I apologized for the fact that I was so ill and unable to think clearly and told her I looked forward to seeing her again as soon as I was well.

Although it must have been obvious to Beccah how ill I was, and I had thought she would be understanding, she instead became furious. She wanted to keep screaming her rage at me, but I was in no mood for it and simply ordered the ambulance personnel to remove her and take her back to Westchester.

That was the last time I ever saw Beccah. Rodger also never saw her again. Although I did not know it at the time, Beccah had fired the both of us.

Since I was never to see her again—and was in no shape to think about the matter at the time—it was a few months before I wondered why she had overdosed on the Elavil I had prescribed her. There is no way to prove it, but the reason psychoanalytically seemed rather obvious. I suspect she overdosed because I was in the hospital. Regardless of the reality of how desperately I needed to be there, she probably felt abandoned by me, angry with me for abandoning her and vengeful because she was angry. What better way to express her desire for revenge and her sense of hurt by me than to attempt to kill herself—or at least appear to do so—with the medication I had prescribed for her?

I did, however, hear from Beccah by phone one more time. It was approximately two years after my pneumonia and three after her exorcism. The phone rang in our kitchen one evening, and I recognized Beccah's voice immediately. "I hope I'm not bothering you," Beccah said. In truth, I had been in the midst of my dinner,

but I would have interrupted anything, I was so glad to hear from her again.

"Jack has skipped town," she informed me. Then with some of her typical sarcasm she continued, "Surprising, isn't it?"

"Not terribly," I said, "given the fact that we used to make bets about the matter."

"It was almost a year ago," Beccah went on, "when things began to get hot for him in my divorce case. He was a sitting duck, of course. I had enough on him to send him to Sing Sing for three lifetimes. Much as I anticipated it, there was no way I could prevent it. He took close to three million dollars with him to wherever the hell he went. Argentina maybe."

"Well, I'm sorry he took some of the money," I told her. "How much do you have left if you factor in the house and your inheritance?"

"Oh, no more than eleven."

"Eleven million?"

"That's right."

"Well you're clearly on solid ground financially," I said after gathering my wits. "How about spiritually?"

"That's one of the reasons I called," Beccah said. "I wanted to apologize to you. You were quite right all along that I was repossessed. I just didn't want to make you feel that you had failed. That's why I couldn't tell you."

Three years of training in psychiatry will give anyone at least a bit of cynicism, and my more than two years with her had been an entire education in itself. I imagined a little more was involved than her not wanting to hurt my feelings, but I would never know for sure. I asked after Catherine, and Beccah told me enthusiastically she was doing fine. She went on to tell me that she had found a psychiatrist in New York City whom she was seeing twice a week. "He's a good man, but he's not like you. I told him about the exorcism. He looked you up in some big book he had that told him all about you. He told me he couldn't understand it because you had perfectly good credentials."

"I can imagine it," I responded. "But why are you calling me now, Beccah?"

"I told you. I wanted to let you know that you were right about me being repossessed. That's all."

"Thank you. But I still think there's more," I said.

"Well, I've still got that damn bone infection. It's pretty much all over my body. Of course the doctors won't tell me. But I've got a pretty good idea that it will kill me within another couple of years. It's a horrible disease."

"Yes, it certainly is," I agreed, still not knowing where all this was going. "I'm very sorry you've still got it. Does that have anything to do with you calling me tonight?"

"Well, I know I owe you twelve thousand dollars for my therapy. I wasn't paying it because I wanted Jack to. But Jack can't pay it now, can he? So I wanted to talk with you about making a deal."

"A deal?" I repeated rhetorically.

"Yes, I thought maybe we could work something out, something that would be a little less hard on me."

"Beccah, I can't imagine it being too hard on you when you've got eleven million. Nonetheless, I will go easy on you and not try to collect any interest on it as many people might ordinarily with a bill that's more than two years overdue. Is there anything else?"

"Well, I'd just like to see you again, Dr. Peck."

"I'd very much like to see you again too, Beccah, but it would have to be a social visit. That means I wouldn't charge you for it at all, but it also means that I cannot take you back as a patient, if that is what you were thinking about. It has nothing to do with you. You know how busy I was. Now I'm three times busier, travel twice as much, and have a staff to manage. I just could not do justice to you, Beccah. I'm sorry."

"I understand."

"Do you still want to see me then, purely for a social visit?" I asked.

"Oh yes."

"How about four o'clock this Saturday afternoon? Would that be convenient for you?"

"Yes, that's fine."

"Okay, I'll see you then, Saturday afternoon at four."

Beccah never showed up for the appointment.

There is a very loose sort of grapevine among mental health professionals that can extend all the way across the country, although in this case a hundred miles was sufficient. I was having lunch with a close friend and colleague a year before I began to work on this book. Over our salads, still making small talk, she said, "Oh, I'm quite good friends with a psychiatrist in New York City who treated a patient of yours. It was someone in whom you were quite invested. God, it's been a long time. Fifteen or twenty years ago maybe. Armitage. Rebecca Armitage. Yes, that was the name of your patient. My friend treated her very gently—right up until she died."

I felt a very brief shock to hear that Beccah had died, but it was hardly any surprise to me. This brilliant woman who had been born in the shadows was almost doomed to be a captive of the spirit of death. "You know, I think I'm going to be writing a book that will in part be about that patient," I said. "You don't happen to know the address or phone number of your friend offhand, do you?"

My colleague did and wrote down his name and phone number for me. Although I thanked her profusely, she probably had no idea how grateful I was to learn the doctor's name and number. I called him later that very afternoon. He was busy, but we made a phone appointment for that evening.

I began that appointment by telling him that my colleague had informed me that he had probably treated one Beccah Armitage some years back—indeed that he had treated her very kindly.

Dr. Ruben immediately said, "Oh, are you the psychiatrist who performed the exorcism on her?"

I acknowledged I was and told him that he must think me quite an odd duck.

"Well," he said, "it's the odd ducks who often lead us into the odd places we need to learn about. Certainly, I know nothing about this possession and exorcism business, but she was nobody's fool and she admired you greatly. She told me she was not possessed when she saw me and I didn't delve into the matter further. She struck me as being a very sick lady, but in a way that I could never put my finger on. Perhaps I should have contacted you and tried to find out more about this exorcism business, but I decided that what she needed was not any kind of deep therapy. Just supportive therapy. She was not only ill psychiatrically, you know, but also with osteomyelitis."

"Yes, I know," I said. "And it is a terrible disease. I suppose she just got worse and worse the way so many patients do."

"Yes," Dr. Ruben replied, "and in the end it killed her. That was about three years after I had started to see her. Very sad. Very painful."

"So it was that rather than suicide?" I asked.

"Who can tell? She died at home. She had enough morphine to kill a battalion. And she needed it. I suppose we might have done an autopsy to find out whether her blood level of morphine was fatally high. But no one at the hospital, including myself, thought the matter deserved an investigation. She would have died very shortly and very painfully no matter what."

I explained to Dr. Ruben that I was writing a book about the difficult issue of possession and that I wanted to use her as one of my clinical case studies. That was why I was so very happy to have tracked him down. "In the book I'll not use your real name, of course. Is there anything else," I asked, "that you knew about her—any other experience you might have had with her—that you can imagine would possibly be of use to me?"

"Oh, yes," he answered. "When she died, I was concerned about her daughter. I had never met her daughter—Catherine, I believe her name was—but I thought I owed it to her, maybe to God, who knows, to go up to her college to see that she would be taken care of. I found Catherine. She seemed to be doing well under the circumstances. I also met her aunt, who had come to take Catherine home with her. This was a sister of Beccah's. A few years older I believe. She seemed like a very nice lady. We had time to sit down and talk together. That was when I learned that virtually everything Beccah had told me over the three years I worked with her was a lie. Three years and I didn't even know why she needed to lie. I guess I am not a very bright psychiatrist."

"Hardly," I said empathetically. "Most psychiatrists aren't bright enough to acknowledge when they've bought a patient's lies. Humility takes a certain kind of smarts. And going to see her daughter took love. No, Dr. Ruben, I admire you a lot. She was lucky to have you."

If I had it to do over again, I wouldn't.

I do not think that I treated Beccah well. As with a number of my other patients, she deserved a psychiatrist who was not simultaneously on the lecture circuit, always rushed, juggling two careers at once. I also think I was too close to her to be her exorcist, having worked with her for over a year and a half before uncovering her possession. To this day I cannot understand why I did not call up Malachi Martin and ask him to take over. For whatever reason—perhaps my growing fame and the applause of audiences—I think that I was arrogant during that period of time. So if I had it to do over again I certainly wouldn't do it myself.

But the more I have thought about her case, I don't think I would have referred her to Malachi to be exorcised. I don't think that even the greatest exorcist in the world (which I assume is what Malachi was at the time) could ever have exorcised her in such a way as to make her treatment a long-term success. I think the exorcism was bound to fail in the long run for two reasons. The first, as I have briefly touched upon, was the depth of Beccah's possession. It makes a general sort of psychiatric sense to assume that the earlier in life the patient is possessed, the deeper the possession will be. Jersey had become possessed at the age of twelve and had had about fifteen years to continue to cooperate and to allow her possession to become more entrenched. Beccah, we knew, had been possessed by the age of five or six at the latest and thus had had over forty years for her possession to deepen its hold on her. Consider what you would do if you had only one friend for forty years. One friend to love and one to love you, a friend who had carried you through forty years of stress. Do you think you would give up such a friend simply for Jesus, simply because a whole bunch of people ganged up on you, no matter how brilliant the exorcist? Do you think there could have been any kind of brilliance or logic that could have swayed you? No, I never saw Malachi in action. I can easily imagine how brilliant he was. But I do not think that even Malachi could have persuaded Beccah to choose a warmer path permanently. Ultimately Beccah was someone very close to being perfectly possessed. While we suppose Beccah had become possessed around five or six, it just as likely occurred before age two. Remember the story of the little runaway who couldn't even talk yet.

However, I must make note here that I would not have known how close Beccah was to being perfectly possessed were it not for the exorcism. Even when they fail, exorcisms are diagnostic. Only in an exorcism is the truth fully revealed.

I wish Malachi were still alive so I could chat with him about Beccah. In my imagination, were I to have asked him to take on Beccah, after listening to me he would have shrugged his shoulders and refused. I think he would have gotten a better feel than

I had for the case almost instantly. I don't think he would have turned me down because of a detached retina or with any excuse whatsoever. I think he would simply have said, "No, she's too far gone."

Still, if I had it to do all over again, I would not have even referred Beccah to Malachi or to any exorcist. You see, for all intents and purposes she had no family, she had no friends, she had no allegiances. She had absolutely nothing of what we today call a support system. Jersey had a fine support system with parents and siblings and a husband and in-laws who all cared for her. But Beccah had only Satan. A fiend who pretended to be her friend, a fiend whom she believed to be her friend, a friend who did not charge her for visits, a real friend, her only real friend: Satan, her alpha and her omega.

CONCLUSION

———◆———

What Is Possession?

Along about now I imagine many of you are wondering, "But what am I to do with all this?"

There is an impish part of me that is tempted to respond, "Beats me!" Or else, "That's your problem."

But you deserve more. And while it is true that I cannot tell you what to do with this I can at least tell you what I did with it.

Until the day I met Jersey I did not believe in the devil. Or, to be perfectly precise, up until three hours after I had met her I was 99+ percent sure that the devil did not exist. Indeed, I was using Jersey as part of a strategy to prove the devil's nonexistence as scientifically as possible—to myself.

Only my experiment began to backfire the minute I heard Jersey say about her demons, "I feel sorry for them; they're really rather weak and pathetic creatures." When I flew home after that first evaluation I was hardly converted to a belief in the devil; it was fifty-fifty at best. Still, what an extraordinary movement of the mind! From antagonistic to neutral within the course of a single day—certainly enough to keep on investigating.

Three months later, after Terry and I had confronted Jersey, exposing a flagrantly evil personality, and after I'd talked to Malachi and had time to digest the experience, I suppose I had been converted. I was now 95 percent sure, enough to command an exorcism to be performed, even though I knew that my own profession might well seek my excommunication. Two months later, on the eve of the exorcism, having heard Jersey scream at me while simultaneously smiling, my certainty that she was demonically possessed was 99 percent. Four days later it was 100 percent. Total. I would never again doubt the existence of Satan.

Beccah's exorcism did not increase my certainty of the devil's existence; there is no place to go beyond total certainty. All I can say is that it was so confusing—that Beccah/Lucifer toyed with us so viciously—I'm not sure I could have survived it without my total certainty.

As a psychiatrist, I had been converted by Jersey's case alone, from a belief that the devil did not exist to a belief—a certainty—that the devil does exist and probably demons (under the control of the devil) as well. By the devil, I mean a spirit that is powerful (it may be many places at the same time and manifest itself in a variety of distinctly paranormal ways), thoroughly malevolent (its only motivation seemed to be the destruction of human beings or the entire human race), deceitful and vain, capable of taking up a kind of residence within the mind, brain, soul, or body of susceptible and willing human beings—a spirit that had various names (among them Lucifer and Satan), that was real and did exist.

I have attempted to tell the stories of Jersey and Beccah with the greatest possible scientific thoroughness. I have left out no significant detail. Consequently, you and I have exactly the same database to work from. But I do not think it likely at this point in time that we would arrive at the same conclusions.

So I was converted to a belief in the devil. Since you had the same database as I, does that mean that I expect you to also become believers in the devil? No. You see, there is one crucial difference in our experiences. I was there, and you were not. Seeing is believing. I saw directly. You have been able to see only through my eyes, and your experience has been of necessity vicarious. No, the most I can hope for is that as a result of reading about Jersey and Beccah you have been converted from a closed to an open mind . . . that you would be willing to look into some more evidence were it available . . . that you believe the matter to be worthy of further study. In summary, it is my hope that you will envision that matters of possession and exorcism, of demons and deliverance, constitute a proper field of scientific inquiry. Specifically, I wish that you will join me in proposing that "demonology" be made an incipient subspecialty of psychiatry and psychology.

Two cases alone do not a science make. But they do make a beginning of a science, and that's all that's needed to start.

Jersey and Beccah could not have been two more different cases. But besides being possessed, they did have several things in common. For starters they were both very good and very bad.

I have already mentioned their goodness from several perspectives. I noted that I felt there was something potentially holy about each of them. For example, through the ages there has been an association between holiness and light. This association may be the reason that painters of old usually depicted the saints with halos (which I suppose some people today might refer to as auras). At the conclusion of both their exorcisms, Jersey's and Beccah's faces were infused with light. They were almost more than radiant. I have seen light in the faces of many good people, but I have never seen it to such a degree.

Malachi and I were both in agreement about the vital point that possessed people are not evil; they are in conflict between good and evil. Were it not for this conflict we could not know there is such a thing as possession. It is the conflict that gives rise to this "stigmata" of possession. Thoroughly evil people are not in conflict; they are not in pain or discomfort. There is no inner turmoil.

As to the thoroughly evil, Malachi and I were not in agreement.

Malachi thought that thoroughly evil people were rare. He

depicted several of them in *Hostage to the Devil,* but all were vague, shadowy figures. I, on the other hand, believe that thoroughly evil people are quite common—much more common than the possessed—and depicted several of them in *People of the Lie* in considerable detail.

Malachi believed that thoroughly evil people were that way because of demonic involvement and because of their complete consent and cooperation with the demonic. Hence he calls such people the perfectly possessed. He considered them to be unresearchable. I, on the other hand, labeled them the people of the lie and believe that they are researchable, albeit with difficulty. In not ascribing their evil to demonic involvement, I have repeatedly said, "Given the universal dynamics of laziness and narcissism, I do not think that the people of the lie need Satan to recruit them to their evil; I believe that they are quite capable of recruiting themselves."

While Malachi and I agreed that possessed people were not utterly evil, that some part of their souls were still good, this goodness did not seem to be particularly dramatic to Malachi. In both Jersey and Beccah I felt their goodness to be so great as to represent potential holiness. This led me to the hypothesis that possession is such a rare condition because there are far more people around than there are demons. To my surprise this hypothesis happened to coincide with the widespread Christian doctrine that the battle between good and evil was essentially won by Jesus when he died on the cross. While it often doesn't feel that way, this Christian doctrine maintains that all we are now engaged in is a mop-up operation of those hopelessly outnumbered minions of Satan. Being on the run, so to speak, Satan is engaged in frantically trying to put out the fires. It is natural, then, that it and its minions would afflict only those human beings who represent a particular threat to the forces of darkness. In other words, it is this potential holiness, I believe, that is the reason the devil pays them special attention.

But it is terribly important to realize that the potentially holy victims of possession are not simply good. They are also very bad as a result of their possession. Having been partially taken over by the demonic, they manifest the evil of the demonic. Despite her goodness, Jersey had begun to abandon her infant children repeatedly. And Beccah, despite her amazing theological sophistication, was a compulsive, chronic crook.

Most psychiatrists believe that all people have within them a certain badness or evil that they try to hide in that part of the mind Carl Jung called the Shadow. But this is something different from possession. While there may be a modest struggle between good and evil in the soul of virtually every human being, in those humans who are possessed the struggle is titanic.

Finally, let me return to the beginning, where I noted how extremely different Jersey and Beccah were. There are only four other genuine exorcists I have personally known. One of the things all five of us are agreed on is that possessed people are very different from one another. There is no such thing as a typical case of possession, nor a typical exorcism. No matter how experienced, no matter how well he knows the patient, once the invocation has begun, the exorcist has entered unexplored territory and has no idea what will be called forth from him.

———◆———

It seemed quite remarkable that when I got down to the bottom of things, both of my suspicious cases turned out to be cases of satanic possession. I had never read about a case of pure satanic possession, which is why I frantically called for help on that first Sunday afternoon.

For several years after completing Jersey's exorcism, I went to the other end of things and wondered whether there was even such a thing as demonic possession, and whether all cases of possession might not be, at the bottom, satanic possession. It was true that before we got to Satan in Jersey's case we had to go through four demons. But were they really demons? Each represented a false idea or heresy that Jersey had been carrying around for many years, enough for each of these false ideas to develop a kind of personality of its own. They seemed to arise more out of Jersey's psyche than to exist as entities that had invaded her. So I wondered whether they were simply Jersey's ideas that Satan was hiding behind, or rather than being independent demons, whether they weren't simply reflections of the One.

However, at the time of Beccah's deliverance we did seem to find a true demon, Judas—one of the best-known demons, close to Satan in the hierarchy but still separate from Satan. And certainly when we expelled Judas, Beccah's recovery was nothing short of miraculous—for three weeks. Indeed, the fact it lasted for only three weeks did nothing to diminish its miraculous nature. The scientist in me naturally wondered whether it was a placebo cure, but I doubted it. Beccah had been severely and constantly depressed every day for the preceding thirty years. To then not feel the least depressed for twenty-one consecutive days was a healing of far greater magnitude than one would expect from the placebo effect. So I began to believe along with everyone else who has written on the subject that demons are evil spirits in their own right and something more than mere reflections of Satan.

At this point I have only one weak hypothesis to offer as to why both my cases were cases of satanic possession. I approached Jersey and Beccah as a hardheaded scientist and as a very traditional psychiatrist with a national reputation that I did not want to lose. If I was going to make a diagnosis of possession, by god, it had to be right. Consequently, it may be no accident that I chose to diagnose only the most serious cases of possession, and being the most serious they were ultimately satanic cases. The only other possibility I can think of is that for some reason God wanted me to see cases of satanic possession, but that is not a scientifically acceptable hypothesis. No, it wouldn't float at all.

CONCLUSION

Then the matter of names may be important. Jersey never even spoke of herself as being possessed by Satan. I just assumed in the end that what I perceived as the Antichrist was also Satan and addressed it as such when I expelled it.* Beccah, on the other hand, as soon as she was repossessed (after her three-week miracle cure following the expulsion of Judas) immediately named her repossessor as Lucifer. Sometimes we addressed it as Lucifer. More often we addressed it as Satan. Neither it nor Beccah seemed to have any preference of name.

Nonetheless, the possessor of Jersey was very different in appearance and kind from the possessor of Beccah. Beccah, having been raised Jewish, was using the Old Testament name for Satan, the name for the devil of the serpent, the provoker of original sin in the Garden of Eden. Fundamentalist Christians who deny the theory of evolution use biblical dates to identify Adam and Eve's temptation by the serpent at a few thousand years before the birth of Christ. The larger number of Christians who accept the theory of evolution will date Eden to the time of the first human beings some two or more millions of years before the birth of Christ.

Regardless of name, I would with total certainty place Beccah's snakelike demon as belonging to a time several million years ago. I spoke about the qualities of heaviness, hugeness,

---

* As far as I know, the concept of the Antichrist first appeared in John's Revelation, which is the concluding text of the New Testament. That concept of the Antichrist seems in Revelation to be quite different from the concept of Satan. Since the days Revelation was first written, however, it should be pointed out that I am by no means the first Christian to have identified the Antichrist with Satan.

Actually, at the time I made that identification I knew none of this. Rather it was like a revelation that I myself received as soon as the supposed pair of demons said with a smirk, "We don't hate Jesus; we just test him." I knew both instantly and with absolute certainty that it was the Antichrist who had just spoken, and I simultaneously knew with equal certainty that this Antichrist was Satan.

and immobility of Beccah's snake, but I did not mention another distinct feeling I had at the time of her exorcism. In my very guts I felt that snake had to be millions of years old to have grown to such a huge size and state of immobility. I felt helpless before it, because it seemed to me it would have taken dozens of backhoes and cranes moving in concert to remove the beast. It truly felt to me like a beast that had been lying there for eternity.

Jersey's satanic face did not give me a similar feeling of great age. It was a much more humanlike face, although its hideousness was every bit as inhuman as the snake. I have stood before a mirror for hours and hours since the exorcism trying to imitate that satanic face, but there was no way that I, an ordinary human, could distort my face into such a nonhuman expression. It was also a quick-moving sort of face, quite distinct from the sluggishness of the serpent. So it did actually feel to me that Jersey's primary demon, the Antichrist who appeared satanic, more or less belonged to the time of the birth and death of Jesus, while Beccah's snake demon belonged to the time of the birth of the human race.

But all of this is hardly science. The fact is we do not know what it means. We do not know whether Satan and Lucifer are one and the same or whether there is any difference between them. Christian theology would hold that Satan and Lucifer are, in essence, the same. But there is no certainty about this. Questions remain, big questions waiting for science to catch up with them.

———◆———

The family story about how Beccah, between the ages of one and two, just able to walk, crossed ten downtown city streets before she was picked up by the police, was either that of an exuberant child gleefully enjoying her escape from the household or, as I believe, an account of absolutely helpless loneliness. We do not know what drove her to run away, but to simply be returned and dumped back in her home without the slightest intervention or notice breaks my heart.

Overtly, Beccah was certainly lonelier than Jersey, but over the years it has occurred to me how lonely Jersey must have been after being molested by her stepfather. Granted there was the tiniest element of choice in the matter; she otherwise could not talk with her mother or siblings about what had happened. For me there is something lonely indeed about a twelve-year-old girl reading the works of Edgar Cayce when she ordinarily would have been out with her friends.

In the years since, I have spoken with several other psychiatrists who, like me, went out on a professional limb to perform an exorcism on one of their patients. Each of their case histories described the patients as being lonely to a greater degree than one might expect. I can hardly be scientific about the matter, but I have begun to suspect that loneliness may be a precondition for possession, or else a precondition for the deepening of that possession.

———◆———

The Roman Catholic church, by virtue of its tight hierarchical and authoritarian structure, plays a role for the entire Christian church as a guardian of "correct" theology and practice. In doing so, it has been the only church to have maintained over the centuries formal instructions concerning the diagnosis of possession and its exorcism. My experience strongly suggests that a change should be made in the church's criteria for diagnosing possession. Those criteria currently put great emphasis upon the presence of supernatural signs or happenings and tend to insist that such signs be present before an exorcism is attempted. In Jersey's and Beccah's cases there were a great many paranormal signs. Most of them would be called "soft" and were for the most part recognizable as such only well after their occurrence. Listed below are such signs in each case.

Jersey

Pre-exorcism

- Inexperienced priest could not remember his interview.
- Her description of her demons as "weak, pathetic creatures."
- Her apparent pretense of a severe schizophrenic psychosis, which could not have been expected by any layperson.
- The overpowering effect her anger had upon me even though I knew she was enjoying the experience.

Exorcism

- The extremely dramatic appearance of a satanic expression on her face during the presence of each of her demons and Satan.
- The inability of the videotape to pick up this expression.
- The appearance on the videotape of a brief sudden and different but equally inexplicable change in facial expression.
- The emergence of four separate demonic personalities and their timing, which is highly unlikely to would seem impossible to have been created by the patient herself.

Beccah

Pre-exorcism

- The dramatic three-week remission following the expulsion of Judas at her deliverance.

Exorcism

- Her negative response to holy water and her apparent agony when the Book of Common Prayer was placed upon her.
- Her inexplicable ability to distinguish between that book and others, sight unseen.
- Her snakelike appearance for a period of over two days unapparent on videotape but apparent to everyone present.

- Her previously overlooked superhuman strength requiring not only ordinarily effective restraints, but the personal restraint of a team of up to nine during a time when she was severely underweight, malnourished, and sleep deprived.

———◆———

I believe through the cases of Jersey and Beccah we actually have succeeded—at least to my own satisfaction—in answering an interrelated complex of four major questions. Those answers are:

1. Yes, the devil or a demonic world does exist.
2. The phenomenon of demonic possessions of human individuals also does exist, and offers *prima facie* evidence for number 1.
3. That a process of exorcism can, in certain seriously possessed patients, be either curative or strikingly beneficial to an extent beyond that which the remedies of traditional psychiatry can achieve.
4. The study of possession is inextricably interwoven with the study of exorcism since it is only during the process of exorcism that the demonic possession is fully revealed.

So we do have a few major answers, but typical of science we now have a far larger number of questions than we had before. No attempt has been made to delineate all such questions, because in total they could themselves fill an entire book. I have instead delineated only a few of those questions to which, integrating my work with others, I believe I can give trustworthy answers—at least while both religion and science remain separate by default, refusing to work together through research.

- Possession is not an accident.
- In becoming possessed the victim must, at least in some way, cooperate with or sell out to the devil. Such cooperation can

range all the way from consciously and deliberately making an actual pact with the devil (as I described in chapter 1 of *People of the Lie*) to something so seemingly innocent as a twelve-year-old incest victim choosing to believe her stepfather's lie in preference to facing a reality almost too painful to bear.

- Such initial sellouts are probably more often than not made under great duress.
- Thereafter possession is a deepening process over time unless the victim reneges on the pact.
- The victim of possession can choose to renege on the pact at any time, but the longer the possession the more difficult the option becomes without an exorcism.
- An exorcism is a massive therapeutic intervention to liberate, teach, and support the victim to choose to reject the devil.
- Often the victim's age at the time of the initial possession can be accurately guessed before the exorcism, but commonly the victim will not offer the explanation or the why of the possession until after the exorcism has liberated him or her to do so. (Jersey's case was typical in this respect, but I know that only because of other cases I have heard about in depth from their exorcists.)
- The more recent the time of onset of the possession, the more the exorcism is likely to be successful.
- Exorcism of genuinely possessed people should be expected to be combative, meaning that at least some physical restraint will be required.
- The use of at least one deliverance either for healing, diagnosis, or both should be a standard part of the management of a case prior to exorcism.*

---

* This was true of the deliverances attempted on Jersey and Beccah, which were extremely difficult. The subject of deliverance is a confusing one. Unfortunately, a recent book by Michael Cuneo, *American Exorcism*, does not clarify this confusion. Purporting to have witnessed in whole or in part more

- Deliverance should be conducted by a team of at least three, exorcisms by a team of six or more. All exorcisms should be videotaped for the legal protection of the team and hopefully for eventual educational purposes. Elaborate written consent forms should be utilized just as they would be for any major surgical procedure.
- It is highly questionable whether an exorcism should be attempted in a case where the patient has no adequate support system of personal friends or relatives.
- Possession is the most severe but not the only kind of demonic affliction.

I have composed this partial list of things we probably know about possession and exorcism, not only in response to the question of "What is possession?" but also to demonstrate that we already have a body of knowledge on the subject. Not a huge one, but certainly large enough to constitute the foundation of a new branch of science, enough to make demonology a respectable field of research and study.

But the acceptance of demonology into the scientific fold is not going to happen—at least not until history itself is reformed, not until a 350-year-old separation of the world of supposed natural phenomena from the assumed world of supernatural phenomena is revisited, and recognized by all concerned as having been a gigantic mistake.

I conclude with that simple recognition. To write fully about what an enormous difference it would make in our consciousness were we to consider the devil with the seriousness it deserves would have required several hundred more pages—essentially a book in itself. I hope that someday someone will write that book.

---

than fifty exorcisms, the author, as far as I can discern, witnessed more than fifty deliverance procedures, but did not witness a single exorcism.

EPILOGUE

It may seem strange to some that I have dedicated this book to Malachi Martin. Many of the accusations about him—that he was a manipulator, sometimes a liar, the seducer of another man's wife, a publicity hound, and especially a proponent of possession and exorcism—are undoubtedly true.

Given all this, it is hardly remarkable that the religious establishment should have looked askance at Malachi, particularly since they knew nothing about the matter of possession and exorcism and, as is so common in the ignorant, were terrified by it.

I had one personally painful experience of the intensity of their vilification. In *Hostage to the Devil*, Malachi had written about how almost magically important it was for an exorcist to proceed only with the blessing of the institutional church. Clearly from the response of the archbishop of Hartford to Terry O'Connor's letter, I was not going to get the blessing of the Catholic church. So I tried to get it from the official Episcopal church for Jersey's exorcism. To this end a friend arranged a meeting between me and the bishop of New York and Westchester. The bishop listened to my story noncommittally but with an intensity and concern that felt supportive. He said that he would like me to tell my story to one of his top lieutenants, Canon Brewster. Consequently, during the busy time I was fishing around the country for an exorcist, I also spent the better part of two days driving down to New York City to meet with Canon Brewster, whom I already knew to be a famous spiritual advisor.

During those two quite lengthy sessions, I not only described Jersey's case and my involvement, but also bared my soul and my spiritual journey to the canon. He too seemed supportive, and raised no question about my spiritual health.

Meanwhile, Jersey's behavior was becoming worse after a month's hospitalization. Dr. Lieberman was under increasing pressure by his hospital to discharge her. The date had to be set, and quickly. The team committed themselves to the four-day period I had selected. Thinking that he might possibly want to be a member of the team, I called Canon Brewster. I told him that the time had come to go ahead and asked, "Do you want to be a participant?"

This seemingly mild-mannered man suddenly screamed at me over the phone. "Are you crazy? Are you really going ahead with this? You must be out of your damn mind!"

With a sense of what was coming, I somehow—perhaps by the grace of the Holy Spirit—had the self-confidence to react appropriately. I responded, "Canon, you've spent a good four hours with me in the past month. Did you get the impression that I was mentally unstable?"

"No, it's not you," he replied, still screaming. "Well, it is you. You've been led down the garden path by Malachi Martin. He's an evil man. Somehow you've fallen under his spell. But I don't blame you. I blame him. Everybody knows he's evil. He's the one that's possessed. He's more possessed than anyone he's written about, and now he's somehow managed to take over your mind."

"May I gather you don't want to be part of the exorcism?" I inquired mildly.

"He's evil, I tell you," the canon yelled. "Stay away from him. He's evil, evil." And at that point the canon hung up on me.

I don't know how much of this was the canon's fault or possibly the bishop's. If the bishop had referred me for an objective evaluation of things, he had chosen the wrong lieutenant. But probably there was no right lieutenant at the time, and it is conceivable to me that the bishop may have thought that I was mad and referred me to the canon with instructions for the canon to bring me to my senses. I don't know.

——◆——

A good decade after our work together on the case of Jersey, Malachi asked me to dinner. That night, Malachi struck me as somehow embittered and slightly over the hill. This was during a lengthy period in which I had allowed myself to become inhumanely busy, and I made no effort whatsoever to reach out to him.

I suppose that one reason I dedicate this book to Malachi is an act of contrition. Malachi served me as a mentor of extraordinary sophistication and dedication. I hope the dedication might somehow find Malachi in God's time to give him a fraction of what he gave me.

In the course of my research I contacted several who had been close friends of his during the years in question. From these people I learned for certain that Malachi did not have any eye trouble and never had a detached retina. Malachi had indeed manipulated me into being an exorcist. I do not ordinarily respect manipulation. In this case I do. My fantasy of handing the case of Jersey over to Malachi and then being allowed to be a detached and uninvolved witness to her exorcism was most unrealistic. I suspect Malachi had guessed it from the beginning. I believe he must have felt a compelling need to see to it that as a legacy he could train some badly needed exorcists, and that the best way he could train me in particular was to corner me into being an exorcist in the way that he did. I could not have learned all that I did as a mere observer. In an exorcism there are only participant observers. Moreover, while I felt that he had practically abandoned me at the time, it was Malachi who found Bishop Worthington to come to my aid, and it was he who would provide me with other forms of support. The reality is that he did not abandon me; he only cleverly pushed me in the direction that I needed to go. He advised me in several dozen ways. In every case his advice was correct. He batted a thousand.

There are reasons Malachi deserves a monument far greater than this dedication. For one, he was a very good writer, and in some instances a truly great writer. *Hostage to the Devil* would not survive were it not so well written. As far as writing goes, however, his previous book, *The New Castle* (which I believe is out of print), is not only a bold book with several innovative and useful concepts, but also one of the best-written books it has ever been my privilege to read. I know Malachi himself regarded it as his best work.

And then there is *Hostage to the Devil.* One is accustomed to reading on dust jackets how the book within is "groundbreaking." The word is often an exaggeration. In relation to *Hostage,* that word is an understatement. Perhaps in the Middle Ages there may have been some kind of guidebook for exorcists. But *Hostage* is the first and only textbook on the subject of possession and exorcism in modern times. It is the only work to describe the stages of an exorcism, and it is obviously based on an enormous amount of personal experience. I have repeatedly argued that demonology should be a new field of medical science. Should that ever come to pass, Malachi will be considered its founder. *Hostage* is a brilliant work of both scholarship and leadership.

It is clear in retrospect that from the beginning Malachi wanted me to become an exorcist. He wanted it badly. But he believed that I should become a Christian before it happened. We Christians ordinarily have a profound need to proselytize. Often it is a selfish need. Since my becoming a Christian was a prerequisite for becoming an exorcist in his mind, one would have expected Malachi to push me toward my baptism in every way possible. The reality is that he appeared to be totally uninterested. He did not push me in the slightest. There was no pressure. I think this can be understood only on the basis that

Malachi was leaving the matter in God's hands. There are few if any greater examples of emotional maturity than for someone to want something to move in a certain direction desperately but yet to be so much in control of himself that in deference to God and to the freedom of the other person he lifts no finger and says no word to further his desires.

Beyond all these things, there is an example of Malachi's greatness that is particularly poignant to me. It will be remembered that Malachi had an elaborate phone system to protect him. It was formidable, and I had never reached him directly. On the afternoon of the fourth day of Jersey's exorcism, when there was little time left, I was suddenly confronted with Satan. At the time I was so intensely involved I had no awareness of the significance of what happened.

It is hardly remarkable that I should have phoned Malachi in desperation for his advice at such a moment. But it was not until I began to write this book that I put the pieces together. In the middle of the very first ring my phone call was answered by Malachi in his brogue with the words: "Is that you, Scotty?" Only two decades later did it occur to me that it was like a miracle for me to be able to reach him. It was a miracle, but one of those rare explicable ones. At least I think so. I believe that Malachi had been sitting in his icon-filled study waiting for my call. How long had he been waiting there? It is my suspicion that he had been waiting for well over two hours on that Sunday afternoon, doing nothing except being in prayer with no other goal than to be available for me if I needed him.

A great many people thought Malachi was evil. Evil people are not capable of love. Oh, they can pretend to be loving as long as the pretense costs them little or nothing. One does not sit for hours to be available to another as a pretense. Evil has a number of opposites. The first to come to my mind are love and goodness. "Is that you, Scotty?" In those four words at that moment both were made manifest.

ACKNOWLEDGMENTS

For a variety of reasons, the years I spent writing this book were perhaps the most difficult of my life. There is simply no way it could ever have been completed had I not been graced with an extraordinary support system of remarkable people who literally bathed me in love. The only problem is their number is so large, I can here do nothing more than merely name them alphabetically without making mention of the particular gifts they gave. I deeply thank:

John Allen, Liz Allen, Shaye Areheart, John Barbosa, Janice Barfield, Melissa Bauman, Steve Bauman, Eve Berry, Ann Boyer, Keith Byler, Hope Childs, Morris Clark, Bernadette Coomaraswamy, Rama Coomaraswamy, Maria Dawson, Jonathan Dolger, Richard Duffy, Valerie Duffy, Armand Eisen, Douglas Evans, Bill Franklin, Danica Gieslin, Kaz Gozdz, James Guy, Mary J. Hatch, Bob Hatcher, Edwina Hazzard, Fred Hills, Margaret Holland, Vester Hughes, Jane Isay, Arthur Jones, Lila Karp, Leslie Khan, Omar Khan, Larry Kramer, Joe Kulhowvick, Kyle Lehning, Ryan Lehning, Michael Levine, Kakia Livanos, Barbara Mahon, Jean Matlack, William McNabb, Phil Mirvis, David Peck III, Heather Peck, Joan Puglia, Earl Puterbaugh, Iraj Rahmati, Mike Reid, Robert Reusing, Richard Sallick, Laura Shackelford, Renee Schwartz, John Severance, Rick Slone, Simon Sobo, Nancy Solley, Everett Spees, Ellen Stephen, Terry Szymanski, David Webster, Fred Welch, Wenden Wiegand, Kathy Yeates, Amy Ziffer.

Still, I must single out for unique mention.

ACKNOWLEDGMENTS

Fred Hills, my editor, who, for twenty years has been a voice of sanity and reason in the complex and complicated world of publishing. Thank you Fred for being so wise in shepherding so many of my works.

AND

Michael Schmidt who, although younger than all the above, I have known for many years and in many ways as a person of unusual courage and wisdom. Michael obtained his doctorate in neuroanatomy in June 2003, and was unclear as to how he might put it to use. I asked what else interested him. "The relationship between religion and science," he replied. So I hired him that afternoon. He agreed to come to my aid in a way no one else could. Although not responsible for any of this book's faults, his delicate footprints are on a number of the pages to follow.

AND

Once upon a time long, long ago a little girl named Gail was born in a manger. Perhaps because of these humble beginnings, she was to develop a severe upward mobility problem (but one symptom of which was a phobia of airplanes). Although she married well (an earl, no less), her problem persisted, which was why she came to see me thirty years ago for psychotherapy and how we met. Alas, hers was a hopeless case, so she fired me after a year. Nonetheless, I remembered her as having nice legs, and I hired her for a menial position a decade later (a psychoanalytic no-no, but in rural areas sometimes ya gotta break the rules to survive). Gail Puterbaugh agreed to work for me only under two conditions: that her position remain utterly menial and that her job description never include the words "growth" or "advancement." But strange things happen in this life (like miracles) and there happened to be an embarrassing (to her) quirk in her personality for which there was no recognized psychiatric label. You see, much as she tried to stomp it out, she cared. She cared for all manner of creatures, great and small (sometimes too much), one of which after a while came to be me. Like children and chipmunks, she could not bear to see me ill-served.

Now, it also came to pass in those years that other employees quit or had to be laid off, and when Gail saw that no potential replacement was as competent as she herself, she was under a compulsion to volunteer "just to fill in for a bit." So it was, without clawing her way, like grade A cream, she naturally floated to the top and into the title of "executive director," meaning I would delegate to her executive-type tasks that she would direct to be done. She ceased worrying about the word "advancement" anymore, since there was no longer anyplace she could advance to (or so she thought). She became so relaxed that there were moments when she forgot about herself and actually became a bit bossy. That was how I discovered that along with everything else, Gail is one of the truly great editors of this world. The final piece of the tale (thus far) is that as I became ever more ethereal with advancing age, it so happened I became a little less competent at managing my earthly affairs—which (you guessed it) has changed the substance of the title, Executive Director, so that she is in all ways my executive director.

Gail Puterbaugh, you will realize I have used a lighthearted tone to acknowledge you lest I weep. And that were this book not meant to be dedicated to Malachi since the time of creation, it would be dedicated to you. Dear Director, Editor, Servant Leader, Counselor, and Friend: you are no sinless lamb. But the next time you come to ask me about Jesus, I shall direct you simply to look in the mirror. Will you dare?

My grateful love,
Scotty

ABOUT THE AUTHOR

Scott Peck's publishing history reflects his own evolution as a serious and widely acclaimed writer, thinker, psychiatrist, and spiritual guide. Since his groundbreaking bestseller *The Road Less Traveled* was first published in 1978, his insatiable intellectual curiosity has taken him in various new directions with virtually each new book: the subject of healing human evil in *People of the Lie* (1982), where he first briefly discussed exorcism and possession; the creative experience of community in *The Different Drum* (1987); the role of civility in personal relationships and society in *A World Waiting to Be Born* (1993); an examination of the complexities of life and the paradoxical nature of belief in *Further Along the Road Less Traveled* (1993); and an exploration of the medical, ethical, and spiritual issues of euthanasia in *Denial of the Soul* (1999); as well as a novel, a children's book, and other works. A graduate of both Harvard University and Case Western Reserve, Dr. Peck served in the Army Medical Corps before maintaining a private practice in psychiatry. For the last twenty years, he has devoted much of his time and financial resources to the work of the Foundation for Community Encouragement, a nonprofit organization that he helped found in 1984. Dr. Peck lives in Connecticut.